BUDGETING DEMOCRACY

BUDGETING DEMOCRACY

*State Building and Citizenship
in America, 1890–1928*

Jonathan Kahn

CORNELL UNIVERSITY PRESS

ITHACA AND LONDON

First published 1997 by Cornell University Press.

Printed in the United States of America

Library of Congress Cataloging-in-Publication Data

Kahn, Jonathan, 1958–
    Budgeting democracy : state-building and citizenship in America,
1890–1928 / by Jonathan Kahn.
      p. cm.
    Includes index.
    ISBN 0-8014-2950-1 (cloth : alk. paper)
    1. Budget—United States—History. 2. Budget—United States—
States—History. 3. United States—Politics and government—20th
century. 4. Municipal budgets—United States—History—20th
century. 5. Municipal budgets—New York (State)—New York—
History—20th century. 6. Political culture—United States—
History—20th century. I. Title.
HJ2051.K34 1997
352.4'973'009—dc21   97-3847

cloth printing   10 9 8 7 6 5 4 3 2 1

for my parents

CONTENTS

CONTENTS

PREFACE

This book is born of my interest in how people imbue particular aspects of their world with distinctive political meanings. I chose to explore budgets as I came to understand them as a system to structure our knowledge and perception of government. In a complex world, budgets provide a political place for everything and put everything in its political place. I focus on the origins of modern budget reform in the Progressive era because it involved a self-conscious effort on the part of a coherent and identifiable band of political elites to change the way Americans saw government and understood their relation to it. In creating our modern budgetary system, these elites articulated an ideology of budgeting that went beyond technical questions of how to make budgets to consider explicitly more fundamental issues concerning the relationship between budgeting and democratic governance in modern society. Today budgets are still with us, but we take them for granted. We have lost sight of how they impose upon us a particular way of viewing our political world.

I began by looking at people who put their intellect in the service of the state. The first think tanks became my initial focus, specifically the Brookings Institution, which was incorporated in 1916 as the Institute for Government Research. The institute was staffed and supported by as good an array of well-credentialed experts and corporate liberal elites as one could ask of any good Progressive era initiative. I soon discovered that the motivating force behind almost all the institute's early activities was its campaign to establish a national budget system. Coming from a background in intellectual and cultural history, I was both baffled and intrigued to find so many well-educated, articulate, and engaged reformers so interested, indeed passionately committed, to something so apparently dry and life-less as budgets. Taking a counterphobic tack, I decided to pursue their ob-session with numbers and charts.

I traced the origins of both Brookings and budget reform back to the New York Bureau of Municipal Research, which was founded in 1906 and led the first campaign for municipal budget reform. As the story be-gan to unfold before me, I came across a reference to a "budget exhibit" in New York City. This in itself seemed odd, but then I found that one such budget exhibit in 1911 attracted over one million visitors in under one month. Further research revealed that the exhibit was not a bland dis-play of accounting ledgers but was an elaborate, even extravagant, pub-lic spectacle. Sponsored by the city government, it filled three floors of a large building on lower Broadway with graphs and charts, models and demonstrations—even motion pictures—all purporting to represent to the citizens of New York precisely what the government was up to.

To the New Yorkers who visited the exhibit, budgets clearly involved more than simple facts and figures. The exhibit featured new techniques of entertainment, display, and public relations to make an increasingly large and complex government intelligible and accessible to the citizenry. The exhibit, and budgets themselves, were an event, an episode of repre-sentation and experience that shaped the political culture of the city. In this light, budgets began to seem very interesting indeed.

As I pursued the phenomenon of budget reform, I soon realized that budgets were (and continue to be) powerful tools that organize and ar-ticulate knowledge about government. In structuring knowledge about government, budgets also structure the political imagination. Between 1906 and 1928, at all levels of government—local, state, and national—budget reform changed the way citizens and politicians, reformers and bu-reaucrats, perceived government and their relation to it.

Ted Lowi helped me define the original focus of this work and stayed with it through its many incarnations. His insights on everything from lo-cal New York City patronage to central clearance in the Bureau of the Budget kept me on track and always challenged me to refine my argu-ments. Stuart Blumin guided me through my early work on budget ex-hibits. After the project had developed into a full-fledged study of the entire campaign for budget reform, Larry Moore provided invaluable help throughout. His consistent support and always constructive criticism pushed me subtly yet persistently to make this a better book. To Larry I owe a special debt of gratitude.

A number of libraries and archives provided helpful support during the course of my research. The staff of Olin Library at Cornell University was consistently helpful in supporting my work. Susan McDonough at the National Archives, Susan McGrath at the Brookings Institution, and Steven Unger at the Institute of Public Administration guided me through their archives with patience and consideration. The staffs at the Columbia Oral History Collection, the Columbia University Rare Books and Manuscript Collection, the Harvard University Archives, the Rockefeller Archive Center, the New York Municipal Archives, and the New York Public Library also provided generous assistance. I also thank the family of Jerome Greene for allowing me to quote from his papers. Portions of Chapter 4 are drawn from my article "Re-Presenting Government and Representing the People: Budget Reform and Citizenship in New York City, 1908–1911," which appeared in the *Journal of Urban History* 19, no. 3 (May 1993): 83–103, and are reprinted by permission of Sage Publications.

Finally to Karen-Sue, the happiest new addition to my life. Writing a book can be a long and solitary endeavor. We had not met when I began this book. Having you with me to share its completion makes it all seem worthwhile.

JONATHAN KAHN

Annandale-on-Hudson, New York

BUDGETING DEMOCRACY

INTRODUCTION: THE POLITICAL CULTURE
OF PUBLIC BUDGET REFORM

Public budgets have become a talisman of modern American politics. Republicans and Democrats, liberals and conservatives—all ritually invoke the budget whenever they are discussing any significant public policy. A program may be good or it may be bad, but if it does not pass budgetary muster, it is dead. Seeking comfort in the illusory certainty of numbers, modern legislators find it far easier to evaluate a law or a program in terms of its fiscal impact than to debate its merits. The budget is their ally or their doom, depending on their ability to bend its terms and categories of analysis to their needs.

A politics circumscribed by budgetary discourse also allows politicians to evade their duties as representatives of the people. To evaluate a program's merits, one must appeal to the values and needs of constituents; to assess its fiscal impact, one need never leave the company of experts. In a political world dominated by bargaining over discrete programs, the budget has become the perfect tool of interest group liberalism.

It was not always so. Before the twentieth century, no government in the United States, local, state, or national, had a coherent budget system. Between 1900 and 1928, a small but energetic band of reformers successfully introduced fundamentally new systems of public budgeting into hundreds of cities, every state, and ultimately the federal government. To all Americans of this time, the fact of having a budget was something new and different. Governments had always had finances, yes, but the idea of a budget itself was alien and had to be learned. Thus, as reformers introduced the techniques of budget reform to the United States, they also constructed its meaning for the citizenry. They "invented" the budget, imbuing it with value and using it to serve very particular purposes distinctive to the demands and ideals of the United States in the Progressive era. To understand our contemporary fixation on budgets and its significance for the promise of democratic politics, we must look back to this time when the idea of public budgets was first introduced into America's political consciousness.

In this book I examine budget reform as a phenomenon that reshaped both the governing institutions and the political culture of the nation. I argue that public budgets are more than simply technical tools for allocating government resources. They are also cultural constructions that shape public life, state institutions, and the relations between the two. As Progressive era reformers used budgets to organize government, they constructed its meaning and structured perceptions of its proper role in society. Budgets came to demarcate the public sphere of government action and thereby became indispensable referents for public discussion of political issues. Through developing systematic analyses of the scope and nature of governmental activities, the movement for public budget reform not only changed administrative practices, it altered the way people perceived government and conceived of themselves in relation to it.

Looked at as a cultural artifact, we can see the budget as a powerful tool of the political imagination. By exploring and mapping terrain of governmental administration, the champions of budget reform allowed prospective state builders and citizen reformers alike to make the conceptual leap from seeing government as a random agglomeration of administrative fiefdoms to envisioning a coherent, interrelated, and unitary state. By thus "imagining" the state, political actors were able to proceed to conceiving of more activist possibilities for the development and application of its power. But even as the budget opened up more activist possibilities for government, it also served to narrow and contain popular engagement with government. Citizens, presented with the budget as the program of government activity, were led to develop new notions of accountability and representation based on passive oversight rather than active political participation. The citizen of the modern "budgetary republic" was to be primarily a passive consumer of information and services.

America's first movement for public budget reform began in New York City at the turn of this century and culminated nationally with the passage and implementation of the Budget and Accounting Act of 1921. The directors of the New York Bureau of Municipal Research—William Allen, Henry Bruere, and Frederick Cleveland—formed the vanguard of the campaign for budget reform. As the campaign moved to the national level in the 1910s, William Willoughby, director of the Institute of Government Research (the immediate precursor to the Brookings Institution), came to the fore to guide the creation and implementation of a national budget system.

Budget reformers' ambitions ranged far beyond the mere restructuring of fiscal administration. First and foremost, they saw in the budget a means to revitalize representative democracy and enable it to meet the demands of urban industrial society. The men of the Bureau of Municipal Research recognized that the varied pressures of urban industrial society had seriously eroded the legitimacy of governing institutions that purportedly derived their authority from the consent of the governed. Government had become more intrusive into the day-to-day lives of citizens while simultaneously growing more distant from them. Similarly, the government had become harder to grasp conceptually because it had grown more complex; citizens no longer had a clear sense of who in government was responsible for what, or even, for that matter, for what activities government as a whole was responsible. More immediately, in large cities with concentrated populations, regular contact between citizen and representative simply had become more difficult. As the sense of shared interests and experience that sustained the fiction of political representation weakened, citizen apathy and disillusionment grew stronger. Into the vacuum had rushed the hated political machines, with their waste and corruption, seducing ignorant immigrants and laborers while alienating well-to-do natives.

Reformers saw in the budget a means to bring the reality of political life back toward the ideal of responsible representative government. A proper budget system, as defined by the men of the bureau, meant accountable and responsible government. The budget would encompass the government as a whole in a single document and clearly identify its duties and functions. A well-publicized budget would serve as a guide to the people, helping them to comprehend the nature and scope of government activities, thereby providing alienated citizens with a much-needed sense of connection to their government. Ironically, these devotees of concrete facts and figures were essentially myth makers, using the budget to reconstruct the foundations of legitimate government in the United States.

As this book shows, budget reformers developed sophisticated theories for an expert audience and actively marketed a more accessible version of their program to a popular audience through massively attended exhibitions, lectures, pamphlets, and press coverage. The men of the bureau also articulated a model of the citizen as a consumer who used an informed vote to purchase services from the government. The good citizen related to the government primarily by using the budget as a vehicle for self-education and oversight, not through more direct forms of political action. By thus presenting familiarity with the budget as an essential precondition to good citizenship, budget reformers interjected the state, via the budget, into all authoritative public discourse.

The Bureau of Municipal Research was remarkably successful. It proved exceptionally adept at adjusting to the give-and-take of municipal politics and convinced even Tammany Hall to accept the basic principles of budget reform. Beyond New York, the movement spread rapidly via comparable bureaus of municipal research to cities across the country. As the movement extended to the national level, however, it developed new meanings and functions for the budget.

By 1916 a new group of reformers, led by William Willoughby, took the campaign for budget reform to the national level. As Allen, Bruere, and Cleveland used budgets to address the relationship between citizens and local governments, Willoughby concentrated primarily on the budget's power to restructure relations of power and authority within the national government. A budget could identify and bind together the diverse and largely autonomous units of the rapidly growing federal bureaucracy. It would, in effect, create a coherent and self-conscious executive branch where before there had been only individual bureaus and departments.

The passage and implementation of the Budget and Accounting Act of 1921 marked a major turning point in federal governance. Before 1921 administrative departments had dealt directly with Congress, largely bypassing the president in their requests for funds and new programs. Requests for appropriations were not coordinated among departments or compared across time. The Budget and Accounting Act changed all this. It established a Bureau of the Budget to compile, compare, and revise departmental estimates into a single budget for presentation to Congress. During the 1920s, the new bureau created a unitary executive branch by promulgating standard accounts and procedures and establishing a variety of coordinating agencies to build a sense of solidarity and common identity among officials throughout the federal government. As it provided the means to create an executive branch, the Budget and Accounting Act also decisively located control over the administrative apparatus of the national state in the hands of the president. Thus, by the time the United States entered the Great Depression, the movement for budget reform had already laid the foundations for the coordinated exercise of national power under presidential direction which came to characterize the New Deal.

The story of budget reform places the idea of political representation at the heart of citizens' questioning of state authority during the Progressive era. For citizens of all political stripes, the basis of all legitimate state action (or inaction) must lie in its connection to the people. Ultimately, the movement for budget reform sought to address fundamental problems of how to maintain a viable representative democracy in a mass society by offering budgets as a new way to connect citizens to the growing state.

Ironically, the budget reformers' very success in getting people to accept the authority of budgets ultimately undermined their deeper goal of revitalizing representative democracy. Budget reform sought to restore governmental legitimacy by giving the people an effective voice in public affairs. The first budget reformers hoped to educate the public, giving it the information necessary to make responsible decisions about public affairs. All too soon, however, the logic of expert authority subordinated popular concerns to the judgment of professionals who looked to the people merely for a plebiscitary ratification of policies determined to be in the public interest. Originally conceived of as an instrument to enhance popular control over government, the budget evolved (or devolved) into a powerful symbol of legitimacy.

Ultimately, the budget eased the crisis of representative democracy by creating a new myth of representation which secured the acquiescence of citizens in the increased exercise of governmental power over their lives without supplying them with any more real control over that government. Today, the budget tells us that politicians are responsible because they must spend our money according to certain rules. Its mere existence reassures us, regardless of any practical realities of its operation. In the recent rise of budgetary jeremiads, predicting the downfall of the nation due to deficits, debt, and unbalanced budgets, we see, per-

haps, the unraveling of the myth of political representation first introduced by turn-of-the century budget reformers. The myth has diverged
too far from reality to sustain itself and we face, once again, a crisis of
representation—a crisis with its roots in the Progressive era's movement
for budget reform.

1

THE EMERGENCE OF MUNICIPAL
ACCOUNTING REFORM

Before the Civil War, Americans had little interest in and even less use for accounting, governmental or otherwise. The war, that cataclysm of blood and fire which saw the unprecedented expansion of public power to mobilize private resources, changed everything except, perhaps, the way Americans kept (or failed to keep) accounts. Revenue and expenditure, receipts and expense, authorization, allocation, and disbursement all mixed together in a largely undifferentiated mass of cryptic ledgers that resisted interpretation or understanding. Lincoln might stir the country with calls to preserve "government of the people, by the people, [and] for the people," but political accountability, literally rendering an account of government activities to the people, rarely entered the realm of political discourse. Accounting, in short, didn't matter.

Modern accounting techniques and the profession of accounting began to take shape after the Civil War in the railroad industry, where the country's first nationally consolidated corporations were emerging. European capitalists invested in the new enterprises and sent the first professional accountants across the Atlantic to audit and secure their monies. Corporate accounting continued to develop gradually in response to pressures to rationalize management and demonstrate competency to outside investors.

America's major cities also grew larger and more complex following the Civil War. Like the great private corporations of the era, cities such as New York (themselves state-chartered corporations) sought "outside" financing to support their growth and continued operations. Like the European railroads investors, new municipal bondholders and taxpayers developed a heightened interest in how city finances (their monies) were administered. Accounting began to matter.

By 1900, accounting had emerged as a recognized profession, and municipal governments had taken steps to adopt the accounting techniques of private corporations. Municipal accounting also took on political significance as a means to legitimate expanded government activity by ostensibly enabling citizens to hold their elected representative "accountable" for their actions. By the 1910s, reformers would claim, without irony, that "accounting is the handmaiden of democracy."[1]

The gradual awakening of local public officials to the value of accounting occurred in fits and starts in various cities across America but was concentrated most consistently and powerfully in New York City. Propelled by rapid demographic expansion and commercial development, New York City grew into America's first modern metropolis during the last third of the nineteenth century. Local government expanded with the city as grand public works and public welfare programs were instituted to keep pace with the demands of urban industrial life. Between 1870 and 1900, the population of Greater New York more than doubled, from 1,478,103 to 3,437,202, and its economy shifted from a mercantile base to banking and corporate ventures. Investment bankers, lawyers, and corporate officers replaced merchants and manufacturers at the forefront of the city's commercial elite. Immigration brought new ethnic and religious groups to New York, and economic development brought organizations and personnel with new and distinct interests into an increasingly complex and diverse commercial environment.[2]

As New York developed, its government undertook a variety of massive engineering projects, both above and below the city streets, that transformed its citizens' day-to-day encounters with city life. Between 1892 and 1902 New York laid over one thousand miles each of water and sewer mains. By 1902 the city had paved almost eighteen hundred miles of street surface and lined those streets with over sixteen thousand electric and nearly forty-three thousand gas lamps. An extensive aboveground streetcar network traversed New York's modern avenues on shiny new tracks that extended for almost thirteen hundred miles throughout

---

[1] Edward A. Fitzpatrick, "Training Accountants for Public Service," *Journal of Accountancy* 23 (January 1917): 36.

[2] Walter Laidlaw, *Population of the City of New York, 1890–1930* (New York: Cities Census Committee, 1932), 11; David C. Hammack, *Power and Society: Greater New York at the Turn of the Century* (New York: Russell Sage Foundation, 1982), 33–46.

the city, while below the streets New York inaugurated its first subway system in 1904.[3]

The government also undertook such major cultural projects as the expansion of public libraries and the centralization of the public school system. In 1890, there were 198,000 children attending New York City's schools. After consolidation, the Greater New York system contained 544,000 students.[4] Between 1880 and 1896, the appropriations for the Manhattan Board of Education alone increased over 75 percent, from $3,422,307 to $6,042,802.[5]

Government taxation and expenditure grew to support these improvements. The 1890s, in particular, saw an exceptional rise in the city's financial activities. After a period of relative stability in the 1880s, both appropriations and the city's funded debt grew rapidly during the 1890s. From 1874 to 1887 the city's debt increased by a little over $6 million, from approximately $118.2 to $124.5 million. The next year it jumped by $4 million and then $10 million more in 1889. By 1896 the debt had risen to over $186 million. Similarly, appropriations for current expenses remained almost level from 1874 until 1894, increasing only $4 million. Over the next three years, however, annual appropriations grew by almost $11 million.[6]

The city's growth culminated in the Greater New York Charter of 1898, which consolidated the boroughs of Manhattan, the Bronx, Brooklyn, Richmond, and Queens under a single civil authority. The size of consolidated New York's finances dwarfed all other government operations in the United States. One contemporary observer estimated that in 1898 the new city would spend five times as much as New York State, more than one and two-thirds as much as all states combined, and nearly one and one-seventh as much as the federal government itself, while its gross debt would exceed the combined debt of all the states.[7] The rate of city expenditures continued to rise after consolidation, increasing 17 percent between 1898 and 1900.[8] By the turn of the century, New York City stood

---

[3]Jon C. Teaford, *The Unheralded Triumph* (Baltimore: Johns Hopkins University Press, 1984), 219–37.

[4]Ibid., 263.

[5]Edward Dana Durand, *The Finances of New York City* (New York: Macmillan, 1898), 288, 377.

[6]Ibid., 372–75; see also Henry Deforest Baldwin, "The City's Purse," *Municipal Affairs* 1 (1897): 329–62.

[7]Durand, *Finances of New York City*, v–vi.

[8]Milo Ray Maltbie, "Cost of Government in City and State," *Municipal Affairs* 4 (1900): 686.

alone as the greatest single institution of public finance in the country.[9]

New York's grand city government, however, was anything but an independent, autonomous actor. To the contrary, like most city governments of the time, New York was a public corporation, chartered by the state in much the same manner as a private business corporation. As such, it traditionally possessed only those powers expressly delegated to it by state government. In effect, the city had a dual identity: both public and private, yet wholly neither.

As a *public* governmental entity, the city exercised traditional police powers to protect public safety, peace, and health. It even had the power to legislate on certain local matters. As a *private* corporate entity, the city engaged in many proprietary activities, including acquiring or leasing utilities and transportation systems, issuing bonds, and contracting for goods and services. In both capacities, New York was engaged in an incessant tug-of-war with the state legislature over the scope of its powers and jurisdiction.[10]

Throughout the nineteenth century the state legislature granted and then retracted a variety of powers relevant to New York City's self-governance. As early as 1857, the legislature enacted the first of a series of statutes (some later repealed) that transferred oversight of such important operations as the police and health departments to the control of state-appointed commissions.[11] In addition, the state legislature repeatedly passed detailed laws intended to foster its direct management of the business affairs of the city. For example, of 1,284 statutes passed between 1884 and 1889 by the state legislature, 390 related solely to New York City.[12]

[9]In terms of revenues and expenditures, local governments as a whole were the largest component of the U.S. federal system at the turn of the century. In an article on city finances, three economists come to the "provisional conclusion" that local government achieved this prominence only toward the end of the nineteenth century. These findings situate New York at the center of a new phenomenon of rapid and distinctive growth in city administration during the last third of the nineteenth century. See John B. Legler, Richard Sylla, and John J. Wallis, "U.S. City Finances and the Growth of Government, 1850–1902," *Journal of Economic History* 48 (June 1988): 347–56.

[10]Joseph L. Tropea, "Rational Capitalism and Municipal Government: The Progressive Era," *Social Science History* 13 (Summer 1989): 140–42. For a general discussion of the development of city–state relations in American law, see Gerald Frug, "The City as a Legal Concept," *Harvard Law Review* 93 (April 1980): 1059–108.

[11]Howard Lee McBain, *The Law and Practice of Municipal Home Rule* (New York: Columbia University Press, 1916), 7, 36–40.

[12]Ibid., 8–10. Gerald Frug makes the provocative argument that in the nineteenth century state governments consistently restricted city power in an effort to eliminate the city as a viable intermediary between the individual citizen and the state; Frug, "City as a Legal Concept," 1101–40.

Such constant meddling led municipal reformers and machine politicians alike to call for greater "home rule"; that is, greater local control over local affairs. To Tammany, home rule might mean the transfer of power from the Republican state legislature to the local Democratic machine, but political reformers saw home rule as a means to address the profound tensions caused by the city's dual identity. Under the existing system, city officials could never be sure of where the state's power ended and theirs began. The lack of clearly defined boundaries to city authority not only allowed the state to intrude upon local governance, it also opened the door for private business interests to usurp certain of the city's proprietary functions. Indeed, the scandals and corruption that periodically plagued New York during the late nineteenth century (beginning with Boss Tweed in the 1860s and culminating in the great utility and insurance scandals of 1905–6) may be seen, in part, as consequences of the ill-defined nature of the city's authority.

Reformers did not view municipal corruption as a simple matter of breaking the law. As Tammany stalwart George Washington Plunkitt observed, there were plenty of opportunities for "honest graft." So many, in fact, that only a fool would bother to break the law to make money.[13] Corruption typically involved municipal corporations making technically legal contracts with private businesses to provide public goods or services, such as sanitation or transportation, which effectively consigned whole areas of public authority to a twilight zone of quasi-public, quasi-private power where grafters could operate free from oversight or accountability. Political reformers hoped that home rule coupled with accounting reform would enable the city to fix the boundaries of municipal government so that whatever power the city had would remain the city's and no one else's. As the nineteenth century wore on, the battle to define the nature and scope of municipal authority centered on the city's system of financial administration.[14]

NEW YORK CITY'S FINANCIAL ADMINISTRATION

Despite structural constraints and repeated state interference, the everyday administration of New York City's finances remained largely in the hands of local officials. New York's principal organs of financial administration were the Board of Estimate and Apportionment and the De-

[13]William L. Riordan, *Plunkitt of Tammany Hall* (New York: E. P. Dutton, 1963), 3–7.
[14]Tropea, "Rational Capitalism," 140–42. Frug, "City as a Legal Concept," 1059–108.

partment of Finance. The Board of Estimate and Apportionment was perhaps the most powerful political body in the city. It controlled all appropriations made from the city's general fund and acted virtually free from
interference by the Board of Aldermen. When established in 1871, the
board was composed of the mayor, the comptroller, the president of the
Board of Aldermen, the president of the Department of Taxes and Assessments, and the corporation counsel (these last two were appointed by
the mayor). The mayor and his appointed officers controlled a majority
of votes on the board.[15]

In 1901 the state legislature amended the composition of the board to
include the mayor, the comptroller, the president of the Board of Aldermen, and the presidents of each of the five city boroughs. The mayor,
comptroller, and president of the Board of Aldermen each had three votes;
the presidents of the boroughs of Manhattan and Brooklyn each had two
votes; and the remaining three members were given one vote each. Under
the new arrangement elective members held a majority of votes on the
board.[16]

The Department of Finance collected and organized estimates from the
various city departments for presentation to the Board of Estimate and
Apportionment. In March of each year the comptroller issued a report de-
tailing the previous year's receipts and expenditures. In 1901 the department was given the power to examine and revise all the accounts from all
other departments when necessary.[17]

The comptroller, as head of the Department of Finance, exercised a
great deal of influence over the city's financial affairs. As an elected official he had a base of power independent of the mayor or Board of Aldermen. The comptroller supervised the accounts of all city agencies,
prescribing their accounting forms and transferring departmental estimates to the Board of Estimate and Appropriations as a basis for the city
budget. During the year the comptroller conducted regular inspections of
agency accounts and published reports on his findings.[18]

The Board of Aldermen, the city's primary legislative body, had little
more than an advisory role in the city's financial affairs. Under the consolidation of 1898, the board was given the power to reduce (but not in-

[15]Durand, *Finances of New York City*, 253–60.

[16]Frederick Clow, *A Comparative Study of the Administration of City Finances in the
United States, with Special Reference to the Budget* (New York: Macmillan, 1901), 41.

[17]Harold D. Force, "New York City's Revision of Accounts and Methods," *Journal of
Accountancy* 8 (1909): 3.

[18]Durand, *Finances of New York City*, 346–48.

crease) the appropriations submitted by the Board of Estimate and Apportionment. The aldermen, however, had only twenty days in which to review and act upon these appropriations, and their actions were subject to a mayoral veto that could be overridden only by a three-fourths majority.[19]

In 1896 taxes on real property provided approximately 82 percent of the city's current tax revenues, with the remaining 18 percent coming from taxes on personal property. This ratio had been relatively constant since 1880. The persistent imbalance resulted largely from a provision in the tax law that allowed individual taxpayers to make public objections to specific valuations of personal property. Wealthy New Yorkers took advantage of the law to obtain remittance or erasure of their tax assessments. In 1889, for example, 26,184 names were listed on the roles as subject to a tax on personal property. There were 13,174 applications for reduction presented to the commissioners of Taxation and Assessment, who proceeded to erase 11,469 names from the tax roles, leaving only 14,715. Commissioners thereby reduced the value of assessed personal property subject to taxation from a potential of $1.6 billion to $204 million. (A later report revealed that in 1905 there was over $30 million of uncollectible arrears of personal taxes—and that was only on property that had actually been assessed.) Further limiting potential revenue was the general practice of assessing real property at about 40 percent of its full value (occasionally assessments would be as high 60 percent and sometimes as low as 10 percent of full value).[20]

Municipal budget systems of the time fell into three general categories: the simple tax levy, the tax levy preceded by detailed estimates, and the

[19]Ibid., 255–60; Teaford, *Unheralded Triumph*, 14–15; Frederick Shaw, *The History of the New York City Legislature* (New York: Columbia University Press, 1954), 5–25.

[20]Durand, *Finances of New York City*, 190–93; Baldwin, "City's Purse," 343–45. John H. MacCracken, "Taxation of City Real Estate and Improvements on Real Estate as Illustrated in New York City," in *State and Local Taxation: First National Conference Under the Auspices of the National Tax Association* (New York: Macmillan, 1908): 375–97. MacCracken noted that "in the case of the personalty tax, more than one half of the names assessed are stricken out before the levying of the tax and only about half of the remainder is collectible" (385). See also "Taxation of Personal Property in New York State from 1880 to 1913: Report of a Sub-Committee of the Board of Taxes and Assessments of the City of New York," in *Proceedings of the Seventh Annual Conference Under the Auspices of the National Tax Association* (Madison: National Tax Association, 1914): 197–204. The phenomenon of tax evasion among the wealthy was common throughout the North during this period. See C. K. Yearley, *The Money Machines: The Breakdown and Reform of Governmental and Party Finance in the North, 1860–1920* (Albany: State University of New York Press, 1970), 37–74.

tax levy accompanied by detailed appropriations. Small cities commonly employed a simple tax levy that approximated a rudimentary pay-as-you-go system and involved little planning or coordination. Many larger cities based their budgets on detailed estimates. Lacking the force of law, however, mere estimates could be disregarded and were often presented informally or without coherent organization. New York's budget system fell under the third category. The Board of Estimate and Apportionment made annual appropriations carrying the force of law, which fixed expenditures for a year and connected them to the levy of taxes for that year.[21]

Each year the Board of Estimate and Apportionment prepared a provisional budget on or before November 1 based on departmental estimates compiled and organized by the comptroller. The provisional budget was then simultaneously submitted to the Board of Aldermen and published in the *City Record*. After fifteen days (twenty days after 1901), the Board of Aldermen returned the provisional budget to the Board of Estimate and Apportionment, which was then required by law to hold special hearings for the public. The hearings, however, came too late in the process to be considered by the Board of Aldermen, even in their limited advisory capacity, and generally occurred long after the Board of Estimate and Apportionment had already decided upon what it considered to be the proper apportionments.[22]

Despite the detailed nature of the original departmental requests, most appropriations were made in lump sums that did not specify the amounts required for the particular functions or activities of an office. Nor did the final budget classify appropriations according to object of expenditure, such as salaries, wages, equipment, or supplies. Contemporary analysts noted that lack of classification and detail greatly hindered the oversight and administration of the budget after its adoption.[23]

The high proportion of fixed expenditures in the budget severely limited the Board of Estimate and Apportionment's discretionary power over the city's purse. State laws fixed annual charges for state taxes, interest, and debt redemption as well as the number and salaries of all departmental heads, their leading subordinates, judges, officers of the city courts, and the police force. In addition, the state legislature required the city to make certain charitable contributions and often required the city to appropriate money for special purposes such as public works projects.

[21]Clow, *Administration of City Finances*, 25–28.
[22]Durand, *Finances of New York City*, 254–60, 267–68.
[23]Ibid., 265; Yin Ch'u Ma, *The Finances of the City of New York* (New York: Columbia University, 1914), 25–26; Force, "New York City's Revision," 285.

Thus, for example, in 1886 Mayor Grace estimated that almost 60 percent of the city's appropriations were practically out of the control of the Board of Estimate and Apportionment, and in 1902 a prominent advocate of home rule asserted that only 17 percent of the budget could be affected by local authorities.[24]

Despite its limitations, local government wielded considerable power, and presented a worthy prize eagerly sought after by New Yorkers from all walks of life. During the last third of the nineteenth century, a proliferation of competing social and economic elites prevented any single group from dominating the city's political or cultural landscape. The fragmentation of elites opened up political space for well-organized groups of non-elites, including neighborhood economic associations, labor, and religious groups.[25] In the midst of this confusion, the type of men who ran the city remained remarkably consistent: members of the business elite tended to dominate the executive branch, well-educated professionals and experts established themselves in civil service and the various departments, while neighborhood merchants and immigrants remained closest to the Board of Aldermen.[26]

THE CORPORATE MODEL OF CITY GOVERNMENT

Both Tammany and the Republicans (and various reform movements) consistently put business elites and professionals into New York's two most powerful offices, those of the mayor and the comptroller.[27] Nonetheless, political reformers and experts throughout the last third of the century repeatedly assailed New York's financial administration as woefully inadequate. Early attacks in the 1870s from the Tilden Commission and civil service reformers focused on corrupt or inept individuals as the root of the problem. Later critics, such as the National Municipal League during the 1890s, came to focus more on the system and apparatus of financial administration rather than on particular administrators as the key to improving New York's government.

In 1877 the governor appointed the Tilden Commission to "devise a plan for the government of cities in the State of New York" in the after-

---

[24]Durand, *Finances of New York City*, 260–61; John G. Agar, "Legislative Interference in New York," *Municipal Affairs* 6 (June 1902): 205.
[25]Hammack, *Power and Society*, 27–36, 103–18.
[26]Teaford, *Unheralded Triumph*, 5–7.
[27]Ibid., 43–60.

math of the Tweed ring scandals. The commission identified soaring municipal debt and the excessive increase in annual current expenditures as two of the chief evils existing in the government of cities. Three principal causes of these evils were "incompetent and unfaithful governing boards and officers," "the introduction of State and National Politics into municipal affairs," and "the assumption by the Legislature of the direct control of local affairs."[28]

The commission proposed that New York restrict urban suffrage to taxpaying property holders and give control over city revenues to a local board of finance. Its members believed that the main object of local government was "to secure faithful administration of financial trusts—to place the control of enormous sums of money in the hands of those who will see that they are applied to their proper uses." The commission viewed the city more as a private corporation than as a body politic and so argued that only "prudent stockholders" with an interest in the corporation should be allowed to choose "guardians" to manage its affairs.[29] Though unsuccessful, attempts to restrict suffrage cast electoral reform essentially as a means to improve the administration of the city's finances (that is, to keep city finances out of the hands of Tammany and its immigrant supporters).

The commission's use of the corporate analogy was not without foundation. New York, in fact, was a municipal corporation, chartered by the state and subject to its strict control. State law defined and protected basic rights. The city's primary purpose, as many reformers saw it, was simply to administer local property interests.

New York's civil service reformers also used the corporate analogy in the 1880s. The Civil Service Reform Association of New York proclaimed that civil service was "the same as the business service of a corporation or a mercantile firm" because it "deals with revenue and expenditure, with accounts, bookkeeping, and records." Public officials therefore needed the same qualities as good businessmen: "capacity, honesty, and experience." The association concluded that "public business differs from private business only in the fact that any pecuniary loss incurred through negligence or dishonesty falls upon a larger number of persons."[30]

28"Excerpts from the Report of the Tilden Commission," *Municipal Affairs* 3 (1899): 434.

29Ibid., 436–38; Durand, *Finances of New York City*, 281–85. For a general discussion of contemporary attempts to restrict suffrage based on analogies to the corporate model, see Yearley, *Money Machines*, 19–34.

30Civil Service Reform Association of New York, *Purposes of the Civil Service Reform Association* (New York: Civil Service Reform Association, 1882).

The association's appropriation of the corporate model was highly selective; its members wished not to emulate the corporation itself so much as the men who ran the corporations. The association had identified accounting methods as a link between municipal and private corporations, but it chose to focus solely on the qualities of individual administrators—capacity, honesty, and experience—as the key to reform. Such admiration for the business executive coincided neatly with the rise of well-educated professionals and experts to positions of control in modern corporations—men of the same background and status as many civil service reformers.[31]

The Tilden Commission and the Civil Service Reform Association, however, aimed less to bring better men into the city bureaucracy than to restrict popular participation in local government. The commission used outright restrictions on suffrage that would limit electoral participation to well-to-do property owners, the association a system of exams and qualifications that would favor the well educated or professionally trained. Since men from the city's social and economic elite already staffed many important positions in local government, the effect of many civil service reforms would be not so much to change the type of men in office as to cut the ties that bound them to society's "less desirable" elements. In effect, both organizations worked to interpose the cultural standards and economic status of the cultivated, property-holding mugwump as a barrier between the common citizen and city government.

Both the commission and the association finessed issues of democratic rights by recasting local government as an essentially private enterprise. They attempted to justify fundamentally antidemocratic policies by arguing that city administration was not wholly of the public sphere. These mugwump reformers wanted to keep elites in office to protect their property from the growing urban masses pressing to enter and influence the system. Suffrage restrictions and civil service requirements insulated well-to-do administrators from the unwashed masses who, reformers asserted, had no right to any say in essentially private matters of property and business.

[31]On the rise of well-educated professionals in modern corporations, see Hammack, *Power and Society*, 52–55; Alfred D. Chandler, Jr., *The Visible Hand* (Cambridge: Harvard University Press, 1977), 377–484. On the social and economic background of mugwump social reformers, see Gerald McFarland, *Mugwumps, Morals, and Politics* (Amherst: University of Massachusetts Press, 1975), 107–25, 201–6. For a general discussion of mugwump views of government as similar to those of business, see Yearley, *Money Machines*, 32–34.

ACCOUNTING, PUBLICITY, AND CORPORATE POWER

The absence of accounting from the agenda of early municipal reform movements evidenced a failure to keep up with current developments in business administration. The period between 1870 and World War I witnessed the emergence of the modern industrial corporation as a large, integrated business enterprise containing many distinct operating units managed by salaried executives. Railroads led the way, devising modern organizational structures and accounting procedures as early as the 1850s. Other enterprises critical to the country's basic infrastructure, such as telegraph and steamship networks, soon followed. To facilitate corporate growth, business leaders perfected the legal form of the holding company during the 1870s and developed intricate managerial hierarchies to control the administration of the sprawling new enterprises. Corporations increasingly looked to outside capital, especially from Europe, to meet the enormous cost of building major communications and transportation systems.[32]

Effective administration of diversified enterprises with complex managerial hierarchies required a steady flow of timely information to evaluate the performance of various departments and their managers. In the 1870s, American railroads began to adopt truly modern accounting practices in response to pressure from European capitalists who sent over independent auditors to compile accurate financial reports before investing. Foremost among the new imports were English and Scottish accountants, who brought with them more sophisticated accounting techniques and a more highly developed sense of professionalism.[33] The new accountants transformed not only the practice but also the practitioners of American accounting, inspiring the creation of professional societies such as the Institute of Accountants and Bookkeepers (founded in 1882) and the American Association of Public Accountants (founded in 1886).[34]

American accountants soon evolved from simple bookkeepers into an organized profession with recognized expertise in financial administration. In 1896 New York became the first state to pass a law providing for

[32]Chandler, *Visible Hand*, 1–2, 90–94, 144–88, 288.

[33]Ibid., 109–17; James Don Edwards, *History of Public Accounting in the United States* (East Lansing: Michigan State University Press, 1960), 47–48; Gary John Previts and Barbara Dubis Merino, *A History of Accounting in America* (New York: Wiley, 1979) 75–86; Michael Chatfield, *A History of Accounting Thought* (Hinsdale, Ill.: Dryden Press, 1974), 273–76.

[34]Chatfield, *Accounting Thought*, 125; Edwards, *Public Accounting*, 50–61, 83; Previts and Merino, *Accounting in America*, 75–94.

the certification of public accountants. By 1905 public accountants had organized twenty-one state professional societies and eight state governments had enacted licensing laws similar to New York's.[35]

As outside capital came to play a more significant role in corporate finance, ownership of large corporate enterprises increasingly became divorced from control. Not only Europeans but also stock- and bondholders throughout America came to "own" business enterprises while professional managers came to control them.[36] Publicity, in the form of accounting reports, became increasingly important for attracting and retaining investment. It presented credible summaries of corporate performance to potential investors and legitimized the ongoing exercise of corporate power by managers who were not themselves owners of the enterprise. Accounting publicity thus facilitated the emergence of integrated industrial enterprises that by the end of the century had come to dominate many of the nation's most vital industries.[37]

The rapid rise of such powerful institutions to preeminence aroused fear and resentment among large segments of American society.[38] To quell popular apprehensions, businesses soon extended the use of accounting publicity to legitimize the exercise of corporate power beyond major private investors to the public at large. Governments, both state and federal, played a significant role in transforming accounts from an instrument of internal bookkeeping into a tool of public relations. In 1887 the Interstate Commerce Act required railroads to file annual reports in accordance with standards set by the statisticians of the newly created Interstate Commerce Commission. By 1900 nearly one-half of the states had passed corporations acts requiring some kind of reporting to stockholders. Simi-

[35]Previts and Merino, *Accounting in America*, 91; Paul J. Miranti, Jr., *Accountancy Comes of Age: The Development of an American Profession, 1886–1940* (Chapel Hill: University of North Carolina Press, 1990), 48. For a complete discussion of the emergence of the movement to gain state certification for public accountants, see Miranti, *Accountancy Comes of Age*, 48–68. Miranti's book is especially helpful as it places accounting in the context of the extensive literature of professionalization; see, e.g., Paul Starr, *The Social Transformation of American Medicine* (New York: Basic Books, 1982); Thomas Haskell, *The Emergence of Professional Social Science* (Urbana: University of Illinois Press, 1977); Burton Bledstein, *The Culture of Professionalism* (New York: Norton, 1976); Mary O. Furner, *Advocacy and Objectivity: A Crisis in the Professionalization of American Social Science, 1865–1905* (Lexington: University Press of Kentucky, 1975); and Laurence Veysey, *The Emergence of the American University* (Chicago: University of Chicago, 1965).

[36]Previts and Merino, *Accounting in America*, 77.

[37]Chandler, *Visible Hand*, 285.

[38]For the classic study of this phenomenon, see Grant McConnell, *Private Power and American Democracy* (New York: Alfred A. Knopf, 1966).

larly, as of 1899, the New York Stock Exchange required all corporations applying for a listing to agree to publish annual balance sheets and income statements.[39]

More than simply gaining passive acceptance, accounting publicity encouraged and sustained broad public participation in the financial markets. By 1893 there were an estimated 1.25 million shareholders out of a population of 62 million in the United States.[40] The expansion of the shareholding public increased the pressure on corporations to continue a steady flow of publicity sufficient to maintain public trust.

Henry Clews, a prominent broker and chairman of the New York Stock Exchange, was acutely aware of the power of publicity and the role professional accountants might play in conferring legitimacy through "scientific" audits. Writing in 1906, he urged any corporations and banking and mercantile firms that became "objects of suspicion" to "speedily clear themselves by inviting the fullest examination and publicity." Clews recommended the use of certified accountants to restore public confidence because their findings "would be accepted as conclusive of the actual conditions being as they stated and described, they would speak with authority." He concluded with an enthusiastic call for "more light—the light of PUBLICITY."[41]

Clews recognized the accountant's potential as a publicist whose expert status could stabilize financial markets by inspiring confidence. For Clews, accounting was not a simple matter of improving fiscal management; it was about presenting the *appearance* of responsible administration to investors and to the public at large.

The Political Uses of Accounting Reform

Rising concern with the public aspects of private corporate accounts fostered a similar interest in the accounts of the public municipal corporation. Reformers who had already adopted the corporation as the mod-

---

[39]Chatfield, *Accounting Thought*, 273–76; Edward Chase Kirkland, *Industry Comes of Age* (Chicago: Quadrangle, 1961), 102–4; Previts and Merino, *Accounting in America*, 87–89. The Massachusetts Board of Railroad Commissioners under the direction of Charles Francis Adams was among the first to require public access to standardized accounts. See Thomas K. McCraw, *Prophets of Regulation* (Cambridge: Harvard University Press, 1984), 23–24.

[40]Previts and Merino, *Accounting in America*, 77.

[41]Henry Clews, "Publicity and Reform in Business," *Annals of the American Academy of Political and Social Science* 28 (July 1906): 143, 144, 154.

el for city administration readily assimilated the techniques of corporate accounting into their analyses of municipal finance. What they discovered with their new skills was a system in disarray; a chaotic jumble of facts and figures masquerading as accounting but providing little, if any, useful information.

In 1898 Edward Dana Durand, a former New York State legislative librarian (and later director of the U.S. Bureau of the Census), published a detailed and highly influential study of New York City's finances, which provided a basis for many contemporary efforts to reform municipal accounting. Durand found that what was technically called the budget (appropriations for current expenses funded by tax receipts) did not include all classes of recurrent income and outlay, especially those connected with street improvement and debt redemption (both significant items)—a fact which, as Durand put it, "keeps many citizens from appreciating the full magnitude of the city's business." Moreover, the figures that the budget did contain were derived from financial statements that employed different accounting methods at different times, making it close to impossible to compile accurate records. Unreliable figures led to repeated irregularities. For example, the comptroller reported recurrent receipts for 1896 as twice what they should have been by Durand's estimate.[42] In short, the city's accounting methods were inaccurate, incomplete, and inconsistent over time. Durand concluded that it was "practically impossible for citizens, or for officers whose duties are not specially connected with the accounts, to understand them and detect errors or frauds."[43]

Durand was generous. An earlier report from the New York State Senate Committee on Cities concluded that "the system of accounting in the several cities is more unintelligible and chaotic even than the laws under which the cities themselves are administered," and that as a result it was "impossible for anyone, either in private life or public office to tell what the exact business condition of any city is in the State of New York."[44]

---

[42]Durand, *Finances of New York City*, vi, 173, 177–79.

[43]Ibid., 352. Among other inadequacies identified by contemporary observers were "salary padding" and unsegregated lump sum appropriations. See Ma, *Finances of the City of New York*, 15–26.

[44]New York Senate Doc., 1891, no. 80, pt. 5, 10, 20–22. Such a primitive accounting system was hardly unique to New York. Most cities and towns in the United States did not issue financial reports. The few cities that did provide for some sort of financial reporting issued confused documents of little use to anyone. For example, in 1895 the Milwaukee comptroller issued a 290-page report in which expenditures were classified only according to the funds on which checks were drawn. Boston's annual report for 1890 lists the trustees of the public library for the past thirty-nine years, yet contains no figures concerning the

Local governments did, on occasion, call on professional accountants for assistance. In 1897, on the eve of consolidation, Brooklyn established the Board of Expert Examiners to report on the financial condition of the city. The board was led by Charles Waldo Haskins, cofounder of the accounting firm of Haskins and Sells and one of the first public accountants to be certified under New York's new licensing law. In form and substance, Haskins's study of Brooklyn resembled a corporate audit; its purpose was to examine the city's books to assess its current financial condition, but it did not examine the efficiency of municipal operations or use the information obtained as a basis for oversight, evaluation, or planning.[45]

Haskins epitomized a new type of relationship between private enterprise and the public municipal corporation: the expert outside consultant. Unlike traction or utility companies, the consultant did not take on public functions under a license or franchise granted by the government. Rather, he provided a service directly to the government itself and influenced public policy. Yet Haskins and his associates remained outsiders, returning to their businesses after completing the report. They did not remain a part of the government they analyzed, nor did their presence permanently alter the balance or structure of power within city government.

Haskins, therefore, did not usurp government functions. He served as a conduit to funnel working knowledge of private business practices into the world of public governmental administration. In contrast to those enterprising capitalists who tried to make government more "businesslike" by directly appropriating its activities through a franchise or contract, Haskins and others like him sought to make government more businesslike by imposing business practices on government administration.

The consolidation of Greater New York in 1898 compounded the problems identified by Haskins and Durand. Integrating the primitive accounting systems of the five boroughs confounded the city's financial officers, bringing them, too, to appreciate the need for accounting reform. The comptroller, unable to issue his report for 1898 until July 31, 1901, complained that "the accounts of the various municipal corporations included within the consolidated territory were so incomplete, and in such

---

new library then under construction. See James H. Potts, "The Evolution of Municipal Accounting in the United States: 1900–1935," *Business History Review* 52 (Winter, 1978): 519–20; for a general discussion of the state of city finances at the turn of the century, see Clow, *Administration of City Finances*, and C. W. Tooke, "Uniformity in Municipal Finance," *Municipal Affairs* 2 (1898): 195–206 (focusing on cities in New York and Illinois).

[45] *Report of Expert Accountants to the Comptroller of the City of New York* (New York: Martin B. Brown, 1898).

bad order as to render it impossible to transcribe them on the books of the new City." As late as 1907 the comptroller was still trying to catch up, issuing his report for 1905 over a year late.[46]

During the 1890s, the sorry state of the city's accounts began to draw the attention of municipal reform organizations. Among the first to integrate accounting into its reform program was the National Municipal League. Organized in 1894 through the efforts of the City Club of New York and the Municipal League of Philadelphia, the National Municipal League acted as an umbrella organization to bring together and coordinate the work of good government associations throughout the country.[47]

In 1900 the league published *A Municipal Program*, which included five proposed state constitutional amendments, a model Municipal Corporations Act, and several essays on particular aspects of municipal reform, including public accounting.[48] In one essay, Leo S. Rowe reasoned that like a business's annual financial report, intelligible municipal accounts would enable the public "shareholders" to enforce responsibility among the public "directors" of the city.[49] Efficiency and economy certainly were goals of the program, but political accountability was primary to both, and the key to accountability was publicity. As Albert Shaw, editor of the *American Review of Reviews*, wrote elsewhere in the *Program*, "There is no check more salutary than the check of publicity."[50]

The publication of *A Municipal Program* in 1900 marked the arrival of accounting reform on the municipal scene. Its recommendations were so well received that the league followed up in 1901 by establishing a standing Committee on Uniform Municipal Accounts and Statistics to further develop an improved system of uniform reporting and continue to spread the gospel of accounting reform. The committee, in turn, sponsored a Conference on Uniform Municipal Accounts that brought together representatives from twelve organizations to discuss and coordinate

[46]New York City, Department of Finance, *Comptroller's Report, 1898* (New York: Martin B. Brown, 1901), 11; idem, *Comptroller's Report, 1905* (New York: Martin B. Brown, 1907), xiii.

[47]Frank Mann Stewart, *A Half Century of Municipal Reform* (Berkeley: University of California Press, 1950), 21.

[48]Ibid., 11–25; Horace Deming, "A Municipal Reform Program," *Annals of the American Academy of Political and Social Science* 17 (1901): 431–32; National Municipal League, *A Municipal Program* (New York: Macmillan, 1900).

[49]Leo S. Rowe, "Public Accounting Under the Proposed Municipal Program," in National Municipal League, *Municipal Program*, 90–91.

[50]Albert Shaw, "The City in the United States—The Proper Scope of its Activities," in National Municipal League, *Municipal Program*, 72.

activities to promote uniform municipal accounts. Among those represented were the American Economic Association (which had itself established a special Committee on Uniform Accounts and Statistics the year before), the American Society of Civil Engineers, the American Society of Municipal Improvements, the American Public Health Association, and numerous public utility associations. By 1904 seven major cities, including New York, Chicago, and Boston, had adopted one or more schedules from the uniform system of accounts developed by the league, prompting Harvey Chase, a prominent Boston public accountant and member of the league's Committee on Uniform Municipal Accounting and Statistics, to remark that "the movement for uniform municipal reports and accounts has now reached the point where it may be considered safely established as a matter which must be reckoned with by every progressive city."[51]

The league's municipal program asserted that publicizing accurate financial reports would serve several purposes. First, accounting publicity would allow the public to make informed decisions about their political representatives. Second, it would provide a means to control public service corporations (grantees of municipal franchises), which seemed to be exercising an ever-increasing influence over city affairs. Third, it would promote financial stability and enhance the credit of the city. Fourth, it would provide a basis of comparison among cities, allowing each to learn from the experience of the others. Fifth, it would facilitate central administrative control by the state over such functions as collecting state taxes, and it would enhance the state's oversight of city activities.[52]

The league saw accounting reform as a means for local governments to obtain public support, business investment, and home rule. Ironically, saving money seemed to be almost incidental to the program's recommendations. Similarly, the municipal program paid little attention to the potential use of accounts as an instrument of internal operational control over the management of city departments. This may be explained, in part, by the fact that although most cities' accounts were unintelligible, their actual financial condition was fairly solid. Indeed, it was under these ar-

---

[51]Edward Hartwell, "Report of the Committee on Uniform Municipal Accounting," and M. N. Baker, "Report of the Conference on Uniform Municipal Accounts," in National Municipal League, *Proceedings of the Rochester Conference for Good City Government* (New York: National Municipal League, 1901), 248 and 255–63; Hartwell, "Report of the Committee on Uniform Municipal Accounts and Statistics," and Harvey Chase, "Practical Application of the Schedules for Uniform Municipal Reports and Accounts," in National Municipal League, *Proceedings of the Chicago Conference for Good City Government* (New York: National Municipal League, 1904), 199 and 228.

[52]Rowe, "Public Accounting," 92–97.

chaic accounting systems that local governments had accomplished the "unheralded triumph" of building the modern metropolis.[53] The successful growth of city administration also indicates that, like Henry Clews, the league was primarily concerned that accounting reform project an *image* of improved administration to potential investors. The league, however, had a much broader view of "investment": beyond the dollars of municipal bondholders, it also hoped to obtain for the city increased confidence from the public at large and ultimately a greater delegation of political power from the state government.

Contrary to much of the campaign rhetoric in turn-of-the-century New York, many accounting reformers acknowledged the limited role Tammany corruption played in the city's finances. They realized that much of the city's budget was not under the control of local politicians but was mandated by state legislation and ongoing obligations such as debt servicing. Thus, for example, in reviewing the administration of Tammany's Robert Van Wyck, the first mayor of Greater New York, Milo Roy Maltbie, editor of *Municipal Affairs* and later secretary of the National Municipal League's Committee on Uniform Municipal Accounts and Statistics, acknowledged that "a large proportion of the increased cost under the Tammany regime is due to mandatory legislation enacted by the state legislature, which is and has been controlled for many years by the Republican Party."[54] Similarly, Edward Durand found that New York's existing financial system, as inadequate as it was in 1897, had "secured a fair degree of official responsibility and honesty, so far as purely financial matters are concerned."[55]

---

[53]New York's experience was fairly typical in this regard. Chastened by the huge debts incurred under the Tweed ring in the late 1860s and the instability wrought by the Panic of 1873, city administrators embarked on a period of retrenchment, reducing the debt 25 percent by 1886. Further aiding the effort to put the city on a sound financial basis was the steady decline of interest rates during the last two decades of the century from an average of 6.1 percent in 1880 to only 3.9 percent by 1895. Although New York's debt began to rise again rapidly during the 1890s, this was due more to the attractiveness of the municipal bond market than to fiscal mismanagement. With retrenchment on debt came a concerted effort to keep taxes as low as possible. After peaking at $2.94 per $100 of assessed value in 1875, the real estate tax rate fell more or less steadily to $1.72 in 1895. Although city spending began to rise thereafter, in part to meet the new demands of Greater New York after consolidation in 1898, assessed valuation of property increased to keep pace with growing expenditures so that the tax rate stabilized and remained nearly uniform after consolidation. See Teaford, *Unheralded Triumph*, 283–306; Durand, *Finances of New York City*, 373–75; Maltbie, "Cost of Government," 686–87.

[54]Maltbie, "Cost of Government," 689.

[55]Durand, *Finances of New York City*, 354–55.

This is not to say that reformers were blind to Tammany's misuse of city funds. To the contrary, both Maltbie and Durand clearly acknowledged that Tammany extravagance, inefficiency, and abuse of official power had wasted "a not inconsiderable" amount of the city's funds. Indeed, they saw the misuse of funds as inextricably linked to the state legislature's persistent interference. The state would not trust local government with more power until it was convinced that such power would be protected from abuse and corruption.

Advocates of home rule argued that a reformed system of accounts would provide just such protection. Exposing accounts to the light of day, they reasoned, would effectively insulate local government from clandestine manipulation.[56] Moreover, matters of local concern could be handled more efficiently by local governing officials, who best understood the needs and concerns of their immediate constituents. A proper system of uniform accounting and statistics would both promote administrative efficiency and "help an intelligent and informed local public opinion to determine the local policy and control the conduct of local government."[57] To advocates of home rule, municipal efficiency was thus in part a function of the responsiveness of the government to local concerns: the more democratic a government was, the more efficient it became. Published accounts furnished both the basic instrument of control for keeping local government responsive to local concerns and the technical apparatus to make it efficient.

Under this scheme, a reformed system of accounts was also to provide a mechanism of ongoing oversight through regular reports made to a state board of audit or similar body. In return for relinquishing a measure of their power, state officials would gain greater access to accurate and reliable financial data.[58] Advocates of home rule argued, in short, that the state should give greater power to the city because accounting publicity would provide sufficient constraints to ensure that the city exercised its new power responsibly. They sought to empower the municipality by limiting it.

[56]For example, accounting publicity would clearly establish the nature and extent of municipal franchises granted to private companies, thereby preventing them from pilfering from the public coffers or corrupting public officials. See Rowe, "Public Accounting," 92–97. See also Maltbie, "Cost of Government," 692–93; Durand, *Finances of New York City*, 355; Agar, "Legislative Interference," 203–5.

[57]Horace Deming, "Public Opinion and City Government under the Proposed Municipal Program," in National Municipal League, *Municipal Program*, 251.

[58]Frank Goodnow, *Municipal Home Rule* (New York: Macmillan, 1897), 20–32; Horace Deming, "The Municipal Problem in the United States," in National Municipal League, *Municipal Program*, 52–57; Tooke, "Uniformity in Municipal Finance," 203.

The National Municipal League's approach to solving the problems of the modern metropolis, especially its emphasis on the democratic character of the reform, diverged significantly from the remedies proposed earlier by the Tilden Commission and civil service reformers. Each group, in its own way, was concerned with the changing relationship between citizen and government brought on by the rapid urban growth of the late nineteenth century.[59] In New York, urban growth and its attendant demographic and economic transformations shook the dominance of traditional mercantile elites while fostering the emergence of the Tammany machine as an avenue of access to political power for new immigrant and working classes. Alarmed by this development, the men of the Tilden Commission and the Civil Service Reform Association proposed reforms that would limit popular access to and participation in government. They responded to the rise of "undesirable" citizens by constricting the boundaries of citizenship.

The accounting reformers of the 1890s and early 1900s responded to the same challenge quite differently. To them the most dangerous consequence of urban expansion was the attenuation of relations between citizens and their government. As R. Fulton Cutting, president of the Citizens Union and first treasurer of the National Municipal League, stated, "[The voter] needs to feel his government is proximate, not alien; that its activity is tangible and fraternal rather than oratorical and remote."[60] To reach out to alienated citizens, accounting reformers began to explore the possibilities not of limiting but of expanding popular participation in government through accounting reform. The information provided by accounts would provide citizens with hitherto unknown access to and control over their government. Accounting information, however, could also domesticate or channel popular participation into ac-

[59]For example, in discussing the benefits of giving the comptroller increased powers under the proposed municipal program, Leo S. Rowe wrote, "With such a combination of powers there is every reason to expect that the office will attract men of the very highest quality" ("Public Accounting," 97). For a consideration of civil service reform and efficiency, see Martin J. Schiesl, *The Politics of Efficiency: Municipal Administration and Reform in America, 1800–1920,* (Berkeley: University of California Press, 1977), 38–39.

[60]R. Fulton Cutting, *The Citizens Union: Its Origin and Purpose* (New York: Winthrop Press, 1903), 5. Jon Teaford argues persuasively that the crisis of late nineteenth-century American cities was more one of image than of structure, that "the system proved reasonably successful in providing services, but there was no prevailing ideology to validate this operation." *Unheralded Triumph,* 10. This crisis, however, was no less real for being one of image. It was very much this problem of popular perception, of citizen apathy and alienation, that Cutting and other accounting reformers sought to address.

ceptable, nonthreatening avenues of expression. The new urban masses would participate in government but would be guided by information provided to them by experts and professionals. Moreover, they would act primarily as voters rather than office seekers or political activists. Accounting reform aimed to displace the immigrant and working class democracy of the machine with a revitalized middle class democracy of educated voters.

From its inception, then, accounting reform involved much more than simply keeping track of money. The logic of urban development may have dictated the adoption of some type of accounting reform, but the time, place, and manner of its adoption imbued this seemingly most transparent of reforms with many and varied shades of meaning and power. In turn-of-the-century New York, accounting reform implicated fundamental issues of political participation, capital investment, city-state relations, and the responsible exercise of power.

In a more general sense, accounting reform of this era concerned redrawing the boundaries of political life. Accounting—and its publicity—were meant to ensure that private corporations operating municipal franchises would not overstep the bounds of their proper authority by recording and reporting to the public the nature and scope of their activities. Accounting would also provide the oversight necessary to convince state legislatures to redefine city–state relations by granting cities greater power. Finally, this distinctively political conception of accounting contained the germ of an emerging vision of comprehensive budget reform that would extend the boundaries of citizenship to include all residents of the metropolis while narrowing the definition of acceptable popular political activity to the casting of an informed ballot.

2 THE NEW YORK BUREAU OF MUNICIPAL RESEARCH

By the end of the nineteenth century, accounting reformers had begun to appreciate the political implications of their work. In relating municipal accounting to home rule and suffrage, reformers had touched upon the broader uses of administrative data in a modern urban democracy, but their ideas were tentative and unfocused. It was not until about 1905 that a new movement for budgetary reform made a systematic and sustained effort to explore fully the political potential of administrative reorganization. By 1912 the movement was well on the way to obtaining nationwide acceptance of a new idea of budgeting as the key to public administration.

Budget reform became a distinctive, coherent, and powerful movement through the efforts of a small band of reformers at the New York Bureau of Municipal Research. More than perhaps any other civic program of the era, budget reform owed its success to a single, clearly defined group. The men of the bureau not only originated the idea of budget reform, they invested the budget itself with meaning and purpose. They created the *idea* of budget reform, which they actively promulgated throughout New York and then throughout the whole country. They distinguished the concept of the budget from that of simple accounting, casting the budget not merely as a tool of efficiency but as the key to maintaining responsible democratic government in modern mass society. In the course of a few short years the men of the bureau transformed the way America viewed and administered government finances.[1]

[1]Between 1911 and 1919, forty-four states passed budget laws, and by 1929, every state but Arkansas had adopted a budgetary system on the executive model. Leonard D. White, *Trends in Public Administration* (New York: McGraw-Hill, 1933), 34.

In 1905 expert accountants campaigning for improved fiscal administration and social reformers combatting corruption in city government came together with the idea of creating an independent citizen agency to apply scientific principles of observation to investigate and reform municipal government. To this end, they joined forces to found the Bureau of City Betterment in 1906, which they formally incorporated in 1907 as the New York Bureau of Municipal Research.

The bureau's staff included both accounting experts and social reformers, several with settlement house experience, and placed accounting and budget reform at the heart of its program to improve municipal administration. Independent of government ties or explicit partisan affiliations, the bureau allowed professional reformers to propose concrete initiatives that directly altered the structure of municipal administration, while capitalizing on their status as experts to maintain a cooperative relationship with government officials as equal partners in municipal reform.

Despite accounting's new prominence, the mechanics of implementing and administering new accounting systems had yet to be worked out. Reform groups such as the National Municipal League drew on accountants' expertise but their recommendations remained abstract; their programs did not directly engage particular municipal governments in any sustained dialogue over how to implement specific recommendations. For their part, city officials, recognizing the need to implement concrete accounting reforms, took some tentative steps to enlist the technical services of local accountants as temporary consultants but had not as yet fully incorporated accounting expertise into municipal administration.

Gradually, certain accountants (and their sponsors) began to make the move from being occasional consultants to acting as full-time participants in municipal administration. By using their newly acquired status as professionals and experts to insinuate themselves into the day-to-day operations of city government, they began to translate general programs of accounting reform into specific practices in particular city governments. Accountants began the century as occasional hirelings responding only when called on for technical assistance, but they concluded its first decade ensconced in permanent positions of authority both inside and outside of government, from which position they actively shaped municipal administration.[2]

---

[2]For general discussions of the development of municipal accounting during the early 1900s, see James H. Potts, "The Evolution of Municipal Accounting in the United States: 1900–1935," *Business History Review* 52 (Winter 1978): 518–36; Potts, "The Evolution of Budgetary Accounting Theory and Practice in Municipal Accounting from 1870," *Accounting Historians Journal* 4 (Spring 1977): 89–100.

With the institutionalization of accounting reform came new definitions of its meaning and purposes.[3] Professional accountants staked their newly acquired authority on their status as nonpartisan, scientific experts. Early advocates of accounting reform, therefore, fit neatly into the division between politics and administration described by Woodrow Wilson as early as 1887 and fully developed into a theory of modern governance by Frank Goodnow in 1900: expert administrators would compile the data and then turn it over to politicians for them to act upon as they saw fit.[4]

Separating politics and administration well served those seeking to promote municipal home rule or obtain investors for city bonds. Both state legislators and potential investors would want a clear, objective picture of a city's finances before surrendering either control or cash to its administrators. Some civic reformers, however, were expressly concerned with accounting's impact on broader issues of democratic governance in a modern metropolis. First in New York City and then throughout the country, they began to subsume the technical problems of municipal accounting within the larger framework of a campaign to reform their cities' entire budgetary systems.

Many cities in the United States had long had some sort of "budget," but it was generally little more than a bare appropriations bill.[5] The campaign for budget reform aimed to transform the budget from mere legislation into a "machine for the administrative control of the City government."[6] Simple accounting reform as propounded by the National Municipal League and others at the turn of the century was a central yet subsidiary component of that machine. Accounting allowed administrators to collect and compile data in accessible and intelligible form, but

[3]The theme of the institutionalization of progressive reform within civic organizations is explored in Richard Skolnick, "The Crystallization of Reform in New York City, 1890–1917" (Ph.D. diss., Yale University, 1964).

[4]See Woodrow Wilson, "The Study of Administration," *Political Science Quarterly* 2 (June 1887): 197–222; and Frank Goodnow, *Politics and Administration* (New York: Macmillan, 1900). These men tried to reconcile a commitment to democracy with growing concerns for efficiency by separating politics from administration. Politics was the realm of democratic action. Administration was the province of trained professionals who applied scientific principles of efficient management. The latter was to be subordinate to, yet free from meddling by, the former.

[5]For a contemporary assessment of the sorry state of municipal financial administration, see Benjamin Parke De Witt, *The Progressive Movement* (New York: Macmillan, 1915), 321–22.

[6]Tilden Adamson, "Budget Making: A Lecture Delivered before the Training School for Public Service Conducted by the New York Bureau of Municipal Research, January 22, 1913," Papers of the Institute of Public Administration, New York.

a modern budgetary system would provide the comprehensive structure and procedure for both politicians and administrators necessary to plan, set priorities, and oversee administration.

Accounting appeared to be an objective system, an administrative creature devoid of political implications. Budgeting, at least as developed during the first decade of the twentieth century, was more problematic. Its authority derived from the supposed separation of politics and administration, yet in practice it seemed to permeate the wall between the two, serving both as an apparently neutral tool of administrative efficiency and as a basis for legislative policy. As early as 1898, in his influential textbook on public finance, Henry Carter Adams recognized the dual nature of the budget when he observed that "in its first stage the budget is a report, in its second stage it becomes a project of law."[7] Budget reformers embraced the budget's duality and elaborated upon it, insisting that a proper system of financial administration was necessary and distinctive to a modern urban democracy.

FROM CONSULTATION TO PARTICIPATION

In 1901 New York passed a law requiring one of the city's two commissioners of accounts to be a certified public accountant (CPA)[8] That same year, revisions to the city charter centralized control over all the "fiscal concerns" of the municipal corporation in the Department of Finance and authorized the department to examine and revise the accounts of the other departments when necessary.[9] Two years later, Comptroller Edward Grout called upon three CPAs attached to the city's Bureau of Municipal Accounts and Statistics to address demands for a more clear and intelligible presentation of the city's financial transactions in the annual comptroller's report. Grout acted largely in response to accounting reforms suggested by the Merchants' Association of New York, which had formed the Committee on Revision of City Accounts to formulate better accounting methods for city departments. Grout's experts derided the Merchants' Association suggestions as incomplete and based on inadequate knowledge of accounting principles. Nonetheless, their report followed

[7]Henry Carter Adams, *The Science of Finance* (New York: Henry Holt, 1898), 105.
[8]Harold Seidman, *Investigating Municipal Administration* (New York: Institute of Public Administration, Columbia University, 1941), 32.
[9]Harold D. Force, "New York City's Revision of Accounts and Methods," *Journal of Accountancy* 8 (May 1909): 4.

the association's lead, making its own suggestions on how to make the city's accounts more uniform and intelligible. Grout implemented many of these suggestions in his report for 1902 (published two years late because of continued difficulties in deciphering the accounts of the various jurisdictions brought together under the 1898 consolidation).[10]

Both the Merchants' Association and Grout used the comptroller's report as an instrument of publicity to provide a clear and intelligible snapshot of the city's current financial condition rather than as a source of information about past performance or future activity. Such a snapshot served primarily to convince potential investors and current bondholders of the city's solvency. The city's business elite, the Merchants' Association, had called for greater "publicity," and Grout had obliged. Accordingly, in conjunction with the publication of his 1902 comptroller's report, Grout sent an outline of the new accounting plan to the presidents of major banking, financial, and other "kindred institutions" throughout the country for criticism and comment.[11]

Grout's actions received high praise from the financial community. *Pit and Post*, a Chicago financial publication, effused, "At a time when so great importance is attached to 'publicity' and candid accounting it would seem as if the work of Comptroller Grout should attract universal attention, and command the careful study of all public and private corporations. . . . Comptroller Grout has done a veritable public service not only to the City of New York, but to the whole country."[12] Grout's "publicity" thus facilitated communication with leaders of commerce and industry, providing a rudimentary public counterpart to Henry Clews' contemporary views of the value of accounting publicity for bolstering the confidence of investors in private corporations.[13]

The comptroller had begun to appreciate the general value of publicity as a tool of promoting investor confidence and legitimating government actions in the eyes of a business elite, but he had not yet learned to tailor publicity to suit particular circumstances or serve specific causes. New York's financial administrators also had yet fully to consider the uses of publicity when directed at the mass of common citizens. Nonetheless,

---

[10]New York City, Department of Finance, *Accountants' Report to Edward M. Grout, Comptroller* (New York: Martin B. Brown, 1903), i–xi.

[11]New York City, Department of Finance, *Annual Report of the Comptroller, 1902* (New York: Martin B. Brown, 1904), xvii.

[12]Quoted in ibid., xvii.

[13]Henry Clews, "Publicity and Reform in Business," *Annals of the American Academy of Political and Social Science* 28 (July 1906): 143–54.

Grout's success provides an early example of the city's calling on the authority of experts both to address and deflect outside criticism.

Despite Grout's repeated attempts at reform following the consolidation of 1898, New York City's accounts remained confused, and delays in collecting and organizing financial data continued to plague the Department of Finance. Significantly, the city's accounts continued to list appropriations in lump sums, with no segregation by function or object of expenditure.[14] In addition, the comptroller's report for 1905 was not submitted to the mayor until April 30, 1907, a delay of well over one full year.[15]

Continued calls for reform and persistent difficulties in effectively assessing the state of the city's finances prompted New York's Mayor McClellan, in February 1905, to appoint a special Advisory Commission on Taxation and Finance composed both of city officers and prominent outside experts in finance, who were directed to examine the financial methods of the city and report a plan for improving them.[16]

[14]Thus, for example, the 1905 appropriation for the Normal College of New York read simply: "For salaries of professors, tutors, and others in the normal college, and the training department of the normal college; for scientific apparatus, books, and all necessary supplies therefor; for replacing and altering the college building, and for the support, maintenance and general expenses of same—$220,000.00." See Yin Ch'u Ma, *The Finances of the City of New York* (New York: Columbia University, 1914), 16.

[15]New York City, Department of Finance, *Annual Report of the Comptroller, 1905* (New York: Martin B. Brown, 1907), xiii.

[16]Among the outside experts were E. R. A. Seligman, professor of political economy at Columbia University, past president of the American Economic Association, and one of the country's foremost authorities on taxation, who served on the commission's Committee on Taxation and Revenue; Frank Goodnow, Eaton Professor of Public Law and Municipal Government at Columbia University and the first president of the American Political Science Association, later known as the "father of public administration," who served on the Committee on the City Debt and Special Assessments; and Frederick A. Cleveland, professor of finance at New York University and also associated with the accounting firm of Haskins and Sells, who served as chairman of the Committee on Accounting and Statistics. Among the city officers serving on the commission were Edgar Levy, former assistant deputy comptroller under Mayor Van Wyck's Tammany administration, who acted as chairman of the commission; Lawson Purdy, of the Department of Taxes and Assessment (he would later serve as president of the Commission on Taxes and Assessments from 1907 until 1918), who acted as secretary; John C. Hertle, one of the city's two commissioners of accounts; and Joseph Haag, a loyal Tammany organization man and secretary to the Board of Estimate and Apportionment. Herman Metz, elected comptroller in 1905 on the slogan "A business man for a business office," joined the commission in 1906. Together, officials and experts were to participate jointly in addressing New York City's financial problems. See Edgar Levy, *Final Report of the New York City Advisory Commission on Taxation and Finance* (New York: Martin B. Brown, 1908). For a brief analysis of Goodnow's theoretical contributions to Progressive urban reform, see Lurton W. Blassingame, "Frank J. Goodnow: Progressive Urban Reformer," *North Dakota Quarterly* 40 (Summer 1972): 22–30.

At once political and nonpartisan, the commission's composition reflected McClellan's increasingly ambiguous attitudes toward Tammany Hall. Tammany first chose McClellan to run for mayor in 1903. When Charles Francis Murphy ascended to the leadership of Tammany Hall in 1902, Seth Low, the antimachine darling of Republican and Fusionist urban reformers, was mayor and New York City's Democrats were in disarray.[17] The party was just beginning to emerge from a prolonged period of struggle and uncertainty in which competing elites repeatedly traded off control over city government, with none ever wholly dominating the political scene.[18] Tammany, however, had built on its strong support among second-generation immigrants during the 1890s to consolidate its power within the party. It soon eclipsed such rival factions as Irving Hall and the New York County Democracy, and gained consistent control over the recruitment of candidates to public office. Thus, by 1903, Murphy was ready to move to retake City Hall.[19]

Sensitive to the need to address the concerns that propelled Low into office in the first place, Murphy carefully crafted an unexceptionable ticket of well-credentialed elites. Thoroughly undercutting the Fusion forces, Murphy convinced comptroller Edward M. Grout and the president of the Board of Aldermen, Charles F. Fornes, both up for reelection on the Fusion ticket, to accept the Democratic nomination for those positions. To head the Democratic slate, Murphy called upon George B. McClellan, Jr. The Princeton-educated son of the eminent Civil War general, McClellan had served Tammany well in Washington as a congressman for several terms. Though reluctant to trade a comfortable life in the nation's capital for the political risks involved with being a Tammany mayor, McClellan recognized his duty to the organization and accepted its nomination.[20]

[17]Robert F. Wesser, *A Response to Progressivism: The Democratic Party and New York Politics, 1902–1918* (New York: New York University Press, 1986), 218. Wesser argues that in 1902 the Democrats were "tentative, insecure, faction ridden, and provincial minded." Although perhaps overstating the case, Wesser paints a convincing picture of a party in need of direction and leadership.

[18]David C. Hammack, *Power and Society* (New York: Russell Sage Foundation, 1982), 27–36, 103–18.

[19]Martin Shefter, "The Electoral Foundations of the Political Machine: New York City, 1884–1897," in *History of American Electoral Behavior*, ed. Joel H. Silbey, Allen G. Bogue, and William H. Flanigan (Princeton: Princeton University Press, 1978), 270–86.

[20]McClellan recalls "protesting vigorously" Murphy's attempts to groom him for the mayoralty. As early as 1896, when McClellan was first mentioned as a possible mayoral candidate, he said: "I don't want the mayoralty. There's nothing about the place I would care for. It's hard work, hard knocks, a hard name, and political death. I want none of it." *New*

From the start, Murphy got more than he bargained for in McClellan. Though a loyal Democrat, McClellan developed ties to Murphy's intraparty rival Patrick McCarren, a Brooklyn Democratic boss with little love for Manhattan's Tammany.[21] Once in office, McClellan immediately began to show unsettling signs of independence, selecting his own corporation counsel, mayoral secretary, and tax board president, as well as commissioners of police, street cleaning, and health—all against Murphy's objections. For the time being, however, McClellan prudently restrained himself from overly antagonizing Murphy, and accepted the boss's recommendations for most other city offices.[22]

McClellan's break with Murphy became nearly complete after his reelection in 1905. With the mayor's term of office newly extended to four years, McClellan saw an opportunity to build his own power base. He placed reform-minded officers in key city departments and made special use of his commissioner of accounts, the young and energetic John Purroy Mitchel, to investigate the administrations of such Tammany stalwarts as John F. Ahearn and Louis Haffen, borough presidents of Manhattan and the Bronx, respectively. Indictments were brought against both men, leading eventually to Governor Hughes's removal of Ahearn from office on grounds of incompetence.[23] McClellan also found a ready ally in the new comptroller, Herman Metz, one of McCarren's political lieutenants, whose nomination the Brooklyn boss had forced on Murphy.[24]

When McClellan appointed his Advisory Commission on Taxation and Finance in February 1905, his bid for reelection lay several months ahead and he still needed Tammany's support. Thus, in composing the commission, McClellan selected a mix of loyal organization men and independent experts. The commission placed experts in formal positions of

---

York Journal, March 15, 1896; quoted in Harold C. Syrett, ed., *The Gentleman and the Tiger: The Autobiography of George B. McClellan, Jr.* (New York: J. B. Lippincott, 1956), 169, n. 21. Syrett's work is the standard biography of McClellan but is largely in the form of McClellan's reminiscences as edited by Syrett; as such it is somewhat uneven and of limited use. Helpful, if brief, analyses of the relations between Murphy and Mitchel can be found in Nancy Joan Weiss, *Charles Francis Murphy, 1858–1924: Respectability and Responsibility in Tammany Politics* (Northhampton, Mass.: Smith College, 1968), 38–42; and John M. Allswang, *Bosses, Machines, and Urban Voters: An American Symbiosis* (Port Washington: Kennikat Press, 1971), 81–84.

[21] Syrett, *The Gentleman and the Tiger*, 222–23, 284–85; Weiss, *Charles Francis Murphy*, 43–44.

[22] Syrett, *The Gentleman and the Tiger*, 181–85; Weiss, *Charles Francis Murphy*, 40.

[23] Syrett, *The Gentleman and the Tiger*, 27, 206–16, 230–34; Weiss, *Charles Francis Murphy*, 42; Seidman, *Investigating Municipal Administration*, 49–52.

[24] Syrett, *The Gentleman and the Tiger*, 222.

authority within the city government. Neither permanent nor full-time employees of the city, the experts were nonetheless something more than mere consultants. They worked together with government officials rather than in the splendid isolation of the typical outside consultant. The commissioners were given a broad mandate to examine and make recommendations for reforming the city's financial administration, which allowed them to take the initiative beyond simply presenting a snapshot of the city's financial condition.

Each committee (Taxation and Finance, City Debt and Special Assessments, and Accounting and Statistics) presented a series of reports to the mayor between December 1905 and October 1908. Most of the reports were technical documents, proposing concrete administrative reforms to limited areas of financial administration and only obliquely addressing the broader political implications of their recommendations. Only the report of the Committee on Accounting and Statistics, prepared under the chairmanship of Frederick Cleveland, then a professor of public finance at New York University, considered the nature of the system of financial administration itself. Cleveland's report provides a clear picture of the general state of the city's finances in 1905 and demonstrates a growing appreciation of financial administration as a tool to establish and assert centralized authority within a growing and increasingly complex governmental bureaucracy.[25]

Cleveland's report found that New York's system of accounting and statistics was woefully inadequate to the task of coordinating and evaluating the city's financial operations.[26] It recommended centralizing administrative control and oversight in the Department of Finance by extending a system of uniform accounts throughout every city department. In addition, the comptroller would be given a freer hand in the removal of accounting heads and chief assistants, while the commissioners of accounts would more aggressively audit departmental accounts and reports, serving "as an inquisitorial branch of the executive for the determination of facts . . . "[27] Cleveland's focus on centralized authority and executive oversight came to characterize subsequent programs to reform municipal accounts throughout the country.

[25][Frederick A. Cleveland], "Report on the System of Accounts and Statistics of the City of New York, submitted June, 1907," in *Final Report of the New York City Advisory Commission on Taxation and Finance*, chaired by Edgar Levy (New York: Martin B. Brown, 1908), 99–124.

[26]Ibid., 101–107.

[27]Ibid., 107–8, 121.

Cleveland's earlier drafts of the report reveal an appreciation of accounts as an instrument of publicity. Like previous advocates of accounting reform, Cleveland proposed to use a revised system of accounts and statistics to win the confidence of potential investors, existing creditors, and other financial elites. (At this point, he took little interest in addressing the mass of citizens.) Cleveland then took the further step of using accounting to address the specific concerns of the city's creditors. He explored in detail the type of financial information the "city's long-term creditor is interested in knowing" and concluded that providing such detailed information was necessary "before the city of New York will be able to sell bonds at their full worth, i.e., without the price being sealed on account of the wide margin of risk that lies in uncertainty as to those corporate facts and conditions which should be revealed by a proper system of accounts."[28]

Cleveland's reports demonstrated a hard-headed recognition that clear and intelligible accounts were essential not only to efficient internal governmental administration but also to maintaining productive external relations with powerful financial elites in the community. Indeed, in light of a bond crisis precipitated by the Panic of 1907, Cleveland's remarks take on the aura of savvy prognostication. During the panic, New York reached the brink of insolvency when financial leaders refused to subscribe to a major issue of municipal bonds. J. P. Morgan came to the rescue, taking upon himself or causing his subsidiary banks to take up over $300 million worth of the city's long- and short-term bonds.[29]

Cleveland certainly would have found such serendipity an untenable basis for scientific financial administration. Later commenting on the panic, Cleveland emphasized that the short-term readjustment that had stabilized the banking system by 1908 was "temporary" and "essentially . . . dangerous" because it was not based on a scientific approach to determining the causes and cure for the panic.[30] His reforms aimed to institutionalize investor confidence through accounting publicity, thereby reducing the likelihood of future crises, while saving the city from reliance on the uncertain hope that some financial deus ex machina would present himself to save the city should another crisis occur.

---

[28]Frederick A. Cleveland, *Report of Mr. Cleveland to the Committee on Accounting and Statistics* (New York: Martin B. Brown, 1907), 11–13. See also Cleveland, *Chapters on Municipal Administration and Accounting* (New York: Longmans, Green, 1909), 251–52.
[29]Syrett, *The Gentleman and the Tiger*, 271–77.
[30]Frederick A. Cleveland, "Neglected Aspects of Currency and Banking," *Annals of the American Academy of Political and Social Science* 31 (March 1908): 426–29.

McClellan received the Advisory Commission's work with high praise and presented it to the state legislature as a basis for legislation to reform of New York's financial apparatus. The final report represented a cooperative effort among political officers and outside experts. The experts here were not the hirelings of the officers; they were central participants in all stages of the investigation. The relationship was temporary but nonetheless marked a significant departure from earlier consultant-type relations between the city and outside independent financial experts.[31]

A Permanent Partner in Municipal Reform

No single person embodied the change from consultant to participant better than Frederick A. Cleveland. Cleveland was born in Sterling, Illinois, in 1865 and did not come to the world of eastern urban reform until he was well into his thirties. For college he stayed close to home, attending Northwestern and Depauw Universities. Upon graduation Cleveland entered the field of law and headed west, not east, to practice in Bellingham, Washington. He returned to the Midwest in 1897 to pursue graduate work in political science at the University of Chicago. He was thirty-four years old before he found his way east in 1899 to enroll as a fellow in finance at the Wharton School of Business at the University of Pennsylvania. He earned his Ph.D. in 1900 and soon thereafter joined Wharton's faculty as an instructor in finance.

The Wharton School was founded in 1881 to provide training in the social sciences for managing practical problems of business. Wharton became a leading exponent of specialized business studies, which sought to develop management as a procedural science. (Harvard, the other major business school of the time, based its program on an approach that utilized case studies to teach more general management skills.) Wharton also emphasized the relationship between business and public affairs and sent many graduates off to establish or staff such organizations as the National Municipal League and the American Academy of Political and Social Science.[32]

In 1902 Cleveland married Jessica England Lindsay, the sister of Samuel McCune Lindsay, a teacher of Cleveland's at Wharton who was then president of the American Academy of Political and Social Science.

[31]*Final Report of the New York City Advisory Commission on Taxation and Finance*, 11.
[32]Steven A. Sass, *The Pragmatic Imagination: A History of the Wharton School, 1881–1981* (Philadelphia: University of Pennsylvania Press, 1982), 30–59, 75–78, 107–14.

Samuel Lindsay was also a prominent reformer, serving on the U.S. Industrial Commission and later on the National Child Labor Committee. He and Cleveland soon became close colleagues in the crusade for budget reform. Lindsay later became secretary of the Bureau of Municipal Research and in 1920 served in the same capacity on the Citizens National Budget Committee.

By 1905, when McClellan named him to the Advisory Commission on Taxation and Finance, Cleveland had firmly established himself at the forefront of the academic study of finance and was well positioned to make the move into government service. In 1902, while still at the University of Pennsylvania, Cleveland became secretary of the National Municipal League's Committee on Municipal Accounts and Statistics. The following year he also served as chairman of the Committee on Municipal Finance and Statistics of the American Economics Association. Charles Waldo Haskins, the first Dean of New York University's recently established School of Commerce, Accounts and Finance, then brought Cleveland to New York as a professor of finance. Cleveland was also affiliated with Haskins's accounting firm, Haskins and Sells, which had earlier served as consultant to Brooklyn. Unlike Haskins, however, Cleveland was not content with the status of temporary consultant to McClellan. Even while serving on the commission, Cleveland was exploring new avenues for creating a more permanent base from which to continue his investigation and reform of municipal government.[33]

Cleveland soon found what he was looking for: a group of like-minded reformers who had been working for several years to establish an independent citizens' agency to examine and report on government activities. Their efforts began in March 1901, when the New York Association for Improving the Condition of the Poor (AICP) asserted that it could maintain a certain public bathhouse for 30 percent less than had been requested as an appropriation by the Tammany politician in charge of the project. In an editorial, the *New York Tribune* concluded that "this incident is doubtless typical of what would happen in every department were there some institution in a position to check official estimates and show what the identical work in question could be done for, with politics

[33]For brief biographical sketches of Cleveland, see Arthur E. Buck, Henry Bruere, and William F. Willoughby, *Frederick Albert Cleveland: A Tribute* (New York: Governmental Research Association, 1946); *The National Cyclopedia of American Biography* (New York: James T. White, 1904), 13:433–34; and *Who's Who in New York* (New York: W. F. Brainard, 1918), 653.

left out."[34] Frank Tucker, general agent of the AICP, seized on the favorable publicity to build support for creating just such an institution. Tucker clipped the editorial and sent it to R. Fulton Cutting, a wealthy New York philanthropist and president of the AICP since 1893, suggesting that Fulton support the idea. Cutting agreed to bring a proposal drafted by Tucker before the New York Chamber of Commerce urging that body to create a bureau or department of civic affairs under its auspices. Tucker's progress stalled at this stage until William Allen joined him at the AICP in 1903.[35]

Like Cleveland, Allen came from a town in the Midwest. He was born in 1874 in Le Roy, Minnesota, and graduated from the University of Chicago in 1897. While at Chicago he was befriended by the brilliant and iconoclastic economist Thorstein Veblen. After Chicago, Allen attended the Wharton School of Business, where he and Cleveland became classmates. They received their Ph.D.s on the same day in 1900.

Beyond the shared timing, Allen's and Cleveland's experiences at Wharton appear to have differed markedly. Cleveland was fascinated by the rapidly growing field of corporate finance. (In 1902 he wrote an influential textbook on the subject, *Funds and Their Uses*.) As a member of the school's faculty he specialized in courses on banking.[36] Allen, in contrast, did not go on to build a career strictly on his economic expertise. He had worked closely with Simon Patten while at Wharton, becoming a protegé of the eminent economist (he later named one of his children after his mentor). Under Patten's influence, Allen chose to broaden his activities to encompass a wide variety of reform efforts.[37] Allen recalled that when it came time to find a job after receiving his Ph.D., "Patten put his arm on my shoulder. I thought he'd never stop looking at me. Finally he said, 'Allen, why don't you help the other fellow?'" With Patten's assistance Allen secured a position as secretary of the New Jersey State Charities Aid

[34]*New York Tribune*; March 11, 1901, quoted in Norman Gill, *Municipal Research Bureaus* (Washington, D.C.: American Council on Public Affairs, 1944), 14, n. 8.

[35]Bureau of Municipal Research, "A National Program to Improve Methods of Government," *Municipal Research* 71 (March 1916): 1.

[36]Sass, *Pragmatic Imagination*, 141–50.

[37]Frederick P. Gruenberg, later a director of the Philadelphia Bureau of Municipal Research, attested to Patten's influence, stating that "the inspiration for governmental research came from Simon Patten. It was Patten who directed the attention of students in the social sciences to the increasing role government in our democracy, particularly government on the municipal level." Gruenberg, "Wharton School and Its Middle Westerners," *The General Magazine and Historical Chronicle* (Spring/Summer, 1955): 109; quoted in Jane S. Dahlberg, *The New York Bureau of Municipal Research* (New York: New York University Press, 1966), 7–8.

Association before joining Tucker in 1903 as general agent for the AICP. From the outset of his professional career, Allen exhibited a concern not only for compiling and interpreting data but also for publicizing the results of his investigations to the public at large. He was trained as one of the new breed of social science professionals but placed his skills as a publicist on a par with his expertise in economics.[38]

In February 1905, Cleveland met with Tucker and Allen and, at Tucker's suggestion, drafted a written prospectus for the organization of a permanent bureau of municipal research. Allen then took on the task of raising money for the new enterprise and, in November of 1905, he prepared a revised statement for circulation to potential donors titled "Brief for the Establishment of an Institute for Municipal Research." Cutting became their first major backer, subscribing $1,000 per month for one year for the creation and maintenance of a "Bureau of City Betterment" to operate on a trial basis as a branch of the Citizens Union, a prominent civic reform organization, of which Cutting was also president. By 1907 the Bureau of City Betterment had proved its worth and left the shelter of the Citizens' Union to incorporate as the Bureau of Municipal Research.[39]

Allen's revised statement called for the creation of an independent agency to collect, classify, compile, and publicize information about government administration. As Allen saw it, the new institute would meet the "supreme need" for an "agency dependent neither upon politics nor upon an average public intelligence that lacks the facts necessary to comprehend the need for such an agency." This new "intelligence center" would "substitute fact for calamity or scandal as teacher to citizenship, and by increasing the number who reason from fact to policy, tend gradually to abolish reactionary, revolutionary or blundering leadership, while progressively diminishing the extremes to which leadership may go in defeating or misrepresenting the protective, benevolent and constructive purposes of government."[40]

[38]William H. Allen, *Reminiscences* (New York: Columbia University Oral History Collection, 1950), 14–30.

[39]Bureau of Municipal Research, "National Program," 1–2; Cleveland's opinion to Allen is included in Cleveland's *Municipal Administration*, 263–303. For discussions of the Citizens Union and its background, see David C. Hammack, *Power and Society: Greater New York at the Turn of the Century* (New York: Russell Sage Foundation, 1982), 150–57; Wallace S. Sayre and Herbert Kaufman, *Governing New York City* (New York: Russell Sage Foundation, 1960), 497; and Robert Muccigrosso, "The City Reform Club: A Study in Late Nineteenth Century Reform," *New-York Historical Society Quarterly* 52 (1968): 235–54.

[40]Allen's "Brief for the Establishment of an Institute for Municipal Research" is reprinted in William H. Allen, *Efficient Democracy* (New York: Macmillan, 1907), 284–85.

Allen's brief reveals a clear intent to create a new type of political space for what would become the Bureau of Municipal Research, situating it between the people and the government, serving both yet dependent on neither. The bureau would use its expertise in manipulating complex data to facilitate the work of administrators within government and to mediate between the government and the people, providing the latter with accurate and intelligible information about the activities of the former.

To function effectively, the bureau's founders had to define clearly the nature and source of its authority. First, they set it apart from and above other municipal reform efforts by declaring that it met a "supreme need" in the field of government. Second, they insisted on its independence from "politics." Such concerns were common to many municipal reformers of this era who believed that only objective, nonpartisan assessments of community needs could provide the basis for constructive and efficient governance.[41] In the bureau's case, however, nonpartisanship was intended to protect, not to create, its true source of authority—its ability to control and to give meaning to information about municipal administration. Third, the bureau's program connected nonpartisanship to independence from the uninformed "average public intelligence," implying that until the public was educated by the bureau, it would be in no position to judge the bureau—indeed, it would be unlikely even to be able to see the need for a bureau. In this tidy, yet powerful, tautology, to see the need for a bureau was itself evidence of above-average public intelligence, while failure to see such a need showed ignorance; thus, only people who had already accepted the legitimacy and basic principles of the bureau would be in a position to judge it.

Simply informing the public, however, was not enough. The bureau was to be a "teacher to citizenship." Allen, who had earlier served as secretary to the National Municipal League's Committee on Instruction in Municipal Government, was especially concerned with the "educational" aspects of reform. To Allen it was not that education cured all, but that education to *citizenship* was essential to good government and effective democracy. His brief proposed to make citizenship a distinct and specialized field of knowledge, carved out from all other endeavors, such as business, law, or science, with its own peculiar subject matter and discipline.

One critical implication of Allen's view of citizenship, only dimly realized in his early articulation of the bureau's program, was its tendency to

---

[41]See Martin J. Schiesl, *The Politics of Efficiency: Municipal Administration and Reform in America, 1800–1920* (Berkeley: University of California Press, 1977).

turn citizenship into something taught by experts as opposed to something learned through a process of active participation in civic life. Allen's program of citizen education placed the bureau as a patient mediator not only between the citizen and government but also between the citizen and his or her own sense of public identity.

To direct the Bureau of City Betterment, Cutting and Allen agreed to hire the young (twenty-three-year-old) Henry Bruere, with whom Allen had worked at the AICP. Bruere was also a midwesterner, born in St. Charles, Missouri, in 1882. Like Allen, he graduated from the University of Chicago, where he, too, worked with Thorstein Veblen, as well as Charles Merriam and Charles Zeublin. After college Bruere attended Harvard Law School for one year and then headed back to the Midwest to work at the International Harvester Company in Chicago, where he oversaw the welfare projects of the McCormick family, including the McCormick Work Men's Club and the Gad's Hill Settlement House. While in Chicago, Bruere regularly visited Hull House, where he met and worked with Jane Addams, Graham Taylor, Raymond Robbins, and other members of the city's social reform community, from whom he absorbed the ethos and the methodology of the settlement house movement. It is revealing that he oversaw the welfare projects of one of the major industrialists of the era rather than working at a more independent organization such as Hull House. Bruere had a genuine concern for those less fortunate than himself but also felt at ease with inequality.[42]

Bruere immediately distinguished himself as director of the Bureau of City Betterment by successfully conducting an investigation of John F. Ahearn, president of the Borough of Manhattan. Late in 1906 Bruere published his findings in a pamphlet titled *How Manhattan Is Governed*. Bruere's report revealed such gross inefficiency that it compelled the city to investigate and eventually prompted Governor Hughes to remove Ahearn from office on grounds of "incompetence." Bruere considered the introduction of competence as a measure of an official's performance to be a landmark in the cause of efficient government.[43]

Bruere's success led to the incorporation of the New York Bureau of Municipal Research later that same year, with Bruere as its first director.

[42]Henry Bruere, *Reminiscences* (New York: Columbia University Oral History Collection, 1949), 14–17; Donald T. Critchlow, *The Brookings Institution, 1916–1952* (De Kalb: Northern Illinois University Press, 1985), 18–19; Allen F. Davis, *Spearheads for Reform: The Social Settlements and the Progressive Movement* (New York: Oxford University Press, 1967), 185–86.

[43]Bruere, *Reminiscences*, 32–35.

Cleveland was brought in as technical director, and Allen left the AICP to become secretary, with primary responsibilities for publicity and fund-raising. The new bureau's staff included William Patterson, who, like Cleveland, was an accountant at Haskins and Sells with a Ph.D. in political science from the University of Pennsylvania; Rufus Miles, an investigator with the Bureau of City Betterment and previously head worker at Goodrich House and social settlement; and Paul Wilson, who, like Bruere, had previously performed elfare work for the International Harvester Company. All told, the bureau's field staff during its first year of operation numbered sixteen, five being certified public accountants with three to fifteen years of experience. Several others had backgrounds in social settlement work, including one woman, a graduate of Smith College who had formerly been engaged in district inspection and statistical work for the city's tenement house department.[44]

The chairman of the bureau's founding board of trustees was E. R. A. Seligman, a prominent professor of political economy at Columbia who was then serving with Cleveland on the mayor's Advisory Commission on Taxation and Finance. Tucker became vice-chairman and Cutting, treasurer. The other trustees were Richard Watson Gilder, editor-in-chief of *The Century* magazine; George McAneny, president of the City Club, a journalist, and later president of the Borough of Manhattan; Albert Shaw, editor of the *American Monthly Review of Reviews* and author of several works on constitutional history and municipal government; and Carroll D. Wright, president of Clark College and former United States Commissioner of Labor. Of note here is the number of trustees directly involved in journalism. They were both reformers and publicists, experienced in crafting and disseminating information to a mass public. The bureau's program reflected this same combination of reform and publicity, and its members would frequently make use of both Shaw's and Gilder's magazines to publicize their work.[45]

Allen surpassed himself in obtaining financing for the new bureau. Andrew Carnegie and John D. Rockefeller joined Cutting in underwriting its first year of operation. Over the next few years the list of major contributors to the bureau grew to include E. H. Harriman, J. P. Morgan, Kuhn, Loeb & Co., Henry Morgenthau, Jacob Schiff, and Felix Warburg, among other prominent members of New York's financial elite.[46] These busi-

---

[44]Bureau of Municipal Research, *Purposes and Methods of the Bureau of Municipal Research* (New York: Bureau of Municipal Research, 1907), 4–5.
[45]Ibid., 2–3.
[46]Bureau of Municipal Research, "National Program," 14.

nessmen naturally sympathized with the bureau's attempts to introduce business methods into city government. Allen's success, however, was also due to the perceived role the bureau in protecting these men's increasing investments in New York City bonds. Though not part of its stated purpose, the technically independent bureau nonetheless served financial elites as outside municipal auditors who could ascertain the city's financial status. Support from this veritable who's who of corporate capital would eventually lead to internal disputes and accusations of excessive outside interference of "corporate interests" in the bureau's work. At the outset, however, their support proved an undeniable boon to the newly formed organization.

In an era awash in civic reform groups, the bureau was something new and different. The historian Charles A. Beard, later himself a director of the bureau, noted that "the Bureau of Municipal Research marked a new epoch in the growth of the science of administration" because it was among the first and foremost advocates of applying the techniques of firsthand "scientific" observation to the study of government.[47] In his work on Progressive era reform in New York City, Richard Skolnick observed that structurally "the Bureau differed from other civic groups in that it bore no resemblance to a social organization. It maintained a paid staff of trained professional engineers, accountants, economists and administrators, most of whom worked full time for the Bureau. It was not a part time leisurely reform organization of professional citizens, but an industrious group of technicians avoiding the florid rhetoric of reformers, yet dedicated to the same objectives."[48]

THE "ABCs"

"It was a fortunate condition that these men were of different temperaments, or shall I say approaches to life and its tasks."[49] Thus did William Prendergast, who succeeded Herman Metz as New York City's comptroller in 1909, recall the unique combination of qualities that Allen, Bruere, and Cleveland—known as the "ABCs"—brought to the Bureau of Municipal Research. More than anyone else, they defined the meaning

[47]Charles A. Beard, "The Advancement of Municipal Science," May 1919, typed manuscript, p. 3, Papers of the Institute of Public Administration, New York.
[48]Skolnick, "Reform in New York City," 329.
[49]William Prendergast, *Reminiscences* (New York: Columbia University Oral History Collection, 1948–50), 948.

and purpose of the budget and campaigned for its adoption across America, beginning in New York City.

Allen, the publicist, focused on using budgets to create an educated citizenry capable of exercising intelligent control over their elected officials. Cleveland, the technical expert, concentrated more on educating public officials and devoted his time to the mechanics of administrative reform. Whereas Allen was an advocate, exhorting the general public to educate itself to full citizenship, Cleveland was a dispassionate investigator, addressing fellow experts and bringing the tools of scientific reasoning to bear on discrete problems of administration.[50] Bruere, the administrator, sought to maintain a balance between the two tendencies (and the two men). He demonstrated a facility neither for publicity nor for technical reform, but instead succeeded at building bridges between the bureau and government officials. During the first five years of the bureau's existence, these three men creatively coordinated their different temperaments and skills into a powerful force for change.

Allen had the intense energy and fierce commitment of a man sure of his course and secure in his beliefs. E. R. A. Seligman captured the force of Allen's character when he noted that "his energy and enthusiasm are unlimited. Dr. Allen is a very positive nature, and like most positive men, has the power of attracting as well as repelling. . . . [I]t is undoubted that his very strength of character has made him a bit unyielding and masterful."[51] Seligman's assessment was often echoed, though occasionally in less flattering terms, by Allen's co-workers and associates. William Prendergast called Allen a "zealot" (though he asserted that he meant the term "in its most complimentary sense") and quoted an associate who had said, "Allen was apt to use a meat axe when a much smaller and less dangerous instrument might suffice."[52] Bruere himself characterized his co-director as "a man of extraordinary mental agility . . . [and] passionate conviction," but also remarked that "he lacked . . . balance and tolerance

---

[50]On the distinction between advocacy and objectivity in the social sciences, see Mary O. Furner, *Advocacy and Objectivity: A Crisis in Professionalization of American Social Science, 1865–1905* (Lexington: University Press of Kentucky, 1975). Furner argues for a general progression during the last third of the nineteenth century from advocacy to objectivity among professional social scientists. Cleveland generally fits this mold, but Allen (who, like Cleveland, earned a Ph.D. from the University of Pennsylvania) would seem to be something of a throwback, or rather, less of a "modern social scientist," eschewing extreme reliance on his expert knowledge in favor of a less specialized and more popular approach to social problems.

[51]E. R. A. Seligman to C. R. Van Hise, August 5, 1914, Seligman Papers, Box 5.

[52]Prendergast, *Reminiscences*, 948.

in his views" and "was very impatient of persons who didn't agree at once that *now* is the time to set things right." Finally, Bruere noted that Allen's "perpetual bombardment" of his co-workers with ideas and suggestions "often led him into unnecessary conflict."[53]

Despite his arrogance, Allen was a democrat at heart, wary of relying too much on technical experts to guide civic affairs. He believed that a "socialism of intelligence" was the key to efficient democracy because "without intelligent control by the public, no efficient, progressive, triumphant democracy is possible."[54] His model citizen was an attentive and intelligent middle class taxpayer who was willing to make an effort to inform himself (or herself—he did see an important role for women in civic affairs) about government operations.

Allen's "socialism of intelligence," however, had a double edge. He saw an "active few" public-spirited citizens as essential to maintaining modern democracy. His elite, however, was based not on class but on adherence to principles of efficiency and democracy. As he stated in *Efficient Democracy*, "Given a hundred so-called best citizens in a millionaire's parlour, and a hundred frequenters of a Bowery saloon, it would be a rash man who would feel sure that the average intelligence as to government is higher in the parlour than in the saloon."[55] In contrast both to old mugwump ideas about rule by the "best men" and to the simple meritocracy of many civil service reformers, Allen's scheme placed efficiency and a commitment to the public good above both elite breeding and technical ability.

Allen also saw socialized intelligence as a means to defuse or coopt the general popular unrest that had greeted the rise of corporate capitalism. "It is probable," he argued, "that when common intelligence is achieved the disquieting socialism of capital will have less cogent reasoning to support it."[56] Rather than condemning or suppressing socialism outright, Allen chose the subtler, less confrontational approach of spreading information about "efficient democracy"—information compiled, interpreted, and disseminated by men such as himself—in order to undermine socialism's appeal.

Allen's approach to reform reflected the influence of his mentor from the University of Pennsylvania, the eminent economist Simon Patten. Pat-

[53]Bruere, *Reminiscences* (New York: Columbia University Oral History Collection, 1949), 20, 39–40.
[54]William H. Allen, *Efficient Democracy* (New York: Macmillan, 1907), vii.
[55]Ibid., 263–64. Allen clearly believed that efficient citizen intelligence transcended class.
[56]Ibid., vii.

ten, convinced that the problems of production in the modern economy had been solved, developed an "economics of consumption" during the 1890s. Fearing that the new age of abundance might lead to intemperate gluttony, hedonistic consumption, and the subsequent impoverishment of social, aesthetic, and moral life, Patten asserted that it was necessary to educate the masses to more elevated tastes. Properly educated consumers would restrain their baser urges and act with temperance to consume in a manner that would perpetuate abundance and spread its benefits throughout society. Like Allen's "socialism of intelligence," however, Patten's "economics of consumption" also had a double edge. Patten believed that sustained abundance required shaping attitudes and restraining evil passions. Thus, in Patten's model, as Mary Furner notes, "Education for consumption was also social control." Allen, too, sought to "educate the consumer," but he conceptualized the consumer as primarily a political, not an economic, actor, who would be educated to participate responsibly in a democratic state.[57]

The Bureau of Municipal Research was to be Allen's ultimate tool of socialized intelligence. He saw the bureau's experts as servants of the people. They would actively disseminate their specialized knowledge among the people to create an intelligent and informed citizenry able to responsibly exercise democratic power. Again, publicity was the key. But whereas others saw publicity as a means to manipulate the masses, Allen saw it as the basis of citizen empowerment. Home rule reformers such as the National Municipal League used publicity to convince wary state legislators to surrender greater power to the cities. Wall Street promoters such as Henry Clews used publicity to convince wealthy investors to surrender more money to corporations (both public and private). Clews and the league sought to persuade; Allen sought to educate. The difference may be tenuous, yet it is significant. Allen had a true faith in the aroused citizenry even as he had a profound distrust of the mob. Some might use publicity to control the mob; Allen would use it to transform the ignorant masses into a responsible public. This was socialized intelligence. It was manipulation. It was social control. But it also aimed to entrust the people with real power.

Cleveland's dispassionate technical approach to reform stood in

---

[57]Daniel M. Fox, *The Discovery of Abundance: Simon Patten and the Transformation of Social Theory* (Ithaca: Cornell University Press, 1967), 44–59; Furner, *Advocacy and Objectivity*, 309–10. For Patten's own highly popular and influential discussion of "education for consumption" in the new world of economic abundance, see his *The New Basis of Civilization* (New York: Macmillan, 1906).

marked contrast to Allen's exuberance. Cleveland, the former professor of finance, was an expert who spoke mostly to other experts. Allen used simple, hard-hitting language set off with boldface headings and complemented by easy-to-read charts and graphics, neatly presenting the complex issues of municipal reform in an accessible and inviting package.[58] Cleveland, by contrast, published detailed technical treatises on banking and public finance. He was a methodical and disciplined thinker who approached problems with great deliberation and had little consideration for more theatrical approaches to reform. Allen valued expert knowledge as a means to enhance popular intelligence. Cleveland, while always appreciating the importance of publicity for democratic governance, valued expert knowledge as an end in itself.[59]

Cleveland utterly lacked Allen's charisma and popular touch. Indeed, he proudly disdained such qualities. Simplifying his work for popular consumption, he believed, would cheapen its value. His analysis, no matter how arid or complex, would stand on its own. As one colleague put it, Cleveland had a "rather involved" way of expressing himself which was "often baffling to a person seeking the simple facts of a case. . . . He needs to realize that a report can be interesting, indeed popular, without destroying its scientific value."[60] Cleveland commanded respect, even loyalty, from his colleagues, but little affection.

Whereas Allen owed much to Patten, Cleveland's work reflected the influence of a later role model, the accountant Charles Waldo Haskins. Haskins was a pioneer in the professionalization of accounting and one of the country's foremost accountants.[61] The two served together on the National Municipal League's Committee on Uniform Municipal Ac-

[58]As one reviewer of Allen's book, *Civics and Health* (Boston: Ginn, 1909), remarked, "The style is so attractive, so simple, so alive, that one reads it not because he feels he ought to, but because he can't help doing so." See "Review of *Civics and Health*," *American City* 2 (May 1910): 242. Ivy Lee, one of the foremost pioneers of public relations, employed similar pamphleteering techniques when he served on the Citizens Union Committee on Press and Literature in 1901, while R. Fulton Cutting was chairman. Although there is no evidence of direct contact between Allen and Lee at this time (they would meet in 1915), Allen's close association with Cutting and the Citizens Union during the early 1900s would likely have familiarized him with Lee's work.

[59]For a brief consideration of Cleveland's character, see Buck et al., *Frederick Albert Cleveland*.

[60]Raymond B. Fosdick to John D. Rockefeller, Jr., August 25, 1915, Rockefeller Family Archives, North Tarrytown, N.Y., RG III 2 D, Box 2, Folder 6.

[61]Cleveland himself later characterized the development of professional accounting as a "monument on which may be found [Haskins's] name in conspicuous letters." Cleveland, introduction to *Business Education and Accountancy*, ed. Charles Waldo Haskins (New York: Harper, 1904), 17.

counting and Statistics and formed a close professional relationship that lasted until Haskins's untimely death from pneumonia in 1903.[62]

Haskins promoted accountancy as a "science" that could help perfect society by fostering efficiency and honesty. "Scientific accountancy," he wrote, "is the hub of the universe of commerce, trade and finance; the pivot as it were of the wheel of fortune; the point, if truly centered, about which the business world revolves with the velocity and ease and restful silence of a spinning top."[63] Cleveland fully accepted Haskins's view of accountancy but adapted it to public affairs by placing a broader vision of "scientific budgeting" at the hub of the universe of governance.

Cleveland's scientific approach to public administration naturally harmonized with Frederick Winslow Taylor's then-current theories of scientific management. Taylor and his circle developed scientific management as a means to rationalize and improve the efficiency of private industry. Its basic principles (adopted and perverted in varying degrees by different industries and organizations since first elaborated by Taylor around the turn of the century) included specialization, planning, quantitative measurement, and standardization as basic ingredients to promoting efficiency. Taylor, it is less commonly remembered, also emphasized the importance of cooperation between worker and manager in developing a productive work environment.[64]

As one recent student of Taylor's work has noted, its primary lesson for the men of the bureau was its "implicit assumption that questions of organizational planning and implementation are researchable, that information collection and use is both possible and salutary for future performance."[65] Of the ABCs, Cleveland was most receptive to Taylor's

[62]For a brief account of Haskins' career, see Paul J. Miranti, Jr., *Accountancy Comes of Age: The Development of an American Profession* (Chapel Hill: University of North Carolina Press, 1990), 36–62.

[63]Haskins, quoted in ibid., 38.

[64]The standard work on Taylor's role in Progressive reform is Samuel Haber's *Efficiency and Uplift: Scientific Management in the Progressive Era, 1890–1920* (Chicago: University of Chicago Press, 1964). Martin Schiesl's *Politics of Efficiency* also contains an interesting discussion of Taylor's work in relation to the development of municipal reform. Hindy Lauer Schacter, in *Frederick Taylor and the Public Administration Community: A Reevaluation* (Albany: State University of New York Press, 1989), provides an insightful and provocative analysis of Taylor's work and includes an entire chapter on his relation to the Bureau of Municipal Research. Schacter attempts to rehabilitate Taylor, emphasizing his concern for workplace democracy, and argues that the bureau's appropriation of his ideas was subtle and sophisticated, consistently subordinating principles of efficiency to concerns for accountability and democracy. See pp. 91–110.

[65]Schacter, *Frederick Taylor*, 93.

message, although he selectively appropriated it to support ideas he had already developed. In 1912 Taylor and Cleveland both participated in a conference on scientific management held at Dartmouth College. Cleveland presented a speech titled "The Application of Scientific Management to the Activities of State and Municipal Government," which, though it employed the term most commonly associated with Taylor's work, contained little that Cleveland had not said in his earlier publications.[66] Indeed, Cleveland privately complained that Taylor "has given little attention to the affairs of large institutions as a whole, and he has not seen the advantage of accounting devices and methods" in promoting efficient management. Cleveland's scientific approach to reform clearly owed more to the accounting theories of his old friend Haskins than to the work of the more eminent Taylor.[67]

Finally, there was Henry Bruere, the youngest of the three and the only one without a professional degree. Bruere balanced and guided the work of his two colleagues while reaching out to establish good working relations with government officials. His background and temperament suited him well to this task. On the one hand, he was deeply influenced by his work in the settlement house movement and he always seemed more comfortable with the "human side" of reform issues, leaving the technical analysis to Cleveland. On the other hand, he lacked Allen's crusading zeal, preferring instead to maintain a more dispassionate perspective on the work of municipal reform. In his roles as mediator and diplomat, Bruere succeeded remarkably well, demonstrating a facility for conciliation and a knack for winning over wary politicians.[68]

Bruere established solid working relations with important officials in city government. New York City's comptroller, Herman Metz—who, upon his retirement from that post in 1909, donated $10,000 to the bureau to establish a fund to promote municipal accounting reform—and his successor, William Prendergast, both counted themselves among Bruere's friends and admirers.[69] Bruere's close friendship with John Purroy Mitchel formed the strongest link between the bureau and the city government. The two met after Mayor McClellan appointed Mitchel as

[66]Frederick A. Cleveland, "The Application of Scientific Management to the Activities of State and Municipal Government," in *Scientific Management: Addresses and Discussions at the Conference on Scientific Management* (Hanover, N.H.: Amos Tuck School of Administration and Finance, Dartmouth College, 1912), 313–35.

[67]Frederick A. Cleveland, *Efficiency Commission Diary, 1910–1911*, entry for January 16, 1911, William Howard Taft Papers, Library of Congress, Reel 375, Series 6, no. 215.

[68]Davis, *Spearheads for Reform*, 185–86.

[69]Prendergast, *Reminiscences*, 948, 957–58.

special counsel to investigate charges brought against Manhattan borough president John F. Ahearn by the bureau in 1906. Their friendship deepened as Mitchel became commissioner of accounts in 1907 and rose to become the youngest mayor in the city's history in 1914. Raymond Fosdick, who served as Mitchel's assistant in the Office of Commissioner of Accounts and later succeeded him at that post, asserted that Bruere "was perhaps more responsible than any other man for providing Mitchel not only with technical advice but with a philosophy of social action."[70]

Together Allen, Bruere, and Cleveland comprised a formidable trio, capable of addressing professionals, politicians, and the public at large in each group's own language. Their particular blend of skill and temperament served them well as they proceeded to establish their position on the municipal scene.

FILLING A POLITICAL VACUUM

As Allen, Cleveland, and Tucker were trying to drum up support for a bureau of municipal research in 1905, they were aided by two major scandals involving influence buying and corruption, one in gas and electric franchises, the other in the life insurance industry. In response to each scandal, New York's state legislature appointed special investigatory committees. Charles Evans Hughes served as special counsel to both committees and effectively launched his political career through his adept conduct of the investigations. The committees recommended, inter alia, that the state government establish new regulatory commissions and devise improved accounting and reporting methods to supply the information necessary for the commissions to oversee business activities.[71]

[70]Raymond B. Fosdick, *Chronicle of a Generation: An Autobiography* (New York: Harper, 1958), 84.

[71]Richard L. McCormick, *From Realignment to Reform: Political Change in New York State, 1983–1910* (Ithaca: Cornell University Press, 1981), 193–218; Robert F. Wesser, *Charles Evans Hughes: Politics and Reform in New York, 1905–1910* (Ithaca: Cornell University Press, 1967), 18–44; William E. Mosher, "Public Utilities and Their Early Regulation," in *History of the State of New York,* ed. Alexander C. Flick (New York: Columbia University Press, 1935), 201–30. For contemporary accounts written by men of or close to the Bureau of Municipal Research, see Henry Bruere, "Public Utilities Regulation in New York," *Annals of the American Academy of Political and Social Science* 31 (May 1905): 1–17; John J. Murphy, "Franchise Grants in New York City," *Annals of the American Academy of Political and Social Science* 31 (May 1908): 78–84; Henry C. Wright, "Development of Transit Control in New York City," *Annals of the American Academy of Political and Social Science* 31 (May 1908): 18–41.

The first scandal erupted when McClellan's Tammany administration awarded a contract for city lighting to the Consolidated Gas Company. The previous reform administration, under Seth Low, had rejected a similar contract on the grounds that it was arbitrary and excessive. Public outcry led Republican Governor Odell to call for an investigation. The legislature responded by naming a joint committee chaired by Senator Frederick Stevens. The Stevens committee uncovered a broad array of corrupt practices, including overcapitalization, fraudulent bookkeeping, tax evasion, and the illegal monopolization of the city's utilities. In one particularly egregious example of capital inflation, the committee found that Consolidated Gas had a book value of $21,942,632 but was capitalized at $37,971,419—a 173-percent overcapitalization of the stock.

The second and larger scandal developed around charges of bribery, graft, and the misuse of policyholders' funds by the giant Equitable Life Assurance Society. Rumors flew about the involvement of J. P. Morgan and E. H. Harriman (both later to become staunch supporters of the Bureau of Municipal Research). The investigating commission discovered that the life insurance industry had regularly been making secret contributions to Republican presidential candidates. (Under Hughes's skillful questioning, George Perkins, a former vice president of the New York Life Insurance Company, and later a member of the Bureau of Municipal Research's board of trustees, admitted that his company gave $48,000 to Theodore Roosevelt's 1904 election campaign.)[72]

Richard McCormick persuasively argues that these scandals transformed New York politics, awakening a spirit of reform and catalyzing changes in attitudes toward government which had been in the making for many years. Before 1905 New Yorkers saw government primarily as an agency to promote economic development by distributing general benefits to a variety of interests. As businesses organized to obtain more effective and interest-specific support, the public gradually came to understand government action to benefit one group as coming at the expense of some other group. This in turn led to rising public unease over the growth of corporate power. Of particular concern were abusive grants of franchises and a general fear of "trusts."[73]

Though they had an impact throughout the state, the scandals of 1905 were centered primarily in New York City, where they forced the issue of business and political corruption to the fore. The resulting rise in citizens'

[72]McCormick, *From Realignment to Reform*, 199–203; Wesser, *Charles Evans Hughes*, 33–44.
[73]McCormick, *From Realignment to Reform*, 138, 153–77.

skepticism about the motives of businessmen and their antipathy toward party bosses eroded party loyalties, leading to lower electoral turnouts and higher rates of ticket-splitting. From 1906 to 1910, Hughes, now governor, sought to rebuild the government's credibility by promoting a model of the state as an activist regulator, administrator, and planner in the public interest. Hughes also turned increasingly to experts and independent commissions rather than to party organizations to resolve political conflicts and rebuild legitimacy.[74]

The men of the bureau reflected and promoted the new political order. Cleveland rejected the laissez faire politics of the nineteenth-century government as a spoils system designed to distribute public resources and promote private enterprise. He declared that the twentieth century demanded a new vision of politics in which government actively promoted the welfare of all citizens.[75] Similarly, Allen asserted that "there will never come a time when the most direct means of promoting health, education and opportunity will not be through government."[76] Cleveland and Allen, like many of their contemporaries, no longer viewed government primarily as a distributor of resources but as an instrument to meet public needs.

The scandals of 1905 ultimately centered around defining the proper relation between public and private power. The gas and insurance companies appropriated essentially public functions to further their private interests. The citizens could understand that private corporations might supply certain public services, but they could not accept private corporations effectively usurping the government's power to decide the terms and conditions under which such services would be provided.

Hughes's investigations revealed that the suspect corporations threatened to deprive the citizenry not only of its hard-earned money but also of its inalienable right to effective political representation. Hughes's solution, increased regulatory oversight and publicity, attempted to shore up the boundary between public and private power. By subjecting corporate operations, both private and governmental, to increased scrutiny, new public service commissions would ensure that each remained within its proper sphere. Publicity and oversight would not create the boundary, but they would make it more difficult to cross.[77]

---

[74]Ibid., 219–35.

[75]Frederick A. Cleveland, *Organized Democracy* (New York: Longmans, Green, 1913), 22, 448.

[76]William H. Allen, *Woman's Part in Government* (New York: Dodd, Mead, 1912), 166.

[77]See Miles M. Dawson, "Publicity of Accounts of Industrial Corporations," *Annals of the American Academy of Political and Social Science* 42 (July 1912): 98–107. This article

Businessmen initially resisted the imposition of regulatory controls, but they soon realized that new laws providing for greater publicity of corporate accounts could be used to deflect demands for more direct state supervision of affected industries. Making the best of a bad situation, businessmen came to understand that reinforcing the boundaries between public and private not only protected government from corporate influence, it also protected corporations from governmental meddling.[78]

Cleveland had an intimate knowledge of the circumstances surrounding the scandals of 1905. While working with the accounting firm of Haskins and Sells, Cleveland took part in the investigation of various life insurance institutions implicated in the scandals.[79] In November 1905, Cleveland wrote an article, "The Relation of Auditing to Public Control," in which he argued against government interference in corporate affairs, insisting that adequate measures for public control resided in state charter provisions and ongoing accounting and reporting requirements. Cleveland asserted that government's primary purpose should not be to uncover malfeasance, but rather "to provide for the means whereby corporate integrity may be established."[80] Betraying his business orientation, Cleveland's first thought was to ensure that government regulation would not be too intrusive. He did not share the popular suspicion of corporate power. Rather, he believed that "the corporation is the modern instrument of private and public welfare, and any consideration to be given the subject of control by the government should proceed from the point of view of welfare to the corporation, rather than opposition to it."[81]

Cleveland clearly opposed those reformers who called for outright municipal ownership of utilities. Bruere, taking a typically more diplomatic tack, argued that municipal ownership wasn't really the issue; it was merely a means (perhaps no more effective than simple regulation) to the

---

deals primarily with questions of national regulation but draws extensively on the example provided by the Armstrong Commission (on which Hughes served as special counsel) in its investigation and recommendations concerning the life insurance business scandals in New York.

[78] See Bruce W. Dearstyne, "Regulation in the Progressive Era: The New York Public Service Commission," *New York History*, July 1977, 331–47. Dearstyne examines the commission's regulation of transportation in particular and concludes that, although cloaked in progressive rhetoric, regulation actually served conservative business interests.

[79] Testimony of Frederick A. Cleveland, *Proceedings of the Joint Committee of the Senate and Assembly of the State of New York Appointed to Investigate the Finances of New York City*, Documents of the Assembly of the State of New York, vol. 29, no. 50, 1909, pt. 1, 268.

[80] Frederick A. Cleveland, "The Relation of Auditing to Public Control," *Annals of the American Academy of Political and Social Science* 26 (November 1905): 669, 678.

[81] Ibid., 665.

greater end of "adequate service at reasonable rates . . . [and] efficient and economical management of corporate affairs." Bruere did not oppose calls for municipal ownership; he simply implied that they were irrelevant.[82]

Similarly, Allen believed that moral outrage at the corruption of particular officials was beside the point when a reasoned analysis of relevant information would cure the ills of maladministration. People had to understand that "government *cannot* be *good* unless it is *efficient*." Access to facts, a "socialized intelligence" as to the workings of the utilities, was far more important to Allen than replacing a few "bad" men through a socialized ownership of the utilities.[83]

Legislative reforms passed in the aftermath of the scandals did much to restore public confidence in business. Restoring public trust in government, however, was another matter. As party identification weakened and voters became more difficult to mobilize, new forms of political discourse and participation were needed to buttress the authority of the changing political order. The men of the Bureau of Municipal Research came on the scene at the right time to take advantage of the political vacuum (long in the making) precipitated by the scandals of 1905. To fill the vacuum they developed a model similar to that of the state regulatory agency, based on oversight and publicity as the means of restoring the government's legitimacy in the eyes of the public.

Just as independent auditing of businesses would restore their legitimacy with a minimum of direct government interference, so too would the bureau's program of budget reform restore government's legitimacy with a minimum of direct citizen interference. In each case, the bureau embraced the idea of a more activist role for government but also sought to contain and channel that activism to preempt any fundamental challenge to the existing structure of governmental or business administration.[84]

---

[82]Henry Bruere, "Public Utilities Regulation," 536–37.

[83]William H. Allen to Starr J. Murphy, 15 December 1905. Rockefeller Family Archives, Record Group III 2 D, Box 2, Folder 5.

[84]Writing about public utilities regulation in New York in the aftermath of these scandals, Bruere took a typically noncommittal tone, simply describing New York's new Public Service Commission law and the establishment of two new oversight committees. Bruere did, however, note approvingly the spirit of "harmony" and "cooperation" that existed between the commissions and the gas and lighting industry in implementing a standard uniform system of accounts. He, too, wanted to avoid excessive government interference in business affairs. Cooperation, not confrontation, allowed for a reasoned interaction between the state and business. Harmony ensured that businesses' fundamental interests would be protected. See Bruere, "Public Utilities Regulation," 535–51.

The men of the bureau proceeded to use their expertise to insinuate themselves into the operations of New York City's government. They steadily gained greater control over compiling and classifying administrative information and established the bureau as a critical mediator both between different departments of government and between government and the people. While the bureau vociferously tried to convince the city that budget reform was essential to efficient and democratic government, it left unspoken the implication that the bureau itself was essential to budget reform.

3 INVENTING THE BUDGET

During their first years of activity, the men of the Bureau of Municipal Research fully articulated a basic program of budget reform. In doing so, they created a new language of public administration and developed new techniques of political accountability that swept the country and transformed relations of power and accountability both within government and between government and the people. Drawing on the raw material of corporate accounting and certain European governmental budget systems, the men of the bureau invented a distinctively American budget whose significance lay less in its techniques of financial administration than in its vision of political power and citizenship in a representative democracy.

Inventing the budget alone, however, was not enough to ensure success. The idea of the budget was something new, and the need for it was not self-evident. New York's government had managed its affairs since colonial times without a budget system. The bureau, therefore, had to convince members of the political community that New York urgently needed this new thing called a "budget system." Like a good advertiser, the bureau created a need for its new product in the mind of its targeted consumer—the government. The transaction, however, did not end with the sale. The new budget system needed maintenance and upgrading that could be supplied only by the experts who originally manufactured the product, in effect forcing the consumer to depend continuously on the retailer for support and guidance.

THE IDEA OF BUDGET REFORM

The idea of budget reform did not spring full grown from the head of Allen, Cleveland, or Bruere; it emerged gradually as the bureau gained acceptance from the government and the public. Bruere recalled that when he had completed the bureau's first major administrative survey (of the Health Department in 1906), he did not originally conceive of his recommendations in terms of budget reform. It was Thorstein Veblen, while paying a visit to his former student Bruere and his friend Allen in the fall of 1906, who first suggested to Bruere that he was, in fact, proposing for New York a budget system on the British model.[1]

As later defined by Cleveland, the budget was "a plan for financing an enterprise or government during a definite period, which is prepared and submitted by a responsible executive to a representative body (or other duly constituted agent) whose approval and authorization are necessary before the plan may be executed."[2] Though typically prosaic, Cleveland's bare-bones description of the budget nonetheless articulated some central principles of budget reform that distinguished it from earlier simple accounting reforms.

First, the budget was a "plan"; it was prospective and connected to policy making, whereas simple accounting reform was retrospective, a means of collecting data on events that had already occurred. Such a prospective outlook differentiated budget reformers from their mugwump predecessors, who were more concerned to preserve and protect an established and fundamentally static notion of good government than to plan for its future development.

Second, the budget was to provide the basis for assigning political responsibility by enabling the legislature and the citizenry to hold the executive and his officers accountable for their actions. The budgetary system was to be a means of promoting representative democracy, whereas accounting reform applied to all enterprises, public or private, democratic or not.

Within government, Cleveland saw a pressing need to determine precisely what various departments were doing and to assign responsibility for results. He found that city government "had been carved up into lit-

---

[1] Henry Bruere, "A Forward and a Backward Glance," Speech presented at the 1947 Annual Conference of the Governmental Research Association (New York: Governmental Research Association, 1948).

[2] Frederick A. Cleveland, "Evolution of the Budget Idea in the United States," *Annals of the American Academy of Political and Social Science* 62 (November 1915): 15.

tle jurisdictions," each jealously guarded by some officer or subordinate. A budget was to be used "as a means of breaking down these many petty jurisdictions and requiring information on standard lines to come to a central office where it could be summarized and coordinated."[3] To fight corruption, the budget would formalize boundaries between public and private spheres; to promote efficiency, it would erase boundaries within them, forcing diverse departments to place themselves under the centralized gaze of a budgetary overseer.

Finally, the budget would identify and situate power. Accounting merely revealed what people were doing, but a budget would define their activities as public or private. Published budgets, both governmental and corporate, would specify the limits of appropriate activity within each sphere. Bribery of public officials or the unregulated surrender of public franchises to private enterprises would transgress the boundaries set forth by well-wrought budgets.

From Ida Tarbell's muckraking exposé of Standard Oil to Louis Brandeis's fulminations against the dangers of monopoly, the "discovery of corruption" and fear of the excessive power wielded by corporate giants over public affairs lay at the heart of much Progressive era reform. Budget reformers recast corruption as a function of a system with no clear boundaries between public and private authority. Corporations became a threat to democracy primarily when they tried to arrogate to themselves powers that properly belonged to the government. The danger lay not so much in power itself as in its inappropriate application. Corruption was not power in the hands of bad men; it was power asserted where it did not belong. If, as the anthropologist Mary Douglas has argued, dirt is "matter out of place," then to the men of the bureau, corruption was "power out of place." The budget would eliminate corruption by locating power in its appropriate sphere and assigning it openly to specific institutions.[4]

A proper system of budgets, both public and private, would normalize relations between the two spheres, specifying which activities properly fell

---

[3]Ibid., 33.

[4]Mary Douglas, *Purity and Danger* (New York: Praeger, 1966), 29–40. For discussions of contemporary attitudes toward corruption and the relation of public to private power, see Richard McCormick, *The Party Period and Public Policy: American Politics from the Age of Jackson to the Progressive Era* (New York: Oxford University Press, 1986), 311–56; Grant McConnell, *Private Power and American Democracy* (New York: Alfred A. Knopf, 1966), 11–50, 119–55; R. Jeffrey Lustig, *Corporate Liberalism: The Origins of Modern American Political Theory, 1890–1920* (Berkeley: University of California Press, 1982), 194–244.

under the purview of which authority. The very visibility of the budget would discourage attempts to transgress its boundaries and would shield government from excessive corporate influence.

Budgets, however, could also serve the interests of savvy businessmen seeking to protect their interests from government regulation or even outright public ownership. As the insurance companies discovered in 1906, increased reporting requirements could actually insulate corporations from governmental interference. So long as businesses published budgets that revealed activities appropriate to the private sphere of legitimate commerce, the government had no justification for intervening in their affairs. It was little wonder, then, that men such as J. P. Morgan, Andrew Carnegie, and John D. Rockefeller lined up to support the Bureau of Municipal Research in its crusade to bring budget reform to city government.

THE BUREAU, THE BUDGET, AND THE AUTHORITY OF EXPERTS

The men of the bureau worked to establish the authority of their institution and of the idea of the budget in the minds of government officials and the public at large as a basis for restructuring governmental relations.[5] They portrayed themselves as doctors of government administration, diagnosing the ills of the urban polity and proposing remedies based on scientific principles and applied expertise. Just as a medical doctor would use professional judgment to construe the meaning of a patient's particular symptoms, so the men of the bureau would identify and name the ills of city government. In shaping public understanding of governmental problems, the bureau thus created the conditions under which its advice seemed appropriate. Acceptance of the bureau's expert diagno-

[5]The campaign for budget reform involved attempts to establish the cultural authority of the budget as a means of defining political reality. Paul Starr's study of the social transformation of American medicine is relevant here. Starr distinguishes two types of authority: social and cultural. Social authority belongs only to social actors and involves "the control of action through the giving of commands." Cultural authority may reside both in social actors and in cultural objects, such as authoritative treatises, and "may be used without being exercised; typically, it is consulted (even by people in authoritative positions), often in the hopes of resolving ambiguities." The great force of cultural authority lies in its power to establish "particular definitions of reality and judgements of meaning and value . . . as valid and true." Starr, *The Social Transformation of American Medicine* (New York: Basic Books, 1982), 13.

sis would naturally foster deference to its prescribed remedy to the problem.[6]

During the late nineteenth and early twentieth century, government became increasingly intrusive while simultaneously growing more distant from the comprehension and control of average citizens. The men of the bureau perceived that these developments were provoking a crisis of authority. In this new political world, individuals felt alienated from a complex and impersonal process of governance which they could not control. The political scandals of 1905–6 crystallized citizen concerns into specific attacks on the legitimacy of local and state government. The bureau's program of budget reform sought to address the crisis by establishing its own authority as a mediator between citizen and government. Budget reformers argued that a published budget would give the people of New York a full report—in a single, clear document—of their government's activities. A properly constructed and advertised budget could reestablish the bond between citizen and government by providing a basis for holding government accountable to the people. The renewed sense of control would relegitimize the increasingly activist city government in the eyes of its citizenry.[7] In this, the bureau's actions represented a political parallel to the contemporary professionalization of the social sciences, which sought to address a similar crisis of authority brought on by a perceived "recession of causation" in the social world.[8]

---

[6]As Starr notes, "The authority to interpret signs and symptoms, to diagnose health or illness, to name diseases, and to offer prognoses is the foundation of any social authority the physician can assume. By shaping the patients' understanding of their own experience, physicians create the conditions under which their advice seems appropriate." Ibid., 14.

[7]Frederick A. Cleveland, *Chapters on Municipal Administration and Accounting* (New York: Longmans, Green, 1909), 67–79; Henry Bruere, *The New City Government* (New York: D. Appleton, 1912), 180–95; Frederick A. Cleveland and Arthur E. Buck, *The Budget and Responsible Government* (New York: Macmillan, 1920), 37–40, 121–23.

[8]The context and process of the bureau's efforts to establish its authority as an institution conform in many respects to the model of professionalization identified by Thomas L. Haskell, who notes that the complex world of late nineteenth-century America was characterized by rising awareness of the interdependence of social life. People came to see everything as connected to and influenced by everything else, both synchronically ("cultural organicism") and diachronically ("historicism"). At the same time they sensed a "recession of causation," experiencing the feeling that each individual, as an individual, had less and less power to influence events in this complex, interconnected world. This caused a crisis of authority in response to which certain members of the social science community professionalized their disciplines as a means of reestablishing the cultural authority of their class. Specifically, Haskell discusses a three-step process by which the social sciences became professionalized: First, they (or rather, their practitioners) established communities of inquirers with specialized vocabularies. Second, these new communities distinguished themselves

Perhaps the bureau might best be conceived of as a quasi- or paraprofessional organization. It sought to emulate and appropriate the authority of the professions it encompassed without fixing its boundaries as a professional organization. It was composed of experts from a variety of fields and professions, each of whom applied his expertise in novel ways. The bureau maintained a remarkably low profile in light of the wide-ranging goals it hoped to achieve. Rather than overtly dominate public debate on government administration, the bureau sought to define and control the terms of the debate by supplying the information and the vocabulary needed to assess and discuss the city's needs. The bureau thus established its authority indirectly by urging people to defer to and act on the information it provided while presenting itself simply as a neutral conduit of this information.[9]

Just as the bureau attempted to appropriate the authority of established professions, so it sought to imbue the idea of the budget with the existing authority of the principles of efficiency and scientific inquiry.[10] The men of the Bureau not only annexed values of efficiency to the idea of the budget, they moralized them. Allen, always the most secure in his sense of the right, unmasked what he called the "goodness fallacy," proclaiming that goodness was a false criterion by which to judge public officials. Instead he proposed efficiency as the primary qualification for public ser-

---

from other groups with similar interests and from society as a whole. Third, by mastering the organization of their own disciplines, social scientists were able to increase their credibility with and authority over the public. Haskell, *The Emergence of Professional Social Science* (Urbana: University of Illinois Press, 1977), vi–vii, 1–47. Starr also identifies these three characteristics, quoting the commonly used sociological terms "collegial, cognitive, and moral" to identify them. Starr, *Social Transformation of American Medicine,* 15. For other attempts to define the attributes of a profession see, Ernest Greenwood, "Attributes of a Profession," *Social Work* 2 (July 1957): 44–55; Ernest Greenwood, "Attributes of a Profession: Revisited," in *Readings in the Sociology of the Professions,* ed. Sheo Kamar Lal, Ambka Chandani, Umed Raj Nahar, and Kirti Khanna (Delhi: Giam, 1988), 4–29; and Harold Wilensky, "The Professionalization of Everyone?" *American Journal of Sociology* 70 (September 1964): 137–58.

⁹In an intriguing essay, Margali Sarfatti Larson writes about the subtlety of expert power, which does not directly confront those subject to it but rather operates beneath the surface by shaping initial perceptions of reality and determining objects of desire. This model certainly seems to fit the bureau's approach to exercising its own expert power. Larson, "The Production of Expertise and the Constitution of Expert Power," in *The Authority of Experts,* ed. Thomas L. Haskell (Bloomington: University of Indiana Press, 1984), 28–80.

¹⁰See Samuel Haber, *Efficiency and Uplift: Scientific Management in the Progressive Era, 1890–1920* (Chicago: University of Chicago Press, 1964), and Martin J. Schiesl, *The Politics of Efficiency: Municipal Administration and Reform in America, 1800–1920* (Berkeley: University of California Press, 1977).

vice.[11] He also wrote on efficiency in religious work, going so far as to subject Christ's life and teaching to his own "efficiency test," which compared "pretense and practice, faith and work, effort expended and results obtained." Allen graciously accorded Christ a high score, but he attributed the decline of contemporary church influence to its failure to apply his test to its own work.[12]

In a striking phrase, Allen asserted that "to be efficient is more difficult than to be good." Efficiency fostered "goodness as the time clock and cash register foster[ed] habits of punctuality." For Allen, surveillance and measurement were essential to true goodness. Mere good intentions might go astray, but efficiency tests in government would "greatly increase" the "goodness that has lasting value to one's fellow man."[13] By repeatedly juxtaposing efficiency with morality (and religion), Allen gave it some of the authority adhering to the latter. He established efficiency as a necessary precondition to goodness; being essential to goodness, efficiency itself became "good"—indeed, it became more important to good government than goodness itself.

The men of the bureau did not abstract efficiency from the social goals it served. Bruere rejected the notion that narrow concerns for economy had inspired the efficiency movement. Rather, he firmly believed that "only through efficient government could progressive social welfare be achieved."[14] Bruere placed efficiency in the service of democratic values, insisting that he was "fighting for the realization of the philosophical concept of robust, real democracy and equality of opportunity, by securing an efficient discharge of the community business."[15]

Cleveland also demonstrated a clear commitment to a normative conception of efficiency in government. "The demand for efficiency," he wrote, "must go farther than to require that the government shall get a dollar for every dollar spent; it must constitute a demand that the government is doing the thing most needed."[16] Cleveland, of course, begged

---

[11]William H. Allen, "The 'Goodness' Fallacy," *World's Work* 13 (November 1906): 8186–89.

[12]William H. Allen, "Efficiency in Religious Work," *Annals of the American Academy of Political and Social Science* 30 (November 1907): 111–12.

[13]William H. Allen, *Efficient Democracy* (New York: Dodd, Meade, 1907), vii–viii.

[14]Bruere, *New City Government*, 1.

[15]Henry Bruere, "The Bureau of Municipal Research," *American Political Science Association: Proceedings* 5 (December 1912): 111.

[16]Frederick A. Cleveland, "The Need for Coordinating Municipal, State, and National Activities," *Annals of the American Academy of Political and Social Science* 41 (May 1912): 27.

the question of who decided what was "most needed," but he made it clear that the budget system was essential to making the determination.

The budget, as a concrete manifestation of efficiency, thus took on moral value. "Wrong budget-making," wrote Bruere, "is a chief sin of inefficient government, and right budget-making one of the first concerns of efficient government."[17] Since right budget making was virtuous, those who made budgets (in the right way) were also virtuous, and presumably worthy of respect and deference. The virtuous men of the bureau, as the foremost authorities on the principles of virtuous budget making, thus sanctified themselves as both advocates and judges of virtuous government.

Ironically, even as they endowed budget making with moral values, the ABCs insisted that their work was grounded on scientific principles of objective observation and neutral evaluation of data. They played down their own role, casting themselves as servants of government and the public, and presenting the budget as a passive object with no force of its own independent of its politically neutral function of efficiently appropriating funds.[18]

The bureau's elevation of the moral significance of budgeting, combined with its limiting of the scope of the budget's power, reveals the subtlety with which the bureau exercised its expert authority. A budget without apparent political force would likely be more acceptable to the members of an established political system who had their own interests and constituencies to maintain. Similarly, a new civic organization presenting itself as a mediator or servant would not appear to infringe directly on established political territory but rather to operate outside of and subordinate to government. The bureau used this nonthreatening approach to establish its position on the municipal scene. It set municipal priorities indirectly, working beneath the surface of things, shaping the flow of information about government administration and interpreting its meaning.

THE LANGUAGE OF BUDGET REFORM

Allen, Bruere, and Cleveland used powerful corporate and medical metaphors to assign meaning and position to the bureau's role in relation

[17]Bruere, *New City Government*, 192.
[18]Cleveland, "Budget Idea," 19.

to citizens and government officials. General comparisons between municipal government and modern business corporations had emerged after the Civil War and were quite common by 1900. The men of the bureau refined the broad corporate theme, identifying specific parallels to support their reform program. As Charles Beard, who became director of the bureau in 1918, put it, "it was the Bureau that first pointed out the analogy between private corporate organization and management and public management, and first brought to the consideration of the public the results of experience in private corporations."[19]

The budget occupied a central position in the bureau's elaboration of the corporate model. "A budget," wrote Cleveland, "is to self-government what the proposals contained in the annual report of the president of a corporation are to the board and stockholders."[20] Both provided the information necessary for democratic control. In his use of the model, Cleveland cast government officials alternately as a board of directors or a board of trustees (or, combining the two, the board of a corporate trust), with voters as shareholders or beneficiaries. Cleveland never explored the implications of his intermingling of the two terms—trust and corporation—but they are significant, especially when applied to the modern democratic state. A corporation is chartered by the state for specific purposes and has as its primary goal the maximization of return to its public shareholders. A trust is not chartered; it does not necessarily have a business or management structure, as does a corporation, and it is administered for the benefit of a restricted and predefined set of beneficiaries. Moreover, the status of a beneficiary cannot be bought and sold in the same way as the status of a shareholder.

As a model for civic society, the corporation implies changing membership, people coming and going, with the government (corporation) responsible only to those currently able to vote (shareholders). The trust model, ironically, can be more inclusive. It implies a responsibility for all people simply by reason of their membership in the polity. They are beneficiaries by reason of their status as citizens, not because they possess a vote.

Cleveland's benign—even admiring—view of the corporation left out several aspects of the model. He did not consider, for example, that in a corporation an elite few with many shares may dominate the enterprise.

[19]Charles Beard, quoted in Jane S. Dahlberg, *The New York Bureau of Municipal Research* (New York: New York University Press, 1966), 47–48.
[20]Frederick A. Cleveland, *Organized Democracy* (New York: Longmans, Green, 1913), 456.

(In fact, this disproportionate exercise of power clearly had parallels in the practical functioning of the democratic model.) Furthermore, Cleveland's use of the corporate model did not address the issue of rights or obligations; the only significant difference between a public and private corporation was that one yielded money dividends and the other yielded improved municipal services.[21]

In pursuing the corporate analogy, Cleveland also failed to consider the place of two critical components of corporate life, labor and the consumer. Cleveland appeared not to have differentiated labor from management or consumers from shareholders. The early 1900s was a period of great labor unrest and union organizing, both in New York and throughout the country.[22] The men of the bureau were aware of this situation, but as they abhorred conflict, they excluded it from their model of democratic government. To them, reasoned cooperation was the way to solve all social and political problems. Cleveland's corporate model of municipal government resolved labor conflict by ignoring it. In the public sphere, Cleveland's approach by implication cast labor (i.e., government employees) as a simple extension of management—just another tool of administration.

Cleveland similarly conflated the roles of consumer and shareholder. In the private sphere the corporation not only provided profit to the shareholder, but it also produced goods and services to a market of consumers. In the public sphere voters were both shareholder and consumers, electing the "board of directors" consuming the goods and services it provided, and sharing the profit of consumer sales. Cleveland does not tell us—nor does he consider the possibility—that the "public corporation" might provide benefits to certain consumers at a cost to its general shareholders. As "citizen consumers," some elites with power and influence may receive disproportionate access to public goods and services.

In spite of Cleveland's embrace of the corporate model, it did not hold a central place for the bureau as a whole. Rather, the men of the bureau turned to another metaphor, a medical one, which portrayed the bureau as a doctor to government, diagnosing its ills and prescribing its cures. In *Efficient Democracy*, Allen included a chapter called "The Business Doc-

---

[21]Cleveland, *Municipal Administration*, 143.
[22]See Melvyn Dubofsky, *When Workers Organize: New York City in the Progressive Era* (Amherst: University of Massachusetts Press, 1968), and Irwin Yellowitz, *Labor and the Progressive Movement in New York State, 1897–1916* (Ithaca: Cornell University Press, 1965).

tor" (also referred to as the "Doctor of Sick Accounts"). This doctor "uses the physician's method in learning what has gone wrong; inspects the business, feels the pulse, looks at the eyes, asks about daily routine, hunts out disturbing causes and prescribes a remedy that will remove, not merely cover up or deaden the pain."[23] Allen here described a special type of auditor who, in addition to compiling data, interpreted it and suggested courses of action based on his interpretations.

As Cleveland put it, the bureau would act toward government as the business doctor acted toward the corporation. As the political equivalent of a medical research laboratory staff, the bureau's experts were to "obtain a scientific diagnosis as a basis for prescription" to cure governmental ills.[24] The men of the bureau used the medical metaphor to position themselves outside the corporate model while establishing authority over it. They were not subject to the discipline of the corporate structure, yet as doctors to government they were essential to its continued good health.

The bureau sustained the metaphor (and the authority it conferred) by characterizing specific governmental defects in medical terms. Allen, for example, referred to the notorious insurance company scandals of 1905 and 1906 as a "cancer,"[25] and Cleveland likened government graft to a disease-causing germ. In an address titled "The Genus Grafter—with Apologies to Bacteriology," Cleveland stated: "Through scourges of 'Black Death,' Asiatic Cholera, and yellow fever we have learned that the only way to successfully protect society is by enforcing a method of living which will protect the individual from disease,—i.e., the remedy of intelligence is sanitation and disinfection as a means of controlling the conditions favoring germ culture. The remedy for graft must have to do with institutional methods, rather than with the treatment of individual cases."[26] Cleveland here demonstrated both a sophisticated grasp of medical theory and a savvy political sense. As Progressive era political reform shifted its focus from individual to structural corruption, so too had recent developments in the germ theory of disease shifted responsibility for disease from the moral habits of the individual to random and amoral germs in the environment.[27] Cleveland's germ analogy directed blame

---

[23]Allen, *Efficient Democracy*, 45.
[24]Cleveland, *Organized Democracy*, 445–46.
[25]Allen, *Efficient Democracy*, 55.
[26]Cleveland, *Municipal Administration*, 23.
[27]Charles E. Rosenberg, *The Care of Strangers: The Rise of America's Hospital System* (New York: Basic Books, 1987), 122–41.

away from individual grafters and focused it on the institutional causes of the disease, thereby allowing existing office holders to embrace budget reform without fearing for their jobs.

When it came to the practical mechanics of budget reform, Cleveland similarly displayed a sophisticated appreciation of the power of language to shape the exercise of authority. In his paper "The Nomenclature and Phraseology of Municipal Administration and Accounts," Cleveland contrasted contemporary municipal administration with the Tower of Babel: God had visited a confusion of tongues upon a presumptuous people in order to hinder the advancement of a "corrupt and wicked generation," but in modern times, municipal corruption depended on obscure and misleading language to succeed. Cleveland argued that "the modern municipal grafter thrives best in silence and darkness. He desires no language that may leaven popular ignorance as to his doings."[28] Just as clear accessible language could illuminate government activities and constrain official power, obscure or misleading language could mask the improper exercise of authority and enable graft to flourish.

The key, for Cleveland, was to find and disseminate a common language of municipal administration. "Words are symbols—," declared Cleveland in a strongly semiotic vein; "they are artificial signs expressing ideas. To convey meaning they must be commonly understood; but a common understanding presumes common ideas which may be similarly expressed in words. Common ideas, in turn, require subjects of thought shall be analyzed; and that object of thought shall be commonly classified. Finally, every classification which takes on the mind of man must proceed from some common, intelligent purpose."[29] Scientific accounting would unify municipal administration with a common language whose precision would insure honest and efficient administration.

Cleveland maintained that "a well devised system of municipal accounts when properly coordinated should give a direct and accurate answer to every question about which the officer and citizen must think."[30] In Cleveland's hands, accounting became a total language that encompassed, defined, and hence controlled "every question" of civic life. But there was a hitch. Although Cleveland wanted "words that are commonly understood and that leave no room for doubt as to the object or subject or class intended," accounting was a technical language that belonged only to those who had mastered it. As keepers of the language, Cleveland

[28] Cleveland, *Municipal Administration*, 175.
[29] Ibid.
[30] Ibid., 179.

and his associates assumed its totalistic and unassailable authority. In the coming years, they extended the discipline of budgets and hence their domain of expertise to cover all aspects of municipal administration and of citizen access to information about that administration—with very mixed results for the democratic process.

Introducing the Budget

The bureau's primary technique for applying "scientific" principles of firsthand observation to investigating municipal administration was the "survey." The social survey emerged in England during the mid-nineteenth century as a technique for compiling statistical information on discrete problems such as public health and housing conditions among the poor. American settlement house workers, so deeply influenced by things British, adapted the technique to American conditions during the 1880s and 1890s. The University Settlement in New York and Hull House in Chicago led the way. In the hands of activists such as Robert Hunter and Jane Addams, the survey became a formidable weapon in the arsenal of middle-class social reform.[31]

Allen had experience with surveys through his work in graduate school and with the Association for Improving the Condition of the Poor. But it was Bruere, ever the intermediary, who brought the method of the social survey to bear on the study of government activities. At the age of nineteen, Bruere worked as the director of the Boys Clubs at the College Settlement in Boston while trying to make a go of Harvard Law School. Bruere never finished Harvard but he stayed with social work. In 1902 he visited the University Settlement in New York, where he met Robert Hunter, who was then engaged in a path-breaking study of poverty in the United States.[32] Hunter was impressed by the eager and able midwesterner and introduced him to the industrialist Stanley McCormick, who brought Bruere to Chicago to oversee his family's welfare activities at the

[31]For analyses of the origins and development of the social survey in both Europe and the United States, see Martin Bulmer, Kevin Bales, and Kathryn Kish Sklar, eds., *The Social Survey in Historical Perspective, 1880–1940* (Cambridge: Cambridge University Press, 1991).

[32]Published in 1904, Hunter's book caused a sensation with its claim that "no less than ten million persons in the United States are underfed, underclothed, and poorly housed." Although denying that the book was a "scientific or exhaustive study," Hunter tried to define poverty analytically and made use of statistical evidence and surveys by other social workers to compose his broad portrait of poverty and destitution in the country at large. Robert Hunter, *Poverty* (New York: Macmillan, 1904), i–iv.

Gad's Hill Settlement House. While in Chicago, Bruere regularly visited Hull House, where he met and worked with Jane Addams, Graham Taylor, and Raymond Robbins, among others in the local social settlement community.[33]

When he returned to New York in 1906, Bruere brought with him a wealth of firsthand experience with social surveys. Over the next few years, Bruere and his new associates at the Bureau of Municipal Research adapted the social survey technique to the study of local government operations.[34] To conduct a survey, the bureau typically put together a team of four men to investigate a particular department. The team worked closely with department officials to compile and organize relevant data while assuring them that the purpose of the surveys was not to undermine them but to help make their departments more efficient. The staff of the bureau was careful to confer with affected officials before commencing investigations of particular departments or operations and always sought to secure promises of cooperation and instructions directing subordinates to cooperate with the bureau's representatives. Ultimately, however, the bureau alone interpreted the information and conveyed its significance.[35]

The bureau's entire program depended on access to government information. To overcome any possible aversion to admitting outside experts into the hidden precincts of government administration, the men of the bureau tried to make themselves of practical use to sitting officials while insinuating themselves into positions from which they could exercise authority independently. First, they did not attack individual members of government, but focused instead on the impersonal structures of administration that allowed inefficiency to flourish. Second, they played down

[33]Henry Bruere, *Reminiscences* (New York: Columbia University Oral History Collection, 1949), 10–17.

[34]James Allen Smith, *The Idea Brokers: Think Tanks and the Rise of the New Policy Elite* (New York: Free Press, 1991), 40–42. Dahlberg, *New York Bureau of Municipal Research*, 54–55; Bureau of Municipal Research, "A National Program to Improve Methods of Government," *Municipal Research* 71 (March 1916): 37–38.

[35]Dahlberg, *New York Bureau of Municipal Research*, 60–64; Bureau of Municipal Research, *Purposes and Methods of the Bureau of Municipal Research* (New York: Bureau of Municipal Research, 1907), 5–7. In an address before the New York Real Estate Board of Brokers in 1909, Cleveland succinctly stated the central position of the bureau: "realizing that true democracy consists in intelligent cooperation between citizens and those elected or appointed to serve, it is hoped that the intelligence gained through systematic and independent citizen inquiry might be used by the mayor, comptroller and heads of departments to correct abuses concerning which a citizen might complain, without waiting for the fortuitous circumstance of a change in administration." Cleveland, *Municipal Administration*, 351–52.

their own importance, casting themselves more as neutral conduits of information than as crusading muckrakers. Third, they showed government officials that well-organized information could bolster their authority both within government and in the eyes of the electorate. Fourth, they made it clear that under existing laws they had a legal right to information and could compel officials to cooperate should they refuse to do so voluntarily. Fifth, the men of the bureau used the information they obtained to establish an ongoing oversight or surveillance of government activities; the more they saw, the more difficult it became for officials to hide information from them.[36]

Bruere's particular skills as diplomat and administrator were first put to the test in 1906 when, as director of the Bureau of City Betterment (the Bureau of Municipal Research's immediate predecessor), he spearheaded a controversial campaign to oust Manhattan borough president John F. Ahearn on grounds of incompetence. Unlike most of its later work, the bureau's initial foray into municipal reform directly challenged a specific politician's administration of various public works, such as street maintenance and upkeep of the public baths.[37]

Ahearn was a formidable target for the fledgling bureau. A Tammany stalwart and leading city official, he had held public office since 1882, the year Bruere was born. Ahearn tried to block Bruere's investigation by denying access to public records in flagrant contravention of both the common law and the New York City charter. Rather than directly contesting Ahearn's withholding of information, Bruere conducted an independent political survey of Ahearn's administration. Working with an assistant, Bruere matched borough repair contracts against work actual-

[36]For a general discussion of the working relationship between the bureau and government officials, see Dahlberg, *New York Bureau of Municipal Research*, 31–51; and Richard Skolnick, "The Crystallization of Reform in New York City, 1890–1917" (Ph.D. diss., Yale University, 1964), 326–52. A good contemporary example of the bureau's early approach to working with government may be found in William H. Allen, "How to Keep Government Efficient," *World's Work* 14 (August 1907): 9255–59.

[37]The following discussion of the Ahearn affair is drawn largely from "The Ahearn Case," *American Review of Reviews* 37 (February 1908): 141; Allen, "How to Keep Government Efficient," 9255–59; Dahlberg, *New York Bureau of Municipal Research*, 12–20; Luther Gulick, *The National Institute of Public Administration: A Progress Report* (New York: National Institute of Public Administration, 1928), 14–17; Harold Seidman, *Investigating Municipal Administration* (New York: Institute of Public Administration, Columbia University, 1941), 48–51; Harold C. Syrett, ed., *The Gentleman and the Tiger: The Autobiography of George B. McClellan, Jr.* (New York: J. B. Lippincott, 1956), 290–93; and Edwin R. Lewinson, *John Purroy Mitchel: The Boy Mayor of New York* (New York: Asta Books, 1965), 39–46.

ly performed. He personally charted public facilities and compared their condition before and after the supposed repairs took place.

On November 23, 1906, the Bureau of City Betterment presented the results of Bruere's investigation in the pamphlet *How Manhattan Is Governed*, which denounced Ahearn's administration of the borough as inefficient and incompetent. In response, Ahearn filed a $10,000 libel suit against R. Fulton Cutting and the Bureau of City Betterment, declared he had "absolutely nothing to conceal," and called for a formal investigation of the charges against him.[38] The initial investigation by the commissioners of accounts was, as Ahearn anticipated, a whitewash amounting to no more than a mild slap on the wrist for the Tammany veteran. Unfortunately for Ahearn, Bruere went to Mayor McClellan and confronted him with evidence that directly contradicted the commissioners' findings.[39] McClellan was at that time engaged in a power struggle against Tammany's boss Charles Murphy. He was only too happy to act on the bureau's findings and appointed John Purroy Mitchel, an independent Democrat, as special counsel to investigate the charges further.

Throughout his investigation, Mitchel worked closely with Bruere, absorbing the mountains of information he supplied together with his philosophy of municipal reform. In July of 1907, Mitchel presented a formal report to McClellan, written with Bruere's assistance[40], that affirmed the bureau's severe criticisms of "inefficiency, neglect, waste and corruption." The mayor forwarded the report to Governor Hughes. Shortly thereafter, Mitchel and Bruere convinced George McAneny, then president of the City Club, to petition the governor to remove Ahearn pursuant to his powers under section 382 of the Greater New York Charter.[41]

As with its appeal to McClellan, the bureau was fortunate in the political timing of the petition to Hughes. Since the beginning of 1907, the new Republican governor had been engaged in a running battle to remove Otto Kelsey, the state insurance commissioner, for reasons that were strikingly similar to the bureau's charges against Ahearn. Hughes had failed in his attempt to remove Kelsey (the senate had blocked him), but following his defeat, he actively supported the Moreland Act, which was passed in May. The Moreland Act empowered the governor to appoint ad hoc in-

---

[38]Bruere also recalled that Ahearn accused him of being "a liar and a thief, and a British spy from Chicago." Bruere, *Reminiscences*, 27.

[39]Ibid., 27–30.

[40]Ibid., 32.

[41]See "Proceedings Against John F. Ahearn," in *Public Papers of Governor Charles E. Hughes* (Albany: J. B. Lyon, 1907), 267–86.

vestigating commissions to examine the administrative practices of any or all departments, boards, bureaus, or commissions of the state. Unable to get the information necessary to remove Kelsey, Hughes wanted to ensure that future governors would not be similarly denied.[42]

Thus when McAneny presented the bureau's brief against Ahearn to Hughes that summer, he found a man uniquely familiar with and sympathetic to the bureau's concerns. Hughes may in fact have viewed the Ahearn affair as a chance to succeed where he had failed with Kelsey. In any case, after holding hearings, Hughes ordered Ahearn's removal on December 9, 1907, on grounds of administrative incompetence and breach of duty.[43]

Bruere and his associates learned several important lessons from the experience with Ahearn. First, it demonstrated the need for regularized and guaranteed access to information about government operations. Second, it confirmed their belief in the efficacy of direct, firsthand investigation of municipal activities. Third, it taught them that even when one government official resisted their interference, others might be willing to cooperate.

Bruere's early success positioned the bureau remarkably well for introducing its program of budget reform. Before the Ahearn affair, corruption and dishonesty had been the markers of a bad politician; with Ahearn's removal, incompetence and inefficiency became equally legitimate measures of a person's fitness to hold public office. The bureau's program of budget reform, first introduced in the fall of 1907 in cooperation with New York City's Department of Health, provided a new mechanism for measuring an official's administrative ability.

The Department of Health presented the bureau with an excellent opportunity to apply its program to city administration. In 1906 the department was in a sorry state. It suffered from inadequate funding, disorganization, mismanagement, and a terrible public image. Bruere capitalized on the department's distress and easily convinced the commissioner of health, Thomas Darlington, that a survey of the department

---

[42]Robert F. Wesser, *Charles Evans Hughes: Politics and Reform in New York, 1905–1910* (Ithaca: Cornell University Press, 1967), 124–45; J. Ellswerth Missall, *The Moreland Act: Executive Inquiry in the State of New York* (New York: King's Crown Press, 1946), 9–23.

[43]Although Hughes's action brought an end to Ahearn's libel suit against Cutting, the matter did not end there. Not one to give up easily, Ahearn engineered his reelection by the Tammany-controlled Board of Aldermen as interim borough president to fill the post he had been forced to vacate. McClellan, demonstrating equal persistence, got the attorney general to institute *quo warranto* proceedings to test the legality of Ahearn's title to his office. The court ruled that Ahearn's reappointment was illegal and finally laid the matter to rest. Seidman, *Investigating Municipal Administration*, 51; Syrett, *The Gentleman and the Tiger*, 291–92.

would be "the best way to increase funds and earn the public's confidence."[44]

Bruere's choice of the health department as a test case was especially adroit because it was highly visible and its work directly affected the entire citizenry. Such problems as contaminated milk, the spread of tuberculosis, and the need for more medical care for children provided a dramatic backdrop to the bureau's work.[45] In addition, the substantive activities of the Department of Health resonated with the bureau's presentation of itself as staffed by "doctors" ready to diagnose and prescribe remedies to cure the ills of maladministration.

The bureau's final report on the Department of Health, published in 1907 as *Making a Municipal Budget*, was the first clear public articulation of the bureau's belief in the central importance of budget reform. Its first words declared that "no document can tell in such condensed form so many significant facts about community needs and government efforts to meet those needs as a properly constructed budget."[46]

The bureau found serious inadequacies in the department's system of records and accounts. Service and cost data were often inaccurate or difficult to find, and accounts were classified not by functions but by "funds" or appropriations. The school inspection fund, for example, paid not only the medical inspectors of schools but also the school nurses and the so-called summer corps, consisting of physicians and nurses who went house-to-house to instruct mothers in how to care for babies suffering from "summer complaint." Furthermore, the bureau found it nearly impossible to determine which function or activity of the department was actually responsible for the money spent.[47]

The report recommended the adoption of detailed functional segregation and classification of accounts and regular record keeping to provide a basis for ongoing administrative oversight of departmental activities.[48] It also argued that similar reports and reforms would be needed for every other department in the city. The bureau emphasized that its services were required both quantitatively, to reach the great number of departments throughout city government, and qualitatively, to perfect the efficient op-

[44]Bureau of Municipal Research, *Making a Municipal Budget* (New York: Bureau of Municipal Research, 1907), 9.

[45]Dahlberg, *New York Bureau of Municipal Research*, 156.

[46]Bureau of Municipal Research, *Making a Municipal Budget*, 5, 9–10.

[47]Ibid., 9–21; Dahlberg, *New York Bureau of Municipal Research*, 158–59.

[48]Bureau of Municipal Research, *Making a Municipal Budget*, 31–32.

eration of the principles of budget making. The bureau had its foot in the door of city government and it was pushing hard to sell its product.[49]

The bureau's first attempt at budget reform set the pattern for its future activities. The Department of Health surrendered to the bureau a degree of internal control and autonomy in return for renewed credibility. The bureau's report secured for the department both its appropriations and renewed public confidence. In return, the bureau received the legitimacy and authority conferred by a formal appeal for assistance from a well-established city department. Through their quiet, supportive approach to municipal reform, the men of the bureau had performed the near-miraculous feat of making the discipline of continuous oversight enforced by clearly fixed lines of accountability appear nonthreatening—even desirable. Their work with the Department of Health demonstrated that submission to their "medical" authority could be empowering.

THE BUREAU AND CITY HALL

To expand its program, the bureau cultivated ongoing contacts with administrative officers and developed an uneasy symbiosis with Tammany Hall and city politicians. The bureau based its relationship with Tammany on a pragmatic recognition of the positive role political machines had played in the development of municipal government.[50] As Bruere said, "When we began this work, the chief obstacle to good government was not villainy but the kind heart. A district leader generally would make a poor department manager and often a corrupt official but he was always a kind friend."[51] Similarly, Allen, even as he battled the machine, acknowledged that "with a Tammany man, there's nothing personal about political controversy; its just a game; whichever way the game breaks, he's a good fellow and you're a good fellow and you're good friends. That comes from training[,] not insisting or theory."[52] Allen admired Tammany men for their practical experience and mastery of the concrete details of politics. Their methods were compatible with Allen's own inductive, experiential approach to municipal administration.

[49]Ibid., 30.

[50]See, for example, Dahlberg, *New York Bureau of Municipal Research*, 37; and William H. Allen, *Reminiscences* (New York: Columbia University Oral History Collection, 1950), 182.

[51]Bruere, quoted in Dahlberg, *New York Bureau of Municipal Research*, 37.

[52]Allen, *Reminiscences*, 182.

Cleveland was the most forthright of the three in his praise of machines. "An American political 'boss,'" he declared,

> is commonly one of the most intelligent and efficient citizens that we have. His guiding motive may not be the public welfare, but he has had a clearer concept of the essential factors of democracy than has the reformer who dreams of high statesmanship in terms of abstract morality, but who lacks the touch and balance of facts about the everyday life of the people. . . . To the Tweed and other "graft" organizations New York owes much that is best in the development of municipal life.[53]

Cleveland did not demonize the machine. He believed it had served an important purpose at a time when government administration was not organized well enough to meet citizens' needs. Nonetheless, he believed emphatically that the time had come for the discipline of budget reform to replace the machine.

The bureau's respect for bosses grew naturally out of its overall strategy to influence municipal administration. Chastened by the defeat of reform mayor Seth Low, the bureau framed its program to be acceptable to City Hall regardless of which party occupied the mayor's office. Access to information and cooperation with government officials were the sine qua non of the municipal research method. It was essential, therefore, that the bureau maintain an open and cordial attitude toward whichever party held the reins of power.

Budget reform allowed for a unique accommodation between old and new in New York politics. The bureau itself periodically drew Tammany's ire, but its basic principles of budget reform were rarely questioned. The *American Review of Reviews* noted in 1909 that despite some attacks on the bureau, "progress is made even with Tammany in office. Tammany officials cannot wholly disregard the demands made by the growing intelligence of the community."[54] The bureau's program tried to apportion the government between professional administrators and machine politicians. The politicians had the legitimacy conferred by public election. This they then transferred to their appointed bureaucrats, who, in turn, maintained or enhanced the initial electoral legitimacy of politicians by providing a mechanism (budgets) of ongoing oversight and accountability. The bureau was a critical intermediary in this cycle of mutual legitimation.

---

[53]Cleveland, *Organized Democracy*, 443–44.
[54]"Progress in Spite of All," *American Review of Reviews* 40 (November 1909): 525.

The Tammany machine, however, was not as accommodating as Commissioner Darlington. It appreciated that budgets could actually bolster political legitimacy, but seasoned party politicians also recognized that widespread publication of an accurate budget might threaten many of their activities. Accepting the fact of budgets was one thing, but they were not about to let a bunch of do-good, overeducated reformers design, implement, and maintain them—at least not without a fight.

In 1909 Tammany launched a sustained attack on the bureau to coincide with the municipal elections that fall. Dubbing it "the Bureau of Municipal Besmirch," Tammany politicians in speeches and leaflets defamed the bureau as unprofessional, self-interested, and impractical reformers who misled the public with inaccurate or unfair presentations of facts about city administration.[55] Tammany also devoted a considerable portion of its campaign handbook, *Our City*, to an attack on the bureau as a slanderous and meddling institution. In addition, Tammany helped to establish an ad hoc organization called "The Great Oaks," which sponsored a campaign exhibit insinuating that the bureau's most prominent backers, including Cutting, Rockefeller, and Carnegie, were using the bureau to manipulate public opinion to further their own financial interests. Finally, the bureau noted that Tammany engaged special writers to contribute regular articles to the press as well as "ten or twelve cart-tail orators" to rail against "the malign influence of the Bureau."[56]

Tammany's vilification of the bureau backfired; it provided immense amounts of free publicity, which brought the bureau's name and methods to the attention of reformers throughout the United States. More important, it also brought in substantial financial support. In the aftermath of the 1909 campaign, Allen, Bruere, and Cleveland were invited to attend a dinner for about fifty prominent New Yorkers who wanted to know more about the organization that had so provoked Tammany's ire. The dinner led to the appointment of a committee to endow the bureau for the following five years, thus ensuring its secure establishment on the municipal scene.[57]

The mayoral election itself was also a great setback for Tammany. Its candidate, the respectable and independent-minded Judge William Gaynor, won, but every other major office with the exception of Queens borough president, went to the Fusion slate. Among the newly elected were several close friends of the bureau, including John Purroy Mitchel,

[55]"The 'Besmirch' Society," *New York Times*, September 2, 1909: 16.
[56]Bureau of Municipal Research, "National Program," 5–6.
[57]Ibid., 6.

elected president of the Board of Aldermen, and George McAneny, a charter member of the bureau's board of trustees, elected borough president of Manhattan.

Mayor Gaynor entered office relatively sympathetic to the bureau. He did not play a significant role in Tammany's election year attacks and actually believed that the bureau had been serving a constructive purpose in city affairs.[58] Mayor Gaynor's feelings toward the bureau chilled considerably during the first part of his term as he grew annoyed at what he considered to be its repeated and petty interferences with his administration of the city's affairs. But his attitude later changed again as he came to appreciate the benefits of maintaining good relations with the bureau. This fluctuating relationship provides a concise and revealing case study of the bureau's willingness and ability to engage in traditional quid pro quo politics to attain its ends.

In 1911 relations between the bureau and Gaynor went from bad to worse as the mayor and his officers repeatedly tried to exclude the bureau from governmental affairs. In March, the corporation counsel went so far as to accuse the bureau of a criminal offense, asserting that the bureau presented a report on a claim of damages directly to the Board of Assessors instead of to the corporation counsel. There is no record of charges having been brought, but the mere threat marked a significant departure from earlier relations.[59] In June the mayor refused to grant the bureau access to conduct an administrative survey of the police department because he found the men of the bureau to "have become officious and troublesome beyond toleration, and disposed to attack in place of helping."[60] In July Commissioner Lederle accused the bureau of violating an agreement with him by publishing an independent (and allegedly misleading) report on the health department that included private correspondence between Lederle and the bureau.[61] The mayor concurred, declaring that the bu-

---

[58] As early as January 31, 1909, then-judge Gaynor wrote that the "Bureau of Municipal Research . . . should be encouraged and helped to go through every department, one at a time, with a fine toothed comb." Quoted in Bureau of Municipal Research, *Six Years of Municipal Research for New York City* (New York: Bureau of Municipal Research, 1911), 70. For discussions of Gaynor's background in New York City politics, see Nancy Joan Weiss, *Charles Francis Murphy, 1858–1924: Respectability and Responsibility in Tammany Politics* (Northhampton, Mass: Smith College, 1968), 44; and Louis Heaton Pink, *Gaynor: The Tammany Mayor Who Swallowed the Tiger* (New York: International Press, 1931).

[59] Henry Bruere to William J. Gaynor, March 22, 1911, Mayoral Papers of William J. Gaynor, 1910–1913, Subject File: Public Relations—Bureau of Municipal Research, New York City Municipal Archives (hereafter cited as Gaynor papers).

[60] William J. Gaynor to Rhinelander Waldo, June 6, 1911, ibid.

[61] Ernst J. Lederle to William J. Gaynor, July 20, 1911, ibid.

reau had "broken faith," and directed Lederle "to exclude from the Department of Health at once any one and every one from the Bureau of Municipal Research."[62] After several other lesser but similar incidents during the remainder of 1911, Gaynor tersely stated, "I have nothing to say about Mr. Bruere because I do not deem him an honest reformer."[63]

Despite its conflicts with the mayor, the bureau continued to work closely with Comptroller Prendergast in implementing a new system of accounting and reporting procedures for the city. Moreover, in Raymond Fosdick, the commissioner of accounts, the bureau had a good friend who retained the mayor's trust and confidence throughout his administration.[64] Nonetheless, the level of antagonism with the mayor was clearly intolerable, and the bureau recognized that something had to be done.

The opportunity to make amends came at the beginning of 1912. As the year opened, Gaynor was entertaining presidential aspirations and so was especially sensitive about his public image. The bureau chose this juncture to issue a public statement reviewing Gaynor's performance which cited no fewer than seventy-four positive achievements of the mayor's administration. This timely bit of favorable publicity was not lost on Gaynor. The mayor's attitude toward the bureau warmed considerably, and by 1913 Gaynor (who had since abandoned his presidential hopes and was in failing health) was actively seeking out Bruere for assistance in framing a city pension system. The mayor reversed his earlier position and granted the bureau complete access to the police department.[65] Gaynor actually declared to Bruere, "I must say to you that you are the one whom I look to, as I have always experienced fairness at your hands, I think."[66] The mayor also arranged for the bureau to conduct renewed work with Commissioner Lederle in the health department.[67] This time, when Lederle again objected to the bureau's publishing an independent report in its own name, Gaynor dismissed his complaints and admonished Lederle to cooperate with Bruere "as he has given me his word that he will work with you and do us no harm by partnership."[68]

Gaynor's radical turnaround demonstrates his appreciation of the

[62]William J. Gaynor to Ernst J. Lederle, July 24, 1911, ibid.

[63]Pink, *Gaynor*, 389.

[64]Raymond Fosdick, *Chronicle of a Generation: An Autobiography* (New York: Harper, 1958), 81–84, 113.

[65]William J. Gaynor to Henry Bruere, June 11, 1913, Gaynor papers.

[66]William J. Gaynor to Henry Bruere, July 2, 1913, ibid.

[67]William J. Gaynor to Henry Bruere, June 25, 1913, ibid.

[68]Ernst J. Lederle to William J. Gaynor, July 16, 1913, and William J. Gaynor to Ernst J. Lederle, July 22, 1913, ibid.

value of having the bureau as an ally. Similarly, the bureau, recognizing the difficulty of carrying out its programs without mayoral support, moderated its criticisms of Gaynor's administration. Although the exchanges of 1911 through 1913 do not reveal direct evidence of self-censorship by the bureau, the mayor's references to the bureau's assurances that it would do "no harm" indicate the bureau's willingness to restrain itself in order to maintain good relations with government officials. Gaynor's greatest objection in 1911 had been that the bureau criticized existing practices rather than simply recommending improvements. By 1913 the bureau seemed more amenable to adopting the mayor's approach and evidently believed it could do so without significantly compromising its integrity.

THE BUREAU'S PUBLIC POSITION

To complete its acceptance among New York's major institutions, the bureau worked to establish its authority in the eyes of New York's substantial community of reform, business, and labor organizations. As in its relations with Gaynor, the bureau's first rule of operation was to avoid antagonizing powerful people. Divisive issues had no place in the bureau's philosophy of cooperation and conciliation. Moreover, as a practical matter, the bureau could not afford to antagonize powerful interests during its first years of operation, while it was trying to establish a presence on the scene of municipal reform.

The bureau shunned controversy from the outset. In early 1907 the bureau (then still operating under the auspices of the Citizens Union as the Bureau of City Betterment) considered conducting a study of municipal franchises but then pulled back because of political considerations. Bruere had gone so far as to enlist the services of George Sikes, an expert on traction questions from Chicago, to come to New York to conduct a study for the bureau. When officials from the Citizens Union got word of Bruere's actions, however, they directed him to rescind his offer to Sikes and cancel the study because it was too politically volatile.[69] R. Fulton Cutting, chairman of the Citizens Union, made it clear to E. R. A Seligman, then chairman of the bureau's board of trustees, that "in the inception of [the bureau's] career, it seemed to us essential that we should avoid any subject that might make us a political body." Cutting denied that the bureau's "patrons" had pressured him to drop the study, but he readily

[69]R. Fulton Cutting to George C. Sikes, July 24, 1907, E. R. A. Seligman papers, Correspondence, Rare Book and Manuscript Library, Columbia University, New York.

admitted that taking a stand on controversial issues, such as the traction question, would inevitably alienate important segments of the political community whose sympathy and support were necessary to the bureau's success. Cutting certainly was not averse to a little self-censorship in order to secure public approval.[70]

Cutting's strategy paid off. The bureau received very favorable press coverage and became a respected and influential member of the city's network of reform organizations. Newspapers in New York and across the nation lauded the bureau's efforts at municipal reform as word of its achievements spread. The bureau collected and published the most laudatory statements in several pamphlets that can only be described as unabashed efforts at self-promotion. Typical of these was an editorial from the *New York Evening Post*: "The Bureau is today the strongest single force working for better government in this city. So marked has been its success that already other cities are striving to follow suit, and the work done here will be of enormous value to similar undertakings elsewhere."[71] The *Brooklyn Eagle* also praised the bureau, which "has thrown the sunlight of publicity on many things, but it has not been run by fault-finders and trouble-makers, and has aroused little antagonism—none from worthy sources."[72] When the public read of the bureau in the press, it was likely to see this sort of positive remarks. Good publicity gave the bureau security and leverage in dealing with other groups in the city.

The bureau also compiled and published testimonials from various public officials with whom it had worked. Mayor McClellan, for example, stated in 1909 that "the service of the Bureau in purely municipal work marks a new departure in city government—the active cooperation of the public with the city administration."[73] Governor Hughes endorsed the bureau during his reelection campaign in November 1908, declaring that, "the character of the Bureau's investigation to aid administration in the city marks one of the most important improvements of recent years. It is striving to get at the facts in an honorable, straightforward way, and is striving to present them so that they will be intelligently comprehended."[74] And George McAneny, admittedly a strong partisan of the bureau,

[70]R. Fulton Cutting to E. R. A. Seligman, July 24, 1907, ibid.

[71]*New York Evening Post*, quoted in Bureau of Municipal Research, "National Program," 61.

[72]*Brooklyn Eagle*, quoted in ibid., 66.

[73]George B. McClellan, Jr., quoted in Bureau of Municipal Research, *Six Years of Municipal Research*, 69.

[74]Charles Evans Hughes, quoted in ibid.

effused: "I regard the institution and the work of the Bureau of Municipal Research as one of the most important economic events that has occurred in the history of the country in the past fifty years."[75] These testimonials did not simply bolster the bureau's reputation; they affirmed the bureau's superior status in relation to other reform groups throughout the city.

New York City during the Progressive era was awash in a bewildering variety of civic reform groups. Every public issue, from tenement housing to parks, child labor, and women's rights seemed to have an association, league, club, or group to promote it.[76] In this jumble of reform organizations, a new bureau might easily be swallowed up and lost, both to the public and to potential contributors. Allen, Bruere, and Cleveland took great pains to distinguish the bureau's work as unique and superior to other progressive reforms.

The bureau's early efforts at reform stood in marked contrast to those of its muckraking contemporaries. The men of the bureau disdained lurid exposés as mere sensationalism which roused the public's emotions without providing any true education or constructive proposals for reform. Upton Sinclair might bemoan that in writing his powerful muckraking novel about the Chicago stockyards, *The Jungle*, he had "aimed at the public's heart and by accident . . . hit it in the stomach,"[77] but the men of the bureau would likely see Sinclair's problem as a failure to aim at the public's head. Good citizenship, they believed, required a steady flow of reliable information, presented in a clear, accessible form that appealed to the intellect. Compared with Sinclair, the bureau might seem to have a cold, even bloodless, approach, yet Allen and Cleveland, in particular, were every bit as passionately committed to their own cause as Sinclair was to his.[78]

The meticulously documented and publicized references by McClellan, Hughes, and others to the bureau's unique services reinforced the bureau's own characterization of itself as a new and different type of organization: a full-time, professionally staffed research bureau for whose members reform was something more than a hobby. Fundamentally, however, the bureau's attempts to set itself apart from other reform groups depended on its ability to establish the distinctiveness of its budget reform program.

[75] George McAneny, quoted in Bureau of Municipal Research, "National Program," 19.
[76] The literature on this phenomenon is vast. Richard Skolnick, "Civic Group Progressivism in New York City," *New York History* 51 (July 1970): 411–39, provides a good brief discussion of the subject.
[77] Upton Sinclair, *The Jungle* (New York: New American Library, 1906), 349.
[78] Allen, *Efficient Democracy*, 280–86; Cleveland, *Organized Democracy*, 125–27.

Allen recognized that other reform groups served a purpose, but he declared that the "supreme need" in the field of government was for an agency which could act as an "intelligence centre" equipped "(1) to collect, (2) to classify, (3) to compile, (4) to make ready for general publication . . . [and] (5) to establish standards of scientific method in collecting, classifying and publishing facts."[79] That is, the various reform organizations had their place, but most needed was an agency like the Bureau of Municipal Research. Proper reform activity had to be based on information of the type supplied by the bureau. Allen thus tried to position the bureau as an intermediary, supplying information to and coordinating the activities of other reform organizations. As the collector, compiler, and disseminator of this information, the bureau could exercise an indirect control over the agendas of other reform groups and steer them toward particular lines of inquiry. Those groups, in turn, would have reason to defer to the bureau because it could confer legitimacy on particular calls for specific reforms by validating the factual bases of their claims.

The bureau identified the budget as "the indispensable basis for intelligence in city planning"[80] because "the only time in the year when any governmental body tried to picture itself 100% of its task, 100% of the communities needs, 100% of the government's opportunity, is when making up its mind how much money it will spend the next twelve months."[81] As the ultimate articulation of the city's needs, the budget became the preeminent guide to reform activities. Reform organizations could disregard the budget (and budget experts) only at the risk of being declared uninformed, inefficient, and misdirected.

The bureau's emphasis on the "goodness fallacy" and its moralization of budget reform also strengthened its position before the many social reform organizations that emphasized goodness and virtue as the basis of their activities. As the bureau subordinated goodness to efficiency, by implication it subordinated moral reform groups and their goals to organizations such as the bureau and its program of budget reform.[82]

The bureau also enjoyed continually good relations with New York's business community, from whom it obtained generous financial support.

[79]Allen, *Efficient Democracy*, 284–85.

[80]Bureau of Municipal Research, *How Should Public Budgets Be Made?* (New York: Bureau of Municipal Research, 1909), 3.

[81]William H. Allen, *Universal Training for Citizenship and Public Service* (New York: Macmillan, 1917), 114.

[82]See, for example, Allen, *Efficient Democracy*, vi–viii; Bruere, *New City Government*, 1, 192.

New York's corporate elite affirmed and institutionalized its support with a five-year endowment of the bureau's activities in the aftermath of Tammany's anti-bureau campaign of 1909. The bureau's extensive use of the corporate analogy to government and repeated calls for the introduction of business methods into city administration employed terms and ideas familiar to businessmen which undoubtedly resonated with their own conceptions of how the city ought to be run. Furthermore, the bureau's avoidance of controversial issues and its emphasis on cooperation promoted the sort of manageable evolutionary change most favored by major corporate capitalists of the period.[83] As early as May 1908, the New York State Chamber of Commerce expressed the business community's broad support when it passed a resolution praising the bureau for rendering "a most valuable public service by investigating and reporting upon the organization and accounting methods of the Finance Department of the City."[84]

The bureau's relations with labor were far more problematic. The corporate analogy, so favored by the men of the bureau, had no place for labor. Allen's "socialism of the intelligence," perhaps the closest thing the bureau had to a policy toward labor, aimed to ameliorate labor unrest through education—hardly an original or challenging idea. In 1912 Bruere did testify before the New York State Factory Investigation Commission (convened in response to the terrible fire at the Triangle Shirt Waist Factory in which 145 workers, mostly women and girls, lost their lives), but his testimony was limited to suggesting ways the state might consolidate city services to promote the more efficient protection of life, property, and buildings. Bruere professed no expertise in labor matters, readily admitting that his "acquaintance with the industrial situation is only that of an ordinary citizen."[85]

The impact of administrative reorganization upon jobs in municipal government strained bureau-labor relations. The increased economy and efficiency advocated by the bureau threatened union jobs. Anticipating labor resentment, in 1910 the bureau published *Municipal Reform through Revision of Business Methods*, which argued that the "clear economies"

---

[83]See Gabriel Kolko, *The Triumph of Conservatism* (New York: Free Press, 1963); James Weinstein, *The Corporate Ideal and the Liberal State, 1900–1918* (Boston: Beacon Press, 1968).

[84]Chamber of Commerce of the State of New York, *Fifty-first Annual Report—Part I* (New York: Press of the Chamber of Commerce, 1909), 2.

[85]State of New York, *Preliminary Report of the Factory Investigating Commission* (Albany: Argus, 1912), 2:1967–76.

of reorganization would help the entire city, whereas inefficient work helped no one.[86] The bureau hoped to make those workers fired to improve efficiency see that the money gained from releasing an unnecessary or incompetent employee would *"in the end prove a blessing to the discharged person himself."*[87] Though ludicrously insensitive to the individuals discharged, the bureau likely hoped to convince workers as a group that administrative reform was in the best interest of the entire community, including labor.

The Central Federated Union of New York, for one, was not impressed with the bureau's explanation. In 1911 the union attacked the bureau, accusing it of being a tool of Rockefeller and Carnegie, and demanded that the state legislature investigate and outlaw it. (Like Tammany, however, at no point did the union attack the idea of budget reform itself.) In tendering a formal motion to amend the city charter to ban the bureau, delegate Edward J. Hanna of the Blue Stone Cutters' Union voiced labor's concern that "all [the bureau] does is go around and get the number of jobs for workingmen cut down and throw people out of work."[88] Bruere, once again the diplomat, took it upon himself to placate labor. In response to Hanna's charges he reiterated that the bureau was "founded on a programme of promoting the welfare of all the citizens of New York, not at the expense of any one group, nor in the interest of any group." Bruere also welcomed the call for an investigation, volunteering to open the bureau's books to any interested party.[89] In the end, the union's actions came to naught, with perhaps the most tangible result being a strongly worded editorial in the *New York Times* in support of the bureau, stating that the union's attack constituted "one of the finest compliments ever paid to the work of the Bureau of Municipal Research."[90] Like Tammany's anti-bureau campaign of 1909, labor's assault bolstered the bureau's status in the mainstream reform community.

Surprisingly, the *New York Call*, the city's socialist paper, avowedly "devoted to the interests of the working people," did not cover the Central Federated Union's attack on the bureau. The *Call*, in fact, consistently treated the bureau well, providing regular and extensive coverage of its activities, generally in a favorable light. The editors of the *Call* seemed

[86]Bureau of Municipal Research, *Municipal Reform Through Revision of Business Methods* (New York: Bureau of Municipal Research, 1910), 3.
[87]Ibid., 38.
[88]"Unions Would End Bureau of Research," *New York Times*, September 9, 1911, 2.
[89]"Is Not Seeking Injury of Labor," *New York Times*, September 10, 1911, 12.
[90]"Jobs for Workingmen," *New York Times*, September 11, 1911, 8.

particularly inclined to warm to the bureau as it became the target of attacks from Tammany Hall in 1908 and 1909. In addition, they eagerly seized upon the information uncovered by the bureau, declaring that it "furnishes Socialists with arguments galore against capitalism."[91] The *Call*'s socialist editors abhorred capitalism, but the ideal of efficiency caught their fancy.

The bureau also maintained close personal ties to the city's socialist community. Allen's and Bruere's old friend Robert Hunter was a regular contributor to the *Call*. Bruere had also belonged to a luncheon group that met regularly at the Adeline Club which, in addition to Hunter, included Socialist party leader and labor lawyer Morris Hillquit and socialist authors Jack London and Ernest Poole.[92] Finally, there were direct family ties to labor and socialism. Bruere's brother Robert was a member of the Socialist Party, serving in 1910 as chairman of its committee on public affairs. Henry's wife, Jane, as well as his sister-in-law Martha Bensley Bruere served together on the publicity committee of the Women's Trade Union League in 1910. Mary Ritter Beard, whose husband, the historian Charles Beard, became supervisor of the bureau's Training School for Public Service in 1915, also joined the Women's Trade Union League, serving on its legislation committee in 1911. And Charles Beard himself was engaged in a wide array of activities on behalf of labor and social reform. Finally, Cleveland's brother-in-law, the eminent political scientist Samuel McCune Lindsay, before serving during the 1910s as the bureau's secretary, held the position of secretary of the National Child Labor Committee. The men of the bureau may have slighted the concerns of labor in their program, but they were firmly enmeshed in a network of personal relationships that linked them to a broader reform community that included labor.

NEW YORK CITY'S NEW BUDGET SYSTEM

Within this complex political context, the bureau successfully extended its program of budget reform throughout New York's administrative system. Beginning in 1907, the bureau, working in cooperation with comptroller Metz and the city's newly established Bureau of Municipal Investigation and Statistics, helped to prepare accounting classifications

91"Budget Exhibit Exposes System," *New York Call*, October 17, 1910, 4.
92Bruere, *Reminiscences*, 14, 57.

for four major departments. The resulting city budget for 1908 constituted the first budget in the United States based on a systematic classification of work being carried on by departments.[93]

Functional classification formed the core of the bureau's first effort at comprehensive budget reform. Segregation of items by function meant "that the budget should show the amounts requested for each kind of work to be done or public service which it was thought should be rendered."[94] Between 1909 and 1913 the budget became "functionalized" almost to the point of self-parody. By 1913 the budget document had grown to 836 pages (from a mere 122 pages in 1908), and the appropriation act contained a grand total of 3,992 distinct items. The budget had become so complex that it neither imposed internal discipline nor provided a viable tool to educate the citizenry. Excess led to retrenchment. Classification by function or activity (such as "General Administration" or "Division of Communicable Diseases" within the Department of Health) was superseded by "object-item classification," which categorized by items such as personnel services and supplies.[95] Bruere, writing as chamberlain of New York City in 1915,[96] had decided that functionalized accounts unduly constrained administrative discretion. Bruere wanted to move away from the negative, restrictive structure of the early budget system to a more positive approach: "The time has come when the relaxation of restrictions may be safely considered. There has come about in a remarkably short time a complete alteration of the attitude of the public officer to his executive responsibility."[97] The timing of Bruere's newfound trust in public officials coincided neatly with a triumph of Fusion

[93]David Bernstein, "Budgeting in New York City" (Ph.D. diss., New York University, 1961), 40–41. Bernstein's study contains a helpful, complete review of New York City's budget system during the first two decades of the twentieth century. Much of the information in the discussion that follows was drawn from or shaped by Bernstein's work.

[94]Bureau of Municipal Research, "Next Steps in the Development of a Budget Procedure for the City of Greater New York," *Municipal Research* 57 (January 1915): 34.

[95]Bureau of Municipal Research, "The New York City Budget," *Municipal Research* 88 (August 1917): 102; Bureau, "Next Steps," 34–37; Bernstein, "Budgeting in New York City," 42–52.

[96]In 1914, Bruere left the bureau to join the administration of the newly elected reform mayor, John Purroy Mitchel, as chamberlain. The post of chamberlain was appointed by the mayor and his duties were largely ministerial. He was, in effect, the city's banker, handling all deposits and withdrawals of city funds from financial institutions. After two years in the post, Bruere recommended that the office be abolished as unnecessary. See New York City, Office of the Chamberlain, *New York City's Administrative Progress, 1914–1916* (New York: Martin B. Brown, 1916).

[97]Henry Bruere, "The budget as an Administrative Program," *Annals of the American Academy of Political and Social Science* 62 (November 1915): 185.

candidates in local politics under the administration of his close friend John Purroy Mitchel, who was elected mayor in 1913 as part of a Fusion sweep. The principles of budget making might be "objective," but Bruere was only too willing to replace a restrictive set of principles with one that allowed for greater freedom of action when he personally approved of the people who would be exercising this increased discretionary power.

The new budget system required timely access to meaningful information. The bureau, therefore, worked with comptrollers Metz and Prendergast to develop a new system of central accounting which was installed in 1910.[98] To support its accounting reforms, the city government created three staff agencies—the Bureau of Contract Supervision, the Bureau of Personal Services, and the Committee on Education—charged with the study and investigation of work done or to be done.[99] In gathering information, the staff agencies intruded on the domain of existing department heads, provoking conflicts over the scope of their proper authority. As Tilden Adamson, director of the Bureau of Contract Supervision, wrote in 1915,

> the greatest difficulty with which we have had to contend has been the general belief that the head of a department knows more about this department than budget examiners. After several years of repeated proof that intelligent and expert examiners who have given close and detailed study to conditions had a better knowledge than commissioners who rarely understood the detailed working of their departments, we have at last succeeded in having the budget considered on the basis of facts rather than on that of the opinions of department heads.[100]

Adamson was describing nothing less than the displacement of existing administrative authority by experts, trained in the methods and program of the Bureau of Municipal Research, who effectively bypassed department heads to present the "facts" of departmental operations directly to the Board of Estimate and Apportionment.[101] Comptroller Prendergast

[98]William A. Prendergast, "Efficiency through Accounting," *Annals of the American Academy of Political and Social Science* 41 (May 1912): 44–50; Schiesl, *Efficiency*, 154.

[99]Bureau of Municipal Research, "New York City Budget," v.

[100]Tilden Adamson, "The Preparation of Estimates and the Formulation of the Budget—The New York City Method," *Annals of the American Academy of Political and Social Science* 62 (November 1915): 261.

[101]Adamson himself had close relations with the bureau (he delivered lectures to classes at the Training School for Public Service), and as comptroller Prendergast acknowledged, the bureau played a central role in all the accounting and budget reforms instituted under

readily acknowledged the bureau as a "consulting expert" whose reports and recommendations he often gladly adopted.[102] Adamson also admitted his dependence upon the bureau, declaring that in the annual preparation of the budget, "we have put all the force of the Bureau of Municipal Research to work for us. Mr. [Bruere] and Dr. Allen have been very kind, and given us all the assistance they could give, and we have not only appreciated it but need it. In fact, we could hardly get along without their help."[103]

Between 1906 and 1911, the Bureau of Municipal Research established itself firmly within the fabric of New York City's government and profoundly influenced the shape and direction of the city's administrative development. To succeed, the bureau had associated the idea of budget reform with the powerful concepts of efficiency and scientific management, while appropriating to itself as an institution professional prestige and authority. Undergirding the entire enterprise was the bureau's claim that its work served democratic and moral ideals. As government officials came to accept the authority of the bureau, they also came to accept the idea of the budget as central to municipal administration, and they vested authority in the bureau as the prime interpreter of budgeting principles.

The men of the bureau also displayed a sophisticated appreciation of the dynamics of machine government and readily seized opportunities to promote their agenda. More generally, the bureau's approach to administrative reform was consonant with the Progressive era shift from viewing government as a promoter of economic development through the distribution of goods to accepting government as an activist regulator, administrator, and planner. This shift occurred throughout the country during the early twentieth century but was greatly accelerated in New York by political scandals surrounding the exposure of influence buying and

---

his watch (1910–1917). William A. Prendergast, *Reminiscences* (New York: Columbia University Oral History Collection, 1948–1950), 308. In 1915, Prendergast referred to the bureau as a valuable consulting expert in all of his work and wrote that "the Bureau of Municipal Research furnishes a service and an example which has been of great assistance to the city administration." Prendergast, "The Work of the Bureau of Municipal Research in Relation to the Administration of the City's Finances," *Real Estate Magazine* (November 1915): 4.

[102]Prendergast, "Work of the Bureau," 6–8.

[103]Tilden Adamson, "Budget Making: Lecture Delivered before the Training School for Public Service Conducted by the New York Bureau of Municipal Research, January 22, 1913," Papers of the Institute of Public Administration, New York, 27.

corruption in the utility and insurance industries, which came to light in 1905–6, just at the time the bureau was founded.[104]

The road to success was neither smooth nor straight. The bureau worked constantly to maintain good relations with government officials. When they served each other's purposes, mutual interest promoted mutual support. On occasion this uneasy symbiosis broke down, and Tammany erupted into fierce tirades against the bureau. Even at its worst, however, Tammany attacked only the bureau, never the idea of the budget itself. All in all, the bureau's work revolutionized the structure and processes of the city's financial administration, introducing a new vocabulary of accounting and administration which emphasized administrative organization rather than political networks to maintain and extend control within government. As the men of the bureau elaborated the implications of the city's budgetary system, it became clear that they were developing a new concept of democratic government.

[104]Richard L. McCormick, *From Realignment to Reform: Political Change in New York State, 1893–1910* (Ithaca: Cornell University Press, 1981), 138, 153–57, 193–218. McCormick also examines the wider manifestation of this transformation across the country in *Party Period and Public Policy*, 311–56.

4 BUDGET PUBLICITY AND CITIZENSHIP IN THE METROPOLIS

The early successes of the Bureau of Municipal Research were but means to the bureau's larger end of revitalizing an urban democracy threatened by citizen apathy and ignorance. "Revitalization," however, was not intended to promote the free and unregulated flow of political discussion and activity among the general populous. Rather, as the titles of Allen's *Efficient Democracy* and Cleveland's *Organized Democracy* suggest, the bureau's ideal democratic citizen was orderly, well educated, and predictable. He or she (the bureau carefully included women in their discussions of the duties of citizenship) would use information about government, as presented through a well-publicized budget, to form an intelligent opinion about public issues and express that opinion primarily through the vote. The men of the bureau worked assiduously to displace the messy popular politics of the urban machine with an orderly budget-based politics that grounded citizenship in self-education and reduced political action to casting a vote.

In one document, the budget would present to the citizens their government in miniature, revealing the responsibilities and expenditures of every department and official. By providing citizens with the information necessary to hold representatives accountable, the budget bound them to modern government in ways that partisan electoral politics could not. Publicity was the key to accountability. The budget had to be widely advertised so that citizens could readily use its information to judge public officials. The budget reformers therefore developed elaborate schemes to publicize the budget—that is, to educate the people to understand and apply their new political idiom. The bureau, however, did not publicize its implicit assumption that it would control the process of citizen's education and thereby define the scope of their empowerment.

The budget ultimately emerged as an instrument that facilitated, rationalized, and legitimated the expansion of government. It was not intended primarily to constrain government expenditures or to force hard choices about distributing and services. To the contrary, by identifying waste and distinguishing "legitimate" programs from graft, budget reform would enable an activist government to expand to meet all true social needs—as defined by the budgetmakers.

DISPLACING THE PARTY MACHINE

Budget reform shared in a broad Progressive era assault on certain nineteenth-century styles and institutions of political activity. Between the 1830s and the 1890s, a well-developed and vital party system served a critical mediating function, integrating new immigrants into the political system and connecting citizens to an increasingly complex and remote government. Political parties organized citizens and presented them with straightforward partisan choices on political issues. Mass spectacles, rallies, and marches mobilized people from all strata of society and engaged them directly in shaping their civic community. As Mary Ryan notes, the nineteenth century parade "re-presented the urban population, forming a detailed, descriptive portrait of urban social structure." In a time of rapid demographic change and economic transformation, such "democratic theater" became an avenue for publicly asserting and affirming group identities based on class, gender, and ethnicity. The parade also became a medium of communication among these groups, forcing interaction and accommodation among rich and poor, men and women, Irish and native born as each vied for position and control in the spectacle.[1] In tandem with periodic civic displays, urban machines, gaining significant power in the immediate postbellum years, established ongoing networks of personal contacts among immigrant and working classes that bound them to local government.[2]

---

[1]Mary P. Ryan, "The American Parade: Representations of the Nineteenth Century Social Order," in *The New Cultural History*, ed. Lynn Hunt (Berkeley: University of California Press, 1989), 138–39; Michael E. McGerr, *The Decline of Popular Politics: The American North, 1865–1928* (New York: Oxford University Press, 1986), 27–31.

[2]Samuel Hays, "Political Parties and the Community Society Continuum," in *The American Party Systems*, 2d ed., ed. William Nisbet Chambers and Walter Dean Burnham (New

During the last third of the nineteenth century, elites and liberal-minded reformers mounted an assault on these highly partisan and popular avenues of political expression. Prominent New Yorkers (E. L. Godkin and Elihu Root, for example) led the way. Inspired by the watchwords of efficiency and nonpartisanship, they launched an array of programs, from civil service examinations to a myriad of electoral reforms (including the initiative, the referendum, the Australian ballot, and direct nomination), each conceived to undermine the party institutions and processes that had tried to connect citizens to their government.[3]

Compounding the force of these attacks, elites from both parties began "to replace the demonstrative partisanship of torchlight parades with a more deliberative and intellectual canvass of pamphlets and documents."[4] Together with the rise of an independent press that eschewed simple party journalism, the new "educational style" of politics deprived common citizens of familiar and accessible guides to public issues.[5] As politics became less accessible, it also became less palatable, as a wave of graft and influence-buying scandals swept the country, the most notably spectacular being the New York life insurance and public utility imbroglios of 1905–6. Alienated and disillusioned citizens stayed away from the polls as voter turnout declined steadily over the next fifteen years.[6]

Most reformers of the Progressive era continued to see party politics, most notoriously represented by the urban machine, as a barrier to social progress. They advocated reforms to eliminate the machine and reduce party power. Some reforms, such as the Australian ballot and voter regis-

York: Oxford University Press, 1975): 152–81; McGerr, *Decline of Popular Politics*, 3–68; Frances Fox Piven and Richard A. Cloward, *Why Americans Don't Vote* (New York: Pantheon, 1988), 26–63; Martin Shefter, "The Electoral Foundations of the Political Machine: New York City, 1884–1897," in *History of American Electoral Behavior*, ed. Joel H. Silbey, Allan G. Bogue, and William H. Flanigan (Princeton: Princeton University Press, 1978), 263–98.

[3]Richard L. McCormick, *From Realignment to Reform: Political Change in New York State, 1893–1910* (Ithaca: Cornell University Press, 1981), 52–56, 114–18, 261–63.

[4]McGerr, *Decline of Popular Politics*, 69.

[5]Ibid., 3–11, 121–22. For an excellent discussion of contesting ideals of "refined" and "colloquial" public speech in nineteenth-century America, see Kenneth Cmiel, *Democratic Eloquence: The Fight Over Popular Speech in Nineteenth Century America* (New York: William Morrow, 1990), 236–57.

[6]Benjamin Ginsberg, *The Consequences of Consent: Elections, Citizen Control and Popular Acquiescence* (New York: Random House, 1982), 29–62. McCormick, *From Realignment to Reform*, 251–63. For an analysis of the transforming effect of political scandal throughout the country during the first decade of the twentieth century, see Richard L. McCormick, *The Party Period and Public Policy: American Politics from the Age of Jackson to the Progressive Era* (New York: Oxford University Press, 1986): 311–56.

tration laws, directly challenged parties' ability to mobilize voters. Others, such as direct primaries, the referendum, and the initiative, sought to bypass party politics altogether and provide citizens with direct access to their government.[7]

Budget reform was different. The men of the bureau criticized as misguided, even dangerous, reforms that gave citizens direct access to a government they could neither see nor understand. They recognized that in a world of big cities and activist government, citizens needed institutions, such as the party machine, to mediate between themselves and government. Budget reformers insisted that simply eliminating corrupt machines was not the answer. Instead of attacking the machine head-on, Allen, Bruere, and Cleveland tried to displace it, to make it less relevant and less powerful by appropriating its mediating function to the budget.

Where once the ward healer or precinct boss had guided local citizens through the labyrinth of municipal government, a well-publicized and accurate budget would give citizens a true and objective picture of government activities. Budget reformers envisioned that instead of appealing to party hacks for guidance, citizens would look to the budget for the information needed to make educated decisions about matters of public concern. The budget, they hoped, would take over the positive mediating function of the party machine while leaving behind its corruption and inefficiency.

The men of the bureau did not consider, however, that budgets would mediate very differently from machines. Machines provided a connection to government that was at once personal and communal. People's relation to the government involved a network of personal relations and activities through which they formed political identities as part of a group. The budget, by contrast, mediated via publicized information, not personal contact. Citizens who related to government through the budget did so primarily as individual consumers of political information, not as members of any larger group. Group identity was irrelevant in the budget reformers' world of information-driven politics.

Despite holding a guarded admiration for the accomplishments of the political bosses, the men of the bureau competed directly with the machines, not only for control of the administrative apparatus of government, but for the soul of the citizenry. According to Cleveland, the boss had won over the citizenry because he had "made citizenship his business"

[7]Ginsberg, *Consequences of Consent*, 79–87, 152–54; Piven and Cloward, *Why Americans Don't Vote*, 63–96; McGerr, *Decline of Popular Politics*, 64–65; McCormick, *From Realignment to Reform*, 52–56, 115, 261–63.

whereas "with the reformer, citizenship has been only an emotion."[8] (Cleveland's criticism sounds as if it could have come from the mouth of Tammany stalwart George Washington Plunkitt, who referred to reformers as "morning glories—looked lovely in the mornin' and withered up in a short time, while the regular machines went on flourishin' forever."[9]) Budget reform would provide a new means to identify and meet the people's needs, thereby usurping the bosses' role.

Cleveland was especially concerned to engage the apathetic middle-class citizen who, he believed, had "shown himself to be both inefficient and devoid of the ideals which assist honorable political appeals to the electorate." The environment of political disengagement, according to Cleveland, had been "the opportunity of the political boss" and allowed "both campaign managers and candidates for office [to] conspire to misrepresent issues and to influence the electoral jury unduly."[10] Cleveland argued that the citizenry responded to the overtures of the bosses in large part because no viable alternatives existed. He even conceded that "the most effective solution that American democracy has so far offered in citizen organization and control is domination by 'the boss.'"[11]

In the informal, ad hoc administration of the political machine, the worlds of public and private power were blurred. A citizen might not know whether a pothole in the neighborhood had been filled as a personal favor or as a public obligation. On a larger scale, a street car system, installed under public auspices, might be controlled by private interests. Whether the offending institution was Tammany Hall or the Consolidated Gas Company, the logic of budget reform was the same: public power could not be held accountable where it could not be clearly distinguished from private power.

Budget reform thus attacked what might be called the "liminal party," that shadowy part of the party organization that blurred into the world of governance such that the private interests of the party members could not be distinguished from the formal responsibilities of a representative government. A budget system would clearly define the nature and scope

[8]Frederick A. Cleveland, *Organized Democracy* (New York: Longmans, Green, 1913), 443–44.

[9]William L. Riordan, *Plunkitt of Tammany Hall* (New York: E. P. Dutton, 1963), 17.

[10]Cleveland, *Organized Democracy*, 245–46. See also Frederick A. Cleveland, "The Application of Scientific Management to the Activities of State and Municipal Government," in *Scientific Management: Addresses and Discussions at the Conference on Scientific Management* (Hanover, N.H.: Amos Tuck School of Administration and Finance, Dartmouth College, 1912), 327–28.

[11]Cleveland, *Organized Democracy*, 443–44.

of governmental responsibilities, thereby reestablishing a clear boundary between public and private power.[12]

Despite budget reformers' criticisms of past administrations, they provided a positive rationale for citizens to invest city government with more, not less, power. Middle-class citizens (and certainly state legislatures) might be wary of giving the "invisible" government of political machines any but the most basic powers. Budgetary accountability would make it safe to place responsibility for public welfare in the hands of government officials. To succeed, budget reformers emulated the political boss and made citizenship their business. The budget, as a new connection between citizen and government, would take the place of the machine. The bureau, as the primary compiler, interpreter, and disseminator of a well-publicized budget, would take the place of the boss.

Under a proper budgetary system, information, rather than personal contact, would connect constituents and representatives. Mass urban society had undermined the bond of shared interests and experiences that lay at the heart of classical conceptions legitimate representation. The men of the bureau understood that the political machines had developed their power by providing new bonds of patronage and party identification between citizen and government. Budget reform, in turn, would displace the bonds of party by presenting information as a new means of holding distant representatives accountable.[13]

Cleveland believed that the idea of budget reform deserved a place in the canon of democratic literature as an unparalleled instrument of representative democracy.[14] The budget process itself provided a link between the represented and their representatives, enabling and mediating the flow of information between the two. Without a budget, wrote Bruere, "public information regarding government results is lacking, public control over government is blind and groping."[15] Democratic politics thus required that budgets become a part of the common political discourse.

---

[12]Patronage was perhaps the favorite territory of the liminal party. As Martin J. Schiesl notes, patronage in the late nineteenth century "became a means whereby the bosses could induce officials to surrender to them part or in some cases all of their legally vested powers." Martin Schiesl, *The Politics of Efficiency: Municipal Administration and Reform in America, 1800–1920* (Berkeley: University of California Press, 1977), 30.

[13]Frederick A. Cleveland, *Chapters on Municipal Administration and Accounting* (New York: Longmans, Green, 1909), v.

[14]Frederick A. Cleveland and Arthur E. Buck, *The Budget and Responsible Government* (New York: Macmillan, 1920), 40.

[15]Henry Bruere, *The New City Government* (New York: D. Appleton, 1912), 130.

Citizens had to be taught to see their government in and through the budget document.

Creating an informed citizenry would also affect power relationships among public officials. In Cleveland's words, "An informed public is the best insurance that public spirited officers may have against the wishes of the 'grafter boss.'"[16] Information was to be used to define a boundary, in this case a barrier, to protect "good officers" from the "bosses."

Here Allen stepped in, proposing his "socialized intelligence" as the key to breaking the ties between the boss and the people. If the boss received the votes of the "less intelligent electorate," the bureau would use the budget to inform the voters of government activity so that they would be less susceptible to manipulation by the boss. Again distinguishing budget reform from sensationalistic muckraking, Allen proposed that the bureau act as an "intelligence center" that would "substitute fact for calamity or scandal as teacher to citizenship" and serve "officials, volunteers, editors and students [i.e. typically middle-class citizens] in every part of the country."[17]

The bureau's campaign for budget reform also implicitly criticized direct democracy reforms such as the initiative and referendum as noble sounding but useless or even harmful if citizens did not have the information necessary to vote intelligently. Cleveland asserted that "adequate publicity" was the "first thing to be provided as a basis for all of the considerations which bear on questions of public activity. . . . Without this all the laws which must be passed, whether for initiative, referendum recall, short ballot, primaries, universal suffrage, or what not, must prove disappointing." The budget informed the public and therefore was prior and superior to all other reforms.

Though wary of initiatives and referenda, Allen accepted their increasing popularity. In typical bureau fashion, he did not attack them directly, but rather tried to interpose the budget (and budget reformers) between the voter and these reforms. "The chief danger from the initiative and ref-

---

[16]Frederick A. Cleveland, "The Need for Coordinating Municipal, State, and National Activities," *Annals of the American Academy of Political and Social Sciences* 41 (May 1912): 27.

[17]William H. Allen, *Efficient Democracy* (New York: Macmillan, 1907), 284. Allen makes no mention of immigrants, workers, or industrialists as targets of education. Indeed, any consideration of the place of capital and labor in urban reform is markedly absent from the writings of each of the ABCs. For them the critical relation in contemporary society was not between capital and labor but between activist, well-to-do citizens and expanding government. They were more concerned with control of the means of governance than with control of the means of production.

erendum," wrote Allen, "is that people will not see their limitations."[18] Allen effectively made democratic citizenship conditional on education. An uninformed or meddlesome citizenry, though it wielded power, was no friend of democracy. To be truly democratic, a vote had to be "informed and directed" by the budget and by civic agencies such as the bureau. In other words, the budgetary process defined what was and what was not a legitimate expression of the popular will.[19]

In an era of declining voter turnout, budget reform further undermined voting by subordinating it to the duties of self-education and oversight of government activities. Progressive era electoral reforms had begun to erode electoral turnouts by erecting procedural and structural barriers to voting. Budget reform finished the job, making the vote conceptually less accessible. That is, budget reform situated the meaning of the vote in the context of middle-class conceptions of education and oversight that were alien to most working class and immigrant voters, who had commonly viewed the vote as a means to keep one of "their own" in office and obtain favors or even employment from city hall. As an instrument of oversight the vote simply was less relevant to working-class concerns and hence less appealing. Similarly, for middle-class groups who embraced the primacy of education and oversight, budget reform degraded voting into a secondary function of citizenship.

BUDGET PUBLICITY AND POLITICAL DISCOURSE

To function as an instrument of representative democracy, the budget had to be readily available and intelligible to the citizenry. In concert with sympathetic government officials, the men of the bureau publicized the budget through press coverage, mailings, public hearings, and budget exhibits. Budget reformers tailored each type of publicity to different publics. Some targeted business elites and politicians, and others reached out to the mass of New York's citizenry.

"News," wrote Allen, "is the great educator. No cause can afford to avoid being news. If your newspapers have special reporters for describing any cause which is of general public concern you cannot make a better investment than to furnish them news while it is still news."[20] From

18William H. Allen, *Woman's Part in Government* (New York: Dodd, Mead, 1912), 71; see also 74, 144.

19Ibid., 74.

20Ibid., 103.

its inception, the bureau carefully cultivated ties with the press. Its founding board of trustees included Albert Shaw, publisher of the *American Review of Reviews*, and Richard Watson Gilder, editor of *Century*. These two magazines provided regular and favorable coverage of the bureau's activities during its early years. The bureau also sent out literally millions of leaflets and postcards to civic organizations and prominent individuals throughout New York. The mass mailings, issued as a series under the title "Efficient Citizenship," often were no more than reprints of favorable newspaper editorials. Nonetheless, they served as a simple and low-cost way to keep budget reform constantly in the minds of New Yorkers.[21]

The bureau also enlisted the city's clergy and civic organizations such as the YMCA to assist in spreading the word on budget reform. In 1909, the bureau worked with a representative executive committee of twenty clergymen headed by Bishop Greer to organize a series of "Budget Sundays" to provide the clergy of the city and the leaders of church organizations with information "as to the progress of budget requests for social, health and educational needs not met," which they could then pass on to parishioners in their Sunday sermons. Dr. William R. Richards of the Brick Presbyterian Church, for example, delivered a sermon titled "The Day of Pentecost and the City Budget," which was reprinted both by the bureau and by the popular magazine *The Survey*. In his sermon, Richards discussed the work of the bureau and urged his listeners to use the budget to inform themselves as to community needs and to communicate their desires to their representatives. As on the biblical day of Pentecost, the new language of budget reform would presumably enable a common understanding among diverse and cacophonous tongues. Only here, it was the scientific spirit of budgeting rather than the Holy Spirit that would descend upon the people. Similarly, the bureau prevailed upon the New York YMCA to urge their 2,500 voting members to inform themselves about the budget.[22]

Annual budget hearings, held before the Board of Estimate and Apportionment, occupied a central position in the bureau's publicity program. "The success of the representative principle," wrote Cleveland, "depends on having the [budget] proceedings conducted openly in a man-

[21]Bureau of Municipal Research, "A National Program to Improve Methods of Government," *Municipal Research* 71 (March 1916): 8.

[22]William H. Allen, *Reminiscences* (New York: Columbia University Oral History Collection, 1950), 99; William R. Richards, "The Day of Pentecost and the City Budget," *Survey* 24 (June 25, 1910): 511–14; William H. Allen, "'The Business of Citizenship' in New York City," *American Review of Reviews*, 40 (November 1909): 598.

ner to make news of them." Hearings allowed individuals to speak directly to the government. Press coverage of the hearings would keep others "as well informed as if . . . [they had] attended the meeting," providing yet another bond to hold together "a large, populous, widely extended democracy."[23]

The actual impact of the hearings was somewhat different. In identifying what government could do, a well-publicized budget facilitated the rise of lobbying by such interest groups as real estate investors. The budget's specific information about which departments were spending how much money on what projects was valuable to interest groups. Organized interest groups, in fact, overshadowed individual citizen participation in the budget-making process because they had well-defined priorities and the institutional structure to act on them consistently over time. Thus, for example, the *Herald* reported, "thanks to the [budget] exhibit and to the hearings, it will be relatively easy this year for the real estate interests to find out what increases are proposed and to make their judgment known."[24] As early as 1911, one journalist noted that "the general interest in the budget itself was probably not as great as a year ago. Less than twenty-five citizens were present at the first of two public hearings and at this meeting almost the only discussion directly on the budget itself was devoted to a protest by real estate interests against any increase for the Tenement House Department."[25]

By 1913, Tilden Adamson, then serving as supervising statistician and examiner in the Department of Finance, complained to the bureau that he had seen "as many as 500 or 600 crowded around there at a public hearing, but they are the same old people; real estate interests are something they want to push along."[26] The bureau itself admitted in 1917 that its attempt through the hearings "to interest the public continuously in the budget and to stimulate attendance at the taxpayers' hearings . . . [had] proved a failure." Originally intended to give taxpayers an opportunity to offer practical suggestions, the hearings had degenerated into "opportunities for civic agencies and city employees to make special appeals for

[23]Cleveland and Buck, *Responsible Government*, 386.

[24]*Herald*, quoted in Bureau of Municipal Research, *Would a Budget Exhibit Help Your City?* (New York: Bureau of Municipal Research, 1911), 13.

[25]James P. Heaton, "Nearing the $200,000,000 City," *Survey* 27 (November 11, 1911): 1185–86.

[26]Tilden Adamson, "Budget Making: A Lecture Delivered before the Training School for Public Service Conducted by the New York Bureau of Municipal Research, January 22, 1913," Papers of the Institute of Public Administration, New York, 35.

increased expenditures."[27] As Charles Beard put it in 1919, one year after becoming director of the bureau, the budget hearings were "quite commonly monopolized by citizens with more verbosity than enlightenment to exploit their petty lobbies."[28]

Despite the limitations of the hearings, the bureau worked diligently to transform them into "a serious, profitable and illuminating experience for taxpayers."[29] Allen saw budget hearings as an instrument of accountability, forcing government officials to justify their actions before the public. He believed that the hearings would give voice to the people, providing an outlet to act on the budget information obtained from mailings, sermons, and exhibits. Citizens, however, were most definitely not to be allowed to vote directly on budget items. They were not even to influence the agenda for discussion. Allen noted approvingly that "to protect themselves against individuals whose interest is not yet based on definite knowledge," the Board of Estimate and Apportionment passed a resolution that "citizens must discuss specific budget items and not . . . dilate on the State of the Union."[30] Citizens could participate, but only on terms strictly defined and controlled by the content of the preexisting budget as compiled by experts.

The budget hearings epitomized the new information-driven politics that lay at the heart of budget reform. The old party politics was based on personal contacts or money. Other Progressive era reforms, such as civil service or electoral reforms, were based on merit or direct popular access to government. Muckraking reform, so firmly grounded in publicity of outrageous abuses of power, relied more on the righteous indignation of an aroused public than on a mastery of facts. Budget reform, however, aimed to predicate the exercise of all political power upon an acceptance and understanding of information compiled, classified, and interpreted by experts. Those who wanted power in an information-driven political process needed access to experts who could manipulate information toward specific ends. In the politics of budget reform thus lay the foundations of the modern think tank: under the guise of objectivity, corporate-sponsored experts crafted policies based on exclusive mastery of information that they themselves, or their colleagues and counterparts

---

[27] Bureau of Municipal Research, "The New York City Budget," *Municipal Research* 88 (August 1917): 62.

[28] Charles A. Beard, "The Control of the Expert," in *Experts in City Government*, ed. Edward A. Fitzpatrick (New York: D. Appleton, 1919), 341.

[29] Bureau of Municipal Research, "New York City Budget," 61.

[30] Allen, "Citizenship" 598.

in government, had generated. It is no coincidence that the bureau became a model for the Brookings Institution, the first true think tank, which was founded in 1916 for the express purpose of campaigning to bring budget reform to the national government.[31]

The hearings defined the scope of political discourse by the specific items contained in the budget document and excluded citizens without knowledge of these specifics. While encouraging and legitimizing "informed criticism," they marginalized all "uninformed" criticism or all comment that strayed from the budget document itself. The hearings thus served to channel and domesticate popular participation in politics. To Allen, who found political confrontation inefficient, the hearings provided a superior alternative to "mass meetings of protest."[32] They were structured, formal, regular, and regulated events conducted in accordance with set rules of protocol and relevance. They both enhanced and controlled citizen access to government. In the name of protecting them, the government confined citizens to discussing specific budget items and prohibited them from "dilating" on broader public issues. In any event, the hearings reached only a relatively few people. To propagate the ideas of budget reform and information-driven politics throughout the city, the men of the bureau staged massive exhibits that captured the attention not only of New Yorkers but also of the entire nation.

ADVERTISING THE GOVERNMENT: BUDGET EXHIBITS

"Expert government's publicity," wrote Allen, "can nowhere be effective which does not act upon the same principles that private advertising has adopted for the selling of goods."[33] As businesses and markets grew during the nineteenth century, time and distance increasingly separated producers from consumers. To bridge this gap, private advertisers promoted brand name recognition to assure consumers of a product's real or

---

[31]For an account of the founding and development of the Brookings Institution, see James Allen Smith, *Brookings at Seventy-five* (Washington, D.C.: Brookings, 1991); idem, *The Idea Brokers: Think Tanks and the Rise of the New Policy Elite* (New York: Free Press, 1991); and Donald T. Critchlow, *The Brookings Institution, 1916–1952* (De Kalb: Northern Illinois University Press, 1985).

[32]Allen, *Woman's Part in Government*, 118.

[33]William H. Allen, "Interpreting Expert Government to the Citizenship," in *Experts in City Government*, ed. Edward A. Fitzpatrick (New York: D. Appleton, 1919), 175.

perceived quality.[34] Similarly, Allen saw that as citizens became increasingly distant from their representatives, the information contained in the budget might serve to guarantee the "real or perceived quality" of governmental actions. (Allen's model also resembled contemporary trends among campaign managers in electoral politics to advertise candidates themselves as commodities. During the early twentieth century, national campaigns in particular focused increasingly on personality and human interest rather than on partisanship to sell their slates to the electorate. "Product identification" became important in selecting men for office.)[35]

The bureau's greatest innovation in governmental publicity was the annual budget exhibit. The men of the bureau conceived of such exhibits as mediums "for clothing budgets with flesh and blood" which would familiarize the people of New York with a new vocabulary of municipal administration and provide them with the information necessary to exercise popular control over city government.[36] Between 1908 and 1911 four budget exhibits met with an enthusiastic reception from the people of New York. Over one million people attended the final and grandest exhibit, staged by the City of New York, during the month of October 1911.

On October 5, 1908, as visitors entered the splendid arcade of the City Investing Building at 165 Broadway, they encountered a new addition to New York City's political landscape: the country's first budget exhibit. The recently incorporated bureau organized the exhibit without direct government support and sponsored it in cooperation with the Greater New York Taxpayers' Conference. The exhibit displayed fairly rudimentary charts and diagrams, including presentations by such civic organizations as the Tenement House Committee, the City Club, the Association for Improving the Condition of the Poor, and the State Charities Aid Association. Among the most noted displays was one showing six-cent hat hooks tagged to show that the city had paid $0.65 for each hook plus another $2.22 to install each hook in a comfort station. The exhibit also featured noonday addresses by prominent officials and leading citizens.[37]

[34]James D. Norris, *Advertising and the Transformation of American Society, 1865–1920* (New York: Greenwood, 1990), 97–98.

[35]McGerr, *Decline of Popular Politics*, 170–73; Robert Westbrook, "Politics as Consumption: Managing the Modern American Election," in *The Culture of Consumption*, ed. Richard Wightman Fox and T. J. Jackson Lears (New York: Pantheon, 1983): 143–74.

[36]Cleveland and Buck, *Responsible Government*, 75. See also J. Harold Braddock, "Efficiency Value of the Budget Exhibit," *Annals of the American Academy of Political and Social Science* 41 (May 1912): 151–57.

[37]William Allen, "New York's First Budget Exhibit," *American Review of Reviews* 38 (December 1908), 686–88.

In conjunction with the exhibit, the bureau persuaded local ministers to take up the message of budget reform and preach over two hundred sermons on the budget and religious work.[38] Allen also later recalled that publicity for the exhibit was greatly enhanced by a press war that developed between the Hearst and Pulitzer papers to cover this strange new event.[39] The exhibit closed triumphantly on November 2, the day before the fall election, with a visit from Governor Hughes, who chose to make it one of his final campaign stops. In his speech, Hughes praised the bureau for its work in promoting honesty and efficiency in government.[40]

Despite a few attacks,[41] the first exhibit surpassed its planners' expectations. Seventy thousand people visited the exhibit and millions more read about it in newspapers. It galvanized public opinion against waste and corruption in government and took the first step toward teaching New Yorkers to see their government in and through the budget.

In 1909, the bureau followed up its initial success with a second budget exhibit along similar lines, which was also well received. The next year, the city government stepped in to sponsor a budget exhibit that far exceeded the previous two in size and scope. To promote public interest in the budgetary process, the Board of Estimate and Apportionment formed the Committee on Budgetary Publicity and allocated $25,000 to fund an exhibit for October 1910. The bureau's own George McAneny, then Manhattan borough president, served as the committee's chairman. The comptroller, William Prendergast, and Bruere's close friend John Purroy Mitchel, the young, progressive president of the Board of Aldermen, also served on the committee. Francis Oppenheimer acted as their press representative. The committee, in turn, established the special Budget Exhibit Committee, chaired by Robert McIntyre of the Department of Finance.[42]

The Committee on Budgetary Publicity made good use of its press representative. As one magazine observed, "The city has adopted the most modern methods of advertising to show the citizens how [the city's money] is spent."[43] The committee created a special budget news service, which sent bulletins summarizing departmental estimates and any requested increases or decreases to local newspapers and to the various civic

[38] Allen, *Reminiscences*, 99.

[39] Ibid., 97–98.

[40] "Hughes's Honesty Plea," *New York Tribune*, November 3, 1908, 3.

[41] For an account of one borough president's attack, see "Budget Exhibit Cartoons Shed Light on Taxes," *World*, October 9, 1908, 2.

[42] New York City, Board of Estimate and Apportionment, *Minutes*, May 20, June 17, July 29, 1910 (New York: Martin B. Brown), 2048–49, 2889, 3756.

[43] "The New York Budget Exhibit," *American City* 3 (November 1910): 234.

organizations of Greater New York. In addition, the committee made a concerted effort to interest churches, schools, colleges, and taxpayers' organizations in the exhibit.

Over eight hundred thousand people attended the 1910 exhibit, which also attracted nationwide attention as the first publicly sponsored exhibit of its kind.[44] The socialist press also enthusiastically supported the exhibit. The *New York Call* ran a series of columns on the first city-sponsored exhibit. In one column, Mary S. Oppenheimer expressed the hope that the exhibits would "be but the beginning of a long series of such exhibits, which shall be to the people of New York a lesson in the government of the people. . . . Every Socialist," she concluded, "ought to try to see it."[45]

The second and final city-sponsored budget exhibit, held in 1911, occupied three spacious floors of the Taft-Weller building at 330 Broadway in lower Manhattan. It ran from October 2 through October 28 so as to coincide with the consideration of the 1912 budget by the Board of Estimate and Apportionment. The exhibit was open daily from 11:00 A.M. until 7:00 P.M. To accommodate those with long working hours, the doors stayed open until 10:00 P.M. on Tuesdays and Thursdays, and from 2:00 P.M. to 6:00 P.M. on Sundays.[46]

On entering the Taft-Weller building (an old dry-goods warehouse), visitors immediately encountered a series of graphic charts and models. Among the first was a large table on which were arrayed a series of gold cubes of varying sizes selected to show the total estimated expenses of any given department and their relation to the total budget. Where the estimates for 1912 exceeded those of 1911, the gold cubes were augmented by purple cubes, prepared to the same scale, and indicating the increase. Everywhere charts and diagrams hung on the walls of alcoves, giving the organization and accountability of the various departments together with full statistics describing their accomplishments and explaining any increase in appropriations.[47]

The exhibit was no mere recitation of dry-as-dust statistics. To the contrary, it was very much a show, a budget extravaganza designed to enter-

[44]Ibid., 232–34; "The New York City Budget Show," *Outlook* 96 (November 5, 1910): 524–26; "Budget Exhibit by City Officials," *Survey* 27 (November 11, 1911): 1184; Herbert T. Wade, "The New York Budget Exhibit," *American Review of Reviews* 44 (November 1911): 574; Heaton, "Nearing the $200,000,000 City," 1185; "Children Visit Exhibit," *New York Tribune*, October 9, 1911, 12.

[45]Mary S. Oppenheimer, "The Budget Exhibit," *New York Call*, October 5, 1910, 6.

[46]Heaton, "Nearing the $200,000,00 City," 1185.

[47]Wade, "New York Budget Exhibit," 576.

tain as well as educate. As Mayor Gaynor said in opening the exhibit, "the great object in all free government is to enlist the attention and discussion of the citizens."[48] Accordingly, the exhibit displayed photographs, models, and even working machinery in addition to more conventional graphic representations of New York's finances. Among the favorites were a model milk station, a new jail cell, a full-size section of the new Croton aqueduct, and "Brentwood," a twenty-one-year-old horse that had served the fire department faithfully (and, of course, efficiently) for seventeen years. (This last, especially popular with the children, was tethered outside, in front of the building.)

Motion pictures provided the greatest attraction. Shown every noon, afternoon, and Tuesday and Thursday evenings, the movies illustrated the workings of the School Farms, the Volunteer Life Saving Corporation, and of the police, fire, and street cleaning departments, among others. Also, a film, one thousand feet long, showed "every detail of the work on the new $163,000,000 Aqueduct."[49] In short, the exhibit was an elaborate multimedia presentation, employing sophisticated publicity, varied graphic presentations, and the latest technology to attract and hold the public's interest.

The bureau hoped the exhibit would both force officials to eliminate waste and promote a common civic identity. Where the political machines had "provided a method of incorporating working people into politics while keeping their political issues off the electoral agenda,"[50] the exhibits similarly would bind all citizens to their government while defining (if not excluding) political issues for them. The budget would mediate between the masses and the government much as the machine had done, but would function according to principles of efficiency administered by experts.[51]

The peculiar aspiration of the budget reformers was to create an instrument that would serve the same functions as the machine but toward different ends. They recognized the need for some form of mediation between the people and the government which neither electoral reforms nor civil service could accomplish. Mere "closeness" of people to government was not what modern mass democracy demanded. Some mechanism had to make government intelligible to the people. Political machines, by giv-

[48]*Evening Sun*, quoted in Bureau of Municipal Research, *Would a Budget Exhibit Help Your City?* 13.

[49]Committee on Budgetary Publicity, "Father Knickerbocker's Budget Exhibit" (New York: City of New York, 1911).

[50]Piven and Cloward, *Why Americans Don't Vote*, 74.

[51]Braddock, "Budget Exhibit," 151.

ing government a human (if often corrupt) face, had done this. Budgets exhibits were a serious effort to find a proper surrogate. They occupied a central place in the bureau's attempts both to bind the alienated well-to-do citizens to their government and to displace the machines as political mediators for the restive working class.

The same medium that provided the citizen with a new political vocabulary also shaped the political discourse of public officials. Mayors McClellan and Gaynor, both products of Tammany Hall (albeit more independent than most), embraced budget reform as a means to add legitimacy to their exercise of authority. But the bureau intended the budget exhibits to force public officials to "explain clearly and pointedly" the reasons for their actions. The exhibits thus shifted the burden of articulation, requiring "the official and not the citizen to describe salaries and wages so the padding could be discovered."[52]

Budget publicity could also facilitate governmental expansion—provided that it proceeded in accordance with the principles of economy and efficiency articulated in the exhibit. Property owners, for example, had particular interests relating to building inspection and utilities. They wanted government to protect these interests but were perhaps indifferent or even opposed to other programs. The budget exhibit could broaden the scope of their support for government activities by showing them that "it is still feasible . . . to widen greatly the scope of municipal activity, without increased appropriations, because of the money saved by retrenchment. They realize that the best possible reason for reducing a padded payroll is that the money is needed to save babies' lives, to buy food for consumptive patients, to provide truancy officers."[53] The exhibit, then, facilitated the acceptance of the growth of government activities (and intrusions into citizens' lives) first, by giving citizens a sense of what the government could do, and second, by convincing them that these activities would not place any greater burden on them. The bureau presented municipal budget-making as something other than a zero-sum game, arguing that meeting social needs in one area did not necessarily entail cutting back on other needed programs.

The bureau worked hard to educate the business elite (especially powerful real estate interests) because its members had been growing more restive as city expenditures increased steadily during the first two decades of the twentieth century. From 1903 to 1908, the city's total budget in-

[52]Ibid., 153.
[53]Ibid., 153–54.

creased 48 percent. From 1908 to 1913, it increased 34 percent.[54] Although the rate of increase had slowed since the introduction of budget reform, real estate interests were alarmed by the prospect of continued growth with attendant increases in the tax rate. In 1913, the City Economy League obtained the signatures of some thirty thousand real estate owners and businessmen demanding economy in city expenditures.[55]

At this time, the *Record and Guide*, the city's foremost publisher of materials on real estate management, invited Henry Bruere to write a pamphlet for its subscribers explaining the reasons for increasing government expenditures. Bruere seized the opportunity to lobby for acceptance of responsible growth in government. Bruere declared that, to obtain lower taxes and improved government services, taxpayers "must organize upon a positive program of activity instead of a negative program of retrenchment." Simply lowering taxes was not in itself desirable. An enlightened business community, argued Bruere, wants "government to be more efficient, not to lower tax roll, but to save lives, improve the comfort and convenience, and advance the welfare of all the people of the city of New York, and not merely those who directly pay taxes."[56]

To back up its appeals, the bureau provided hard figures demonstrating that the bulk of the city's increased appropriations was due not to expanded services but to poor debt management. In 1916, Cleveland wrote a series of four articles for the *Record and Guide* addressing the continued rise in city expenditures and tax rates.[57] In answer to the question "why have taxes increased?" he stated emphatically that "it is almost entirely due to the city's borrowing policy and not to the increased cost of administration, operation and maintenance."[58]

In an age of growth and new abundance, the budget was not intended to force tough choices between competing demands on governmental resources. To the contrary, it was meant to enable government to meet all true social needs by distinguishing legitimate areas of government activity from wasteful graft and inefficiency. The budget would thus transform competition into cooperation and acceptance of activist government.

[54]Bureau of Municipal Research, "Will Taxes Increase in Greater New York?" *Efficient Citizenship* 660 (December 31, 1913): 3–4.

[55]Henry Bruere, *The Cost of Government in New York City: A Discussion of City Business for Taxpayers* (New York: Record and Guide, 1913), i.

[56]Ibid., 2.

[57]This series of articles, appearing between November 11 and December 2, were reprinted by the bureau as "Some Results and Limitations of Central Financial Control," *Municipal Research* 81 (January 1917): 1–63.

[58]Ibid., 47.

Under this budgetary regime, where a government could meet all legitimate social needs, normative considerations of what government should do lost relevance. Political debate focused instead on looking to the budget to define what constituted "legitimate" government activity. Interest group demands thereby could become legitimized simply through inclusion in a properly constituted budget, regardless of their normative value in relation to some perceived public good.

Budget Exhibits and the New Citizenship

The exhibits were well received largely because they employed common media of display and amusement familiar to mass audiences. By 1908, grand expositions and world's fairs were regular parts of America's repertoire of mass education and amusement. During this period major fairs were staged every four or five years, the grandest being the World's Columbian Exposition, held in Chicago in 1893. Cleveland himself attended the Louisiana Purchase International Exposition in St. Louis in 1904 to deliver a paper before the first International Congress of Accountants.[59]

Fairs and expositions familiarized people with new products and innovations while more subtly conveying ideological messages about America's status in the world. Visitors were guided as tourists through a maze of exhibits representing various cultures, technological innovations, and art. From these fairs, the people learned how to navigate the public space within buildings containing a myriad of exhibits. More important, they learned how to interact with and "read" the messages of staged, re-created realities presented for popular consumption.[60]

[59]The paper, "The Administrative Importance of Distinguishing between Revenues and Expenses and Receipts and Disbursements in Municipal Accounting," was reprinted by Cleveland in his book *Municipal Administration*, 155–74.

[60]The literature on expositions is extensive. For some of the most interesting and helpful, see Robert W. Rydell, *All the World's a Fair* (Chicago: University of Chicago Press, 1984). Rydell analyzes the relation between the Columbian Exposition and concepts of racism and imperialism in America. David F. Burg, *Chicago's White City* (Lexington: University of Kentucky Press, 1976), and R. Reid Badger, *The Great American Fair: The World's Columbian Exposition and American Culture* (Chicago: N. Hall, 1979) provide more general accounts of this fair's place in American culture. In addition, Alan Trachtenberg, in the final chapter of *The Incorporation of American Culture: Culture and Society in the Gilded Age* (New York: Hill & Wang, 1982), and Neil Harris, in "Museums, Merchandising, and Popular Taste: The Struggle for Influence," in *Material Culture and the Study of American Life*, ed. Ian M. G. Quimby (New York: W. W. Norton, 1978), 140–74, provide excellent essays on

Even more fully integrated into the urban landscape, museums and department stores also taught the people of New York to read languages of display and consumption. Many of the country's great museums and department stores were established during the last third of the nineteenth century. Elite sponsors of art museums (like later sponsors of budget exhibits) who wanted to raise the level of public taste tried to reach "a large lay audience, capturing its attention, increasing it knowledge and shaping its sense of possibility."[61] Similarly, department stores became display areas for cultural artifacts. Both taught patrons categories for assimilating the messages of these displays.[62] As Alan Trachtenberg has noted, the department store "taught the social location of goods: trousers as 'men's clothing,' silks as 'women's wear,' reclining chairs as 'parlor furniture.' It systematized, conveniently, the world of goods into discrete names, each with its niche, and in visible spatial relation to all others. . . . [T]he department store organized the world as consumable objects."[63]

In a similar manner, the budget exhibits taught the political location of governmental "goods" and services. They showed citizens what belonged in the public sphere, and where. Public health and safety, for example, were clearly governmental functions. Within this "public" category, however, a function such as building inspection might be classified variously under the health, tenement, or fire department. Other health and safety measures, such as overseeing working conditions, might be implicitly defined as private through exclusion from an exhibit.

Allen hoped the exhibit would attract a broad audience. Noting the appeal of displays, such as the six-cent hooks of the 1908 exhibit, he recalled that "men would come in from the subway, truckmen and longshoremen, to see the free show. They'd pick these things up, nudge the next man, and show him. So they'd go around the floor."[64] Here citizens from all walks

---

world's fairs in turn-of-the century America. Finally, Dean MacCannell, in *The Tourist* (New York: Schocken Books, 1976), provides a broad sociological analysis of the relation between tourism and modernity which contains some provocative insights into the phenomenon of world's fairs. On the related phenomenon of historical pageantry in the early twentieth century, see David Glassberg, *American Historical Pageantry: The Uses of Tradition in the Early Twentieth Century* (Chapel Hill: University of North Carolina Press, 1990).

[61]Harris, "Museums, Merchandising, and Popular Taste," 142.

[62]Ibid., 149–54; Norris, *Advertising*, 16–19; Susan Porter Benson, *Counter Cultures: Saleswomen, Managers, and Customers in American Department Stores, 1890–1940* (Urbana: University of Illinois Press, 1986), 18–21; William Leach, "Strategists of Display and the Production of Desire," in *Consuming Visions: Accumulation and Display of Goods in America, 1880–1920*, ed. Simon J. Bonner (New York: W. W. Norton, 1989): 99–132.

[63]Trachtenberg, *Incorporation of American Culture*, 132.

[64]Allen, *Reminiscences*, 97.

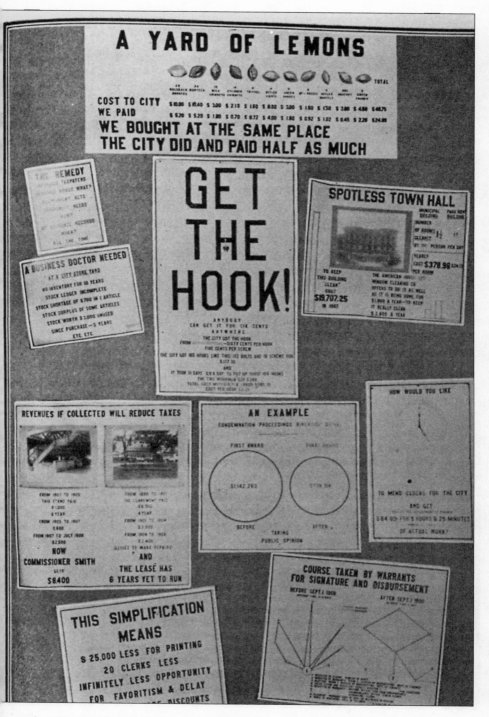

osters from the First New York City Budget Exhibit in 1908. (American Review of Reviews)

Scenes from the 1911 New York City Budget Exhibit.
(American Review of Reviews)

"A model police station with lieutenant's desk. A card attached to the desk stated it cost $544.00, and would be used by the detective bureau at police headquarters."

"Crowds waiting to be admitted to the opening and first noonday meeting held in connection wi budget exhibit, on Broadway, New York City."

"Series of cubes displayed at the entrance of the budget exhibit, to show the total expenses of the several city departments, and their relation to the budget as a whole."

"'Brentwood,' a veteran horse of the New York Fire Department. He has responded to 5,427 alarms in seventeen years of service. Within the coming five years, the city will have disposed of practically all of its fire horses, making way for improved auto-motor apparatus."

of life seemed literally to be manipulating their government. Bruere emphasized that to succeed, the exhibit had to capture the public's imagination and "get inside the minds of citizens" through presentations that were "brief, prompt, explicit and so framed as to throw into prominence significant facts that tell the story of action and efficiency quickly."[65]

The exhibit was a citizen's guidebook to municipal administration. It presented government as something to be assimilated through a leisure activity, associating the exercise of citizenship with amusement and consumption. Indeed, visitors to the exhibit were akin to tourists exploring the terrain of city government. Their "tour" provided them with an "authentic" representation of what the government "really" did, a behind-the-scenes look at the functioning of government as not normally seen by the average citizen. Through this encounter, the budget exhibit itself became, perhaps, more real to citizens than the government itself.[66]

Inescapably, if not intentionally, the budget exhibit cast its visitors in the role of passive spectators. Citizens watched movies and listened to lectures. These activities might engage them, perhaps even inspire them; more likely, though, as with public hearings, they served to persuade them to regard any budgeted government as normal and unproblematic. The spectacle of the exhibit aroused public interest yet domesticated popular participation by directing citizen activism toward consuming budget data and "buying" policies and politicians with the vote.

Budget reform defined citizenship primarily as oversight of government activities. It provided no space for involved interaction among citizens independent of direct reference to the affairs of government through the budget. Citizens were not to offer information directly to one another. If they had something to say, they should speak to the government, either with their vote or at a public hearing. The government would process this information and, if appropriate, pass it on to other citizens through exhibits and published reports. The budget exhibit cast government as a hub from which spokes of information ran to individual citizens. This wheel of information, however, had no rim to connect individual citizens directly to one another.

Despite its atomizing tendencies, budget reform embraced the myriad

[65]Henry Bruere, "Efficiency in City Government," *Annals of the American Academy of Political and Social Science* 41 (May 1912): 19–20.

[66]On the relationship between tourism and the search for "authentic" experience, see generally MacCannell, *Tourist.*

of civic reform groups that proliferated during the Progressive era. The men of the bureau wanted all other groups to refer to the bureau before acting. Here the bureau itself would act as the hub radiating spokes of information to other civic groups. In addition, most civic groups tended to be organized around discrete issues. Like individual citizens, they functioned as atoms with respect to other groups that had different interests. Each group would have to form its agenda by reference to the budget. Ultimately, then, the civic groups would not mediate between citizen and government, the budget would.

For the men of the bureau, twentieth-century democracy, like the modern professions, was to be based on a body of technical information specific to the profession—in this case a budget. To be a citizen in good standing, one had to master this information and use it responsibly. Like the professional career path on which the middle-class careerist relentlessly pursued higher status, the bureau presented citizenship as oriented vertically toward the government standing above the people, not horizontally toward other citizens.

Describing the "culture of professionalism," Burton Bledstein notes that "the vertical vision obstructed any horizontal recognition as middle-class Americans refused to relate to each other as equals. . . . Looking vertically, middle-class Americans lacked a corporate sense of community."[67] Similarly, a "political culture" based on individuals who built their political life around the assimilation of information would foster a citizenry of atomized individuals who looked first to the budget, rather than to a "corporate community" of their fellow citizens, to form their political attitudes and beliefs. The good citizen was to be identified not by any community or even political affiliation but by his or her mastery of objective facts compiled by nonpartisan experts.

As the budget established boundaries between public and private power to fight corruption, it also sought to separate individuals' identity as public actors from any personal ethnic, religious, or class affiliation in order to foster responsible citizenship. In contrast to the partisan spectacles of the nineteenth century, in which citizens celebrated and affirmed their membership in broader ethnic, religious, or class groups, citizens in the budgeted republic were to refer only to scientifically obtained information about government activities to guide and sustain their political action. Ethnic, religious, or class identities were irrelevant, even dangerous:

[67]Burton J. Bledstein, *The Culture of Professionalism: The Middle Class and the Development of Higher Education in America* (New York: W. W. Norton, 1976), 106–7.

they threatened to obscure a clear conception of public needs based on a dispassionate assessment of budget information.

If budget reform thus shared in broader Progressive era attempts to "Americanize" the immigrant and uplift the working classes, it did so with a difference. The men of the bureau did not try to erase ethnic or other affiliations but to locate them in a separate and (echoing the logic of the Supreme Court's logic in *Plessy v. Ferguson*) presumably equal world of private individual concerns. Who people were and what they did or believed in private was their own business, but when they acted politically, they were to leave all private identifications behind. Budget reform attempted to assimilate workers and immigrants less into a specifically "American" world than into the company of the educated middle class, which based its political action on reasoned analysis of objective facts. Nor was assimilation limited to immigrants and workers. The men of the bureau believed that *all* citizens, regardless of status, needed to accept their model of citizenship.

Budget reform thus deracinated citizenship. It told people that intellect alone was relevant to good citizenship. Education replaced one's personal loyalties or affiliations as the basis for acting as a public person. The good citizen in a republic of budgets was not Irish or German, Jewish or Gentile, rich or poor; he or she was only more or less informed about government activity.

In their happy assumption that an informed public acted "right," the men of the bureau begged the questions of who defined what was "right" and why. Clearly, they believed that the right path could be discovered only through applying objective principles of scientific investigation. The unavoidable implication was that "right" meant right in the eyes of the experts, such as themselves, who determined what information was necessary for the people to act intelligently. Popular acts had to be authenticated by experts before being accepted as true expressions of the popular will. The budget, then, although not itself defining the public good, became indispensable to its definition. Without reference to the budget, popular sentiment could not comprehend true public needs and therefore could never rise to the level of an authentic expression of the public will.

The men of the bureau had a deep and abiding commitment to democratic values, yet they distrusted the uneducated and easily manipulable masses. Their basic quarrel with the machine, after all, was not so much with the corrupt politicians who abused their power as with the ignorant citizens who allowed the abuse to take place. For them, the roots of corruption lay not in the black hearts of party hacks but in the ignorance of the people. Their solution was to shift the meaning of democratic citizenship from a public life grounded in the highly partisan community of machine politics toward one in which fundamentally deracinated educated individuals interacted with government through the dispassionate and rational medium of budget information.

As the logic of budget reform extended to all levels of government, it intruded the state, as represented in the budget, into all political discourse. As the ultimate means both to identify social needs and to represent what government could and should do, the budget became a primary reference point for all political discussion. Through the budgetary process the state could define the terms and set the boundaries for all political debate. Insofar as citizens accepted the bureau's model of budget reform, they delegitimized the free flow of public discussion among citizens unmediated by the state. In the political world of budget reform, before one citizen could speak authoritatively to another on a matter of public concern, he or she first had to consult the budget for relevant information.[68] The budget thus mediated and controlled relations both among citizens and between citizens and their government. It made it safe to entrust citizens with power by educating them. But at the same time it impeded the development of informal machine-style communities of political discourse by marginalizing ethnic, religious, or class-based political concerns and requiring reference to the budget as a prerequisite for political discussion. Whereas the bureau had first used budget reform negatively to displace political machines and erode citizens' ties to political parties, it now used it affirmatively to bind citizens to the growing and increasingly activist modern state.

---

[68]As evidenced in their overwhelmingly favorable coverage of the movement for budget reform, popular newspapers and magazines, which might not have considered their communications with the public to be mediated by the state, nonetheless fully accepted the logic of budget reform, that informed political opinions (even when made by the media) required reference to the budget.

5 BUDGET REFORM GOES NATIONAL

"From [Frederick Winslow] Taylor and his associates, on the one hand," wrote Dwight Waldo in his classic study of public administration, *The Administrative State*, "and Allen, Bruere and Cleveland, on the other hand, there extends a firm resolve to enlarge the domain of measurement, an unbroken missionary endeavor to extend the suzerainty of 'the facts.'"[1] Allen, Bruere, and Cleveland subjected all aspects of city administration to the discipline of the budgetary process. Not content to rest on their successes in New York City, they campaigned aggressively to extend budget reform to every governmental entity in the country. Cleveland's pioneering work in municipal accounting led the way, shaping the administrative practices of a generation of experts in public service. The bureau itself inspired similar agencies and budget reform campaigns throughout the country. By 1920, public budgeting was embraced by cities and states which a decade before had been operating on simple pay-as-you-go plans of public finance.

While the bureau's ideas spread, however, the institution itself entered a period of decline as its founding "ABC powers" left to pursue other related endeavors. As early as 1911, the momentum in budget reform began to shift to the national level when Cleveland took a leave of absence to develop a plan for a national budget system as chairman of President Taft's Commission on Economy and Efficiency. By 1915, Allen and Bruere had left for good, and Cleveland was devoting much of his time to forming the Institute for Government Research, soon to be established in

[1]Dwight Waldo, *The Administrative State: A Study in the Political Theory of American Public Administration*, 2d ed. (New York: Holmes and Meier, 1984), 58.

Washington, D.C., as part of the campaign for a national budget system. Nonetheless, even as the first stage of the bureau's existence came to a close, its program of budget reform had attained a formidable "suzerainty" over the domain of public administration.

EXPANDING THE DOMAIN OF BUDGET REFORM

In the opinion of one historian of accounting theory and practice, the revision of New York's accounting system under the bureau's direction was "probably the most significant single event lending impetus to the development of budgetary accounting in the United States."[2] Cleveland oversaw the revision, using it to implement methods he derived from commercial accounting based on strict differentiation between current and capital expenses. In 1909, the Department of Finance, with the assistance of the bureau, formalized his new methods in the *Manual of Accounting and Business Procedure of the City of New York*.[3]

As word of New York's innovations spread, inquiries flooded into the bureau about their nature and implementation. In response, the bureau prepared a series of pamphlets in nontechnical language to summarize the practices and procedures set forth in the manual. The pamphlets, published as "Short Talks on Municipal Accounting and Reporting," were sent to the mayors and accounting officers of over three hundred municipalities, to commercial organizations, and "public spirited men the country over."[4] The "Talks," however, were too fragmentary and incomplete to serve as an actual guide to reform. In 1913, therefore, the bureau, with funding from former comptroller Herman Metz, published *A Handbook of Municipal Accounting* as a comprehensive and publicly available counterpart to the *Manual*." The *Handbook* was the first complete textbook on municipal accounting in the United States and became the generally accepted authority on municipal accounting methods for the next fifteen years.[5]

[2]James H. Potts, "The Evolution of Budgetary Accounting Theory and Practice in Municipal Accounting from 1870," *Accounting Historians Journal* 4 (Spring 1977): 93–94.

[3]New York City, Department of Finance, *Manual of Accounting and Business Procedure of the City of New York* (New York: Martin B. Brown, 1909).

[4]Bureau of Municipal Research, *A Handbook of Municipal Accounting* (New York: D. Appleton, 1913), vii.

[5]Potts, "Evolution of Budgetary Accounting Theory," 96; James H. Potts, "The Evolution of Municipal Accounting in the United States: 1900–1935," *Business History Review* 52 (Winter 1978): 528–29.

The bureau further extended its influence by providing direct assistance to government officials outside New York City. In 1907, Governor Hughes appointed the Charter Revision Commission to study the organization and administration of New York City's government. The bureau seized the opportunity to offer its services to the commission. The commission accepted and later recorded "with pleasure its appreciation of [the bureau's] disinterested service" in preparing an unprecedented analysis of New York City's municipal administration.[6] The bureau thus established close ties with state government early on, demonstrating the value of its unique services and eliciting hearty praise from its new patrons.

The bureau provided similar services in 1909 to a joint committee of the New York State senate and assembly, appointed to investigate the finances of New York City. The committee gratefully acknowledged that "by the advice and suggestions of [the bureau's] experts, and the services of its accountants, all freely rendered, [the] committee has been able to accomplish results which otherwise would have been impossible within the expenditure which your committee has felt at liberty to incur."[7] The bureau readily provided its services for free in order to gain access to government.

The height of the bureau's influence in state government came with the New York State Constitutional Convention of 1915. To prepare for the convention, the legislature created the Constitutional Convention Commission in 1914 and directed it "to collect, compile, and disseminate information and data . . . it may deem useful for the delegates . . . in their deliberations."[8] The newly created State Department of Efficiency and Economy was entrusted with primary responsibility for meeting this need and called on the bureau for technical assistance and support. The bureau responded enthusiastically, supplying a staff of twenty led by Cleveland and Charles Beard. By reason of its experience and expertise, the bureau soon took command of the project and assumed primary responsibility for the overall direction of what became an extensive study of the organization, functions, and personnel of each bureau, department, and office of the state.[9]

Following the publication of the study, the state asked the bureau alone

[6] *Report of the Charter Revision Commission of 1907 to the Governor of the State of New York*, New York Senate Doc. vol. 2, no. 10, 1908.

[7] *Report of the Joint Committee of the Senate and Assembly of the State of New York Appointed to Investigate the Finances of New York City* (Albany: J. B. Lyon, 1909), 10.

[8] New York, *Laws* (1914), chap. 261, quoted in Thomas Schick, *The New York State Constitutional Convention of 1915 and the Modern State Governor* (New York: National Municipal League, 1978), 42.

[9] Schick, *New York State Constitutional Convention*, 42–43; Jane S. Dahlberg, *The New York Bureau of Municipal Research* (New York: New York University Press, 1966), 93–97.

to prepare a briefer "Appraisal" of New York's administrative structure with recommendations for change. Once again, having gained access to government through its reputation as an objective compiler of information, the bureau obtained greater influence and latitude to express prescriptive opinions as government officials came to accept and depend upon the product it provided.

The bureau proposed three reorganization amendments: an executive budget, the consolidation of state administrative agencies, and a short ballot. The budget formed the cornerstone of the recommendations, providing the basic mechanism for ensuring responsiveness and responsibility in government. Specifically, the executive budget amendment directed the heads of all state departments to submit to the governor (instead of to relevant legislative committees) itemized estimates of their needs for the coming year. The governor would then hold public hearings on the estimates, make his own revisions, and submit to the legislature a comprehensive budget plan of proposed expenditures and estimated revenues. Despite some delegates' fears that an executive budget would lead to an "autocracy," the Republican-controlled convention eventually agreed to reorganization amendments almost identical to those drafted by the bureau.[10] The bureau's success owed much to the convention floor leader, former U. S. attorney general George W. Wickersham, who had recently served with Cleveland on President Taft's Commission on Economy and Efficiency and who was also a trustee of the bureau.[11]

New York's voters ultimately rejected the constitutional amendments set before them in 1916. Even so, the bureau's work for the convention was, in the words of one contemporary scholar of public administration, "a remarkable forecast of modern tendencies" in its provisions for the executive branch.[12] Cleveland himself believed that even though "the proposed new constitution was defeated at the polls . . . it has had a marked influence on the political thinking of the whole country."[13] Dwight Waldo went so far as to characterize the bureau's "Appraisal" as the twentieth-century equivalent of the *Federalist Papers*, which provided "a conscious statement of fundamental philosophy and a summary and synthesis of the political thought of the previous decades."[14]

---

[10]See Bureau of Municipal Research, "The Constitution and Government of New York: An Appraisal," *Municipal Research* 61 (May 1915): 1–32.

[11]Schick, *New York State Constitutional Convention*, 75–76, 80–100.

[12]Leonard D. White, quoted in Schick, *New York State Constitutional Convention*, xii.

[13]Frederick A. Cleveland and Arthur E. Buck, *The Budget and Responsible Government* (New York: Macmillan, 1920), 109.

[14]Waldo, *Administrative State*, 34.

To the men of the bureau, Waldo's comparison of the "Appraisal" with the *Federalist Papers* would have seemed especially apt. The bureau was concerned to address fundamental issues about the nature and purpose of political representation in twentieth-century America. The "Appraisal," in many respects, stands as the culmination of the bureau's decade-long endeavor to articulate and disseminate a vision of modern democracy revitalized and maintained by budget reform. In this regard, the men of the bureau were grappling with the same problem addressed so brilliantly by James Madison in the *Federalist Papers*: how to maintain a viable republic over vast spaces and a diverse population. Madison saw diversity as its own solution: numerous factions would prevent any single one from predominating. The men of the bureau used budget reform to update Madison and address the threat to the republic posed by urban industrial society and large complex government in the twentieth century. Budget reform would relegate factions to the private sphere and harmonize all public action through adherence to rational assessment of scientifically obtained data.

The bureau's studies of state operations and reform proposals shaped debate over governmental reorganization across the nation for the next decade. Especially influential were the bureau's arguments for an executive budget, under which the governor, rather than the legislature, formulated the state's financial plan. Between 1911 and 1919 forty-four states passed budget laws, and by 1929, every state but Arkansas had adopted a budgetary system on the executive model.[15]

The bureau publicized its activities through a bulletin service, including the "Efficient Citizenship" series, and extensive correspondence (which, by 1916, had amounted to over sixty thousand individual letters to pubic officers and citizens, not including form letters.)[16] Supplementing its printed publicity, bureau staff members traversed the country presenting their reform program to city councils, commissions, chambers of commerce, boards of trade, and civic organizations.

Allen, as the bureau's chief publicist and fund-raiser, also directly lobbied business elites in personal conferences. Between 1908 and 1914 he traveled the country in answer to requests for talks at meetings about municipal research. Allen spread the word about municipal research to busi-

---

[15]Schick, *New York State Constitutional Convention*, 131–33; Cleveland and Buck, *Budget and Responsible Government*, 124; Leonard D. White, *Trends in Public Administration* (New York: McGraw-Hill, 1933), 34.

[16]Bureau of Municipal Research, "A National Program to Improve Methods of Government," *Municipal Research* 71 (March 1916): 83–85.

ness groups across the country and persuaded them to fund local bureaus on the New York model. He made full use of the prestige of the bureau's trustees and financial backers to gain the favor of reluctant businessmen. In return, he enhanced their reputations by holding them up as models of enlightened business leaders. Allen later recalled that in campaigning for the bureau, he was "selling Mr. Carnegie, Mr. Rockefeller, Mr. Cutting, and by this time I could include Mr. Morgan, Jacob H. Schiff, Frank Vanderlip,—other bankers and business men,—Mr. Harriman." Local business leaders eagerly bought Allen's product. As one Minnesota businessman told him, "I don't believe you realize what it means in these outer cities when you meet a group of business men who are the big business men of their own city and you tell them that in New York, this kind of problem that they're dodging is being met frankly, openly, by J. P. Morgan, John D. Rockefeller, and Andrew Carnegie. I don't believe you have any conception of what that means out here."[17]

The bureau's careful creation of newsworthy budget "events" also ensured extensive media coverage throughout the country. Municipal research and budget exhibits appealed broadly to a population familiar with and receptive to the reform impulse. Newspapers from Boston to Los Angeles covered the bureau's work and praised its accomplishments in editorials. Citizens in Indianapolis, Toronto, Memphis, Atlanta, and Chicago might pick up their papers on any given morning and read of such advances in municipal government as the New York City budget exhibits, or bureau-sponsored administrative surveys. Newspapers in smaller cities, such as Reading, Pennsylvania, North Adams, Massachusetts, Tacoma, Washington, and Mason City, Iowa, carried word of the bureau's activities to people outside major metropolitan areas.[18]

During the 1910s, cities throughout the country followed New York's example and staged budget exhibits of their own. The largest were held in Cincinnati in 1912 and 1913. (The 1912 exhibit alone drew over one hundred thousand people in two weeks.) Organized under the direction of Lent D. Upson, a bureau-trained municipal research expert, the Cincinnati exhibits employed many of the same techniques as the one in New York—to great effect. According to Upson, "the immediate results of this exhibit" were "seen in the attitude of the public to the proposal for an in-

[17]William H. Allen, *Reminiscences* (New York: Columbia University Oral History Collection, 1950), 155.

[18]The bureau kept extensive clippings files and reprinted excerpts from many articles in such publications as *Six Years of Municipal Research in New York*, 72–74, and "National Program," 59–67.

creased tax, which, being granted by a bare majority last year, was renewed this year by a vote of almost two to one."[19] Proper publicity thus paid direct dividends by gaining citizens' acceptance of an increasingly activist government. Other cities holding exhibits during the 1910s included Philadelphia, Chicago, Milwaukee, Hartford, and Hoboken. Nor were these solely big city phenomena. Smaller towns, such as Greenwich, Connecticut, and Dobbs Ferry, New York, also staged exhibits for their citizens. New York City itself maintained a smaller permanent version of the budget exhibit after 1911 at the City College.[20]

In 1915, the bureau's program reached an even broader audience when New York City sent a municipal exhibit to the Panama-Pacific Exposition in San Francisco. Derived from the 1911 show and costing $100,000, New York's exhibit garnered many awards, including grand prizes for the overall exhibit and for the general excellence of its illustrative photography.[21] Henry Bruere, then serving as New York City's chamberlain under Mayor John Purroy Mitchel, chaired the committee that organized the exhibit and presided over its dedication in San Francisco. Bruere reported that "the exhibit will show . . . that New York is in the forefront of civic progress in the United States, and will make available to people the country over a vast amount of suggestive information on the government of a great city."[22]

Beyond New York, the bureau, in cooperation with local civic organizations and public officials, conducted general surveys of governmental administration in twenty-five cities and five counties from Connecticut to Oregon. Men from the bureau also helped to conduct limited surveys of particular departments in an additional twenty-five cities, plus a study of the United States Office of Indian Affairs. The bureau followed up on its surveys by installing completely new systems of accounting and business

[19]Lent D. Upson, "Cincinnati's First Municipal Exhibit," *American City* 7 (December 1912): 530–32.

[20]"Milwaukee's Open Book," *Survey* 27 (January 1912): 1443; J. Harold Braddock, "The Significance of the Dobbs Ferry Idea," *American City* 7 (August 1912): 106–7; William Bennett Munro, "Current Municipal Affairs," *American Political Science Review* 7 (February 1913): 107.

[21]Frank Morton Todd, *The Story of the Exhibition* (New York: G. P. Putnam's Sons, 1921), 3:341–45; New York State, *State of New York at the Panama-Pacific Exposition* (Albany: J. B. Lyon, 1916), 435–36.

[22]Henry Bruere, *Administrative Reorganization and Constructive Work in the Government of the City of New York, 1914* (New York: [Office of the City Chamberlain], 1915), 48–49.

procedures in six cities while overseeing partial administrative revisions in seven others.[23]

The bureau also loaned men from its general staff who actually became employees of the governments they were assisting while remaining subject to the bureau's supervision. The most significant loan involved Cleveland's work as chairman of the Taft Commission on Economy and Efficiency. Other agreements sent bureau men to work installing an accounting system for the Panama Canal Zone, directing school surveys in Ohio and Wisconsin, and investigating city accounting and business methods in Chicago.[24]

To institutionalize the bureau's influence, Allen conceived the Training School for Public Service, which opened in October 1911 with financial support from Mrs. E. H. Harriman.[25] The school aimed "to train men for the study and administration of public business . . . [and] to furnish wherever practicable a connecting link between schools and colleges and municipal or other public departments for practical field work."[26] The school presented a rigorous curriculum that combined classroom instruction with practical clinical experience. The period of training varied according to a student's previous experience and the type of preparation desired. Two years was considered advisable, but many students attended the school for shorter periods.[27]

New York served as a laboratory for the students, who conducted studies on subjects ranging from the city's election machinery to civil service administration to street paving. Budgetary work played a central role in every student's education. Each trainee was required to study and participate in the city's budgetary process. Comptroller Prendergast was especially helpful in this regard, welcoming students into his office to work under his direction.[28]

Applications poured into the school from all over the country. During the first three years of operation, over 1,000 men and women applied for admission from two hundred cities in thirty states and two foreign coun-

[23]Bureau of Municipal Research, "National Program," 25–31.

[24]Ibid., 24.

[25]As Bruere later recalled, "Mr. Allen, about this time, conceived another idea which was entirely his own—that was instituting a school for training for public service." Henry Bruere, *Reminiscences* (New York: Columbia University Oral History Collection, 1949), 51.

[26]Bureau of Municipal Research, *Training School for Public Service: Announcement—1911* (New York: Bureau of Municipal Research, 1911), 2.

[27]Dahlberg, *Bureau of Municipal Research*, 127.

[28]Ibid., 123–25.

tries. Of these, the school accepted a total of 165. In addition to being geographically diverse, the students represented a wide variety of occupations and professions. Applicants to the class of 1914 included teachers, accountants, lawyers, businessmen, engineers, social workers, civil servants, college students, a mayor, a minister, and a librarian.[29]

The school did not train for a distinct profession called "public service"; rather, it took citizens from all walks of life and trained them in the principles and methods of efficient citizenship, which they could then take back and spread among their home communities. As Charles A. Beard stated soon after becoming the school's supervisor in 1915:

> Public service . . . is not a single profession. It calls for persons trained in all professions, and possessing such diverse qualifications and talents that there can be no common education for all divisions of the service although there is undoubtedly a highly desirable type of training in administrative science which should be superimposed upon each of the various special disciplines. . . . It is therefore erroneous to speak of training for public service as a distinct discipline like law, medicine, engineering, or accounting. The public service embraces scores of different types of positions for each of which there are special and local requirements.[30]

The school superimposed its ideas on existing disciplines. The principles of efficient citizenship derived from the work of the bureau and operated above and independent of all other professions. They were flexible, capable of adapting to all aspects of public life. They could go anywhere, extending the domain of measurement to cover all sorts of "special and local requirements."

The training school inspired and directed the early development of the profession of public administration. Later historians of public administration classified it as "the first genuine professional school of public administration" in the country. The school never gave degrees of its own, but Columbia, New York University, and the University of Pennsylvania and of Michigan each passed resolutions in 1914 allowing credit from training school fieldwork to be applied toward graduate degrees. The

[29]Bureau of Municipal Research, "Annual Report of the Training School for Public Service," *Municipal Research*, Extra No. 1 (August 1915): 4.

[30]Charles A. Beard, "The Problem of Training for the Public Service," *Municipal Research* 68 (December 1915): 5–6.

training school also inspired the creation of governmental research agencies and programs in public administration at universities across the country.[31]

The men and women who attended the training school together with members of the bureau's staff spread outward from New York City to found, direct, and staff bureaus of municipal research in other cities. Twenty-five bureau-trained experts went on to direct other research bureaus with another forty-three serving as staff members. By 1926, over forty governmental research agencies had been established in cities, and several for county and state governments. In addition, Cleveland played a central role in establishing the Institute for Government Research in 1916 to study national administration. The model even spread overseas, spawning an institute for municipal research in Tokyo in 1922, and a bureau in China as well.[32] The profusion of research bureaus led to the creation of the Governmental Research Association in 1914 to coordinate activities and facilitate communication among them. The association held annual conferences at which representatives from the various bureaus came together to share ideas and formulate common policies and procedures to guide their work.[33]

Budget reform also became a tool of empire building as America en-

[31]In 1913, Harvard University established a bureau for research in municipal government and by 1931, fourteen governmental research agencies were flourishing at universities across the United States. By 1924, the University of Michigan offered a master's degree in public administration (a program headed by former bureau men), and the University of California at Berkeley, the University of Missouri, Toledo University, William and Mary College, and the University of Wisconsin each granted undergraduate degrees in public administration. Then, in 1924, working in close cooperation with the bureau, Syracuse University opened the Maxwell School of Citizenship and Public Affairs specifically to offer graduate education and preparation for government service. All of these programs drew inspiration and direction from the training school. See Alice B. Stone and Donald C. Stone, "Early Development of Education in Public Administration," in *American Public Administration: Past, Present, Future*, ed. Frederick C. Mosher (University: University of Alabama Press, 1975), 28–34; Dahlberg, *Bureau of Municipal Research*, 132–40.

[32]Governmental Research Conference, *Twenty Years of Municipal Research* ([New York]: Governmental Research Conference, [1927]), 3–8; Dahlberg, *Bureau of Municipal Research*, 66–67, 136–39; Benjamin De Witt, *The Progressive Movement* (New York: Macmillan, 1915), 334–35. The school's more prominent graduates included Raymond Moley and Robert Moses. For an account of Moses's experiences at the school and with the bureau generally, see Robert A. Caro, *The Power Broker* (New York: Vintage, 1975), 59–112.

[33]See Governmental Research Association, *Proceedings: 1914–1924, inclusive* (New York: Governmental Research Association, [1925]), typescript; and Norman Gill, *Municipal Research Bureaus* (Washington, D.C.: American Council on Public Affairs, 1944), 86–96.

tered the world during the first decades of the twentieth century.[34] Henry Bruere's experience as financial adviser to the Carranza government in Mexico vividly illustrates the use of budget reform as an instrument of foreign policy. In 1916, Bruere left his position as city chamberlain to become vice president of the American Metal Company, a mining and metal trading concern with interests in Mexican mining properties. Shortly thereafter he joined a special commission to confer with representatives of the Mexican government concerning the taxation of mining operations. The commission included Frank Lane, secretary of the United States Department of the Interior, and John Mott, director of the International YMCA.[35]

Following the conferences, Luis Cabrera, Mexico's secretary of finance, invited Bruere to study his country's financial system and make recommendations for its improvement. After consulting with the United States ambassador to Mexico, Frank Lyon Polk, and with President Wilson, Bruere accepted Cabrera's invitation and went to Mexico in May 1917. To assist him, Bruere compiled a staff of six Americans, including two professors of finance from Princeton and one from Columbia, and forty-four Mexicans. Bruere's closest associate on this venture was Thomas R. Lill, a certified public accountant on the staff of the Bureau of Municipal Research. Bruere returned to the United States after a few months, but Lill remained in Mexico for nearly two years and compiled an extensive report on the status of its national debt. Lill was paid by the Mexican government and served as acting director of its Commission on Financial and Administrative Reorganization, which Carranza established in the fall of 1917.[36]

[34]The intersections of lives committed both to budget reform and to American expansionism are quite remarkable. President Taft, whose Commission of Economy and Efficiency (directed by Cleveland) blazed the trail for national budget reform, was the first civil governor of the Philippines after the Spanish-American War. William Willoughby, who served under Cleveland on the Taft Commission and later became the first director of the Institute of Government Research, was director of the treasury in Puerto Rico during the early 1900s and later briefly served with his twin brother Westel as a constitutional advisor to the government of China in 1916. Frank Goodnow, president of Johns Hopkins, who also served on the Taft Commission and became the first chairman of the board of trustees of the Institute for Government Research, preceded the Willoughbys as constitutional adviser to the Chinese government. Cleveland himself moved on from budget reform during the 1920s to serve on a commission of financial advisors to the Chinese national government in 1929 and held the powerful position of chief inspector of salt revenue in China from 1931 to 1935.

[35]Bruere, *Reminiscences*, 127–35; Henry Bruere, preface, in Thomas R. Lill *National Debt of Mexico* (New York: Searle, Nicholson & Lill, C.P.A.s, 1919), 1–3; Senate Committee on Foreign Relations, *Investigation of Mexican Affairs*, 66th Cong., 2d sess., 1920, 611–77, (testimony of Thomas R. Lill).

[36]Bruere, *Reminiscences*, 131–33; Senate, *Investigation of Mexican Affairs*, 612–14, 636.

Since 1914 Mexico had paid neither interest nor sinking fund install-ments on its debt, internal or foreign. Maladministration, corruption, and war had thoroughly undermined investors' confidence in the government. Bruere's mission was to help stabilize a financial system thrown into tur-moil by the Mexican Revolution and protect the interests of companies such as American Metal. (Bruere and Lill also helped to arrange a meet-ing in 1918 between Mexico's acting secretary of finance, Rafael Nieto, and the International Bankers Committee, headed by J. P. Morgan.)[37]

In coming to Mexico, Bruere served much the same function as the first accountants sent from England to America in the 1880s. In effect, he was an outside auditor sent to safeguard his employers' investment. As Bruere put it, they were concerned "with whether the Government was to be sta-ble or from the standpoint of the Mining Interests with which I was as-sociated, whether or not its program would lead to a wise administration of public funds. . . ."[38] Rather than simply going over the "company's" books, however, Bruere and his associates made specific recommenda-tions to reform Mexico's system of financial administration. As a direct result of Bruere's recommendations, the Carranza government imple-mented several major reforms: it created a new office of Contralor Gen-eral with powers to collect and oversee the distribution of public funds; it centralized governmental purchasing under a single department of pur-chases; and it introduced a monthly budget and allotment system. These reforms not only helped Mexico regularize its financial administration, they also opened up that administration to the scrutiny of foreign in-vestors. Access to financial information would give the American Metal Company the same type of power that a proper budgetary system was supposed to give to citizens. Only here, the "citizens" were foreign cor-porations that voted with dollars, not ballots.[39]

Triumph and Decline

By the mid-1910s, the bureau was riding high on the crest of what had become a nationwide campaign for budget reform. In 1916, the bureau confidently asserted that "the term 'budget,' like the phrase 'social jus-tice,' or 'Americanism,' has now become one of the staple commodities

[37]Bruere, preface, 1–3; Senate, *Investigation of Mexican Affairs*, 636–37.
[38]Bruere, *Reminiscences*, 131.
[39]Thomas R. Lill, "The Contralor General De Mexico," *National Municipal Review* 8 (November 1919): 601–6.

of politics."[40] As the public incorporated the terms of budgeting into its political discourse, however, the bureau's once distinctive voice as a vanguard publicist became only one of many clamoring for reform. As the momentum in the campaign for budget reform shifted to the national level, new organizations and individuals came to the fore to eclipse the bureau, which had begun fundamentally as a *municipal* research agency. Finally, the bureau's very success brought out long-simmering personal and ideological tensions between Allen and Cleveland that eventually fractured the ABCs.

The first intimations of decline came masked in the guise of honor and recognition. In 1910, President Taft invited Allen and Cleveland to his "Summer White House" at Beverly Farms to discuss a proposed inquiry into the administration of the national government. Following a second meeting with Cleveland, Taft asked the bureau to make a preliminary study of some of the problems such an inquiry might encounter. Favorably impressed, and with the strong support of his secretary, Charles D. Norton, Taft then appointed Cleveland chairman the President's Commission on Economy and Efficiency, which was formally established in 1911 pursuant to a congressional appropriation.

Through the commission, Cleveland carried the campaign for budget reform directly from the local to the national level. (State budget reform would not get off the ground until the New York State Constitutional Convention in 1915.) The commission, in effect, conducted a bureau-style survey of the federal government. The commission's report, *The Need for a National Budget*, set the agenda for national budget reform until the passage of the Budget and Accounting Act in 1921.[41]

Cleveland's work for the commission took him away from the bureau for nearly three years. In his absence, Allen became more active in the technical and research sides of the bureau's activities, showing a special interest in problems of pedagogy and school administration. When Cleveland returned to the bureau in 1913, he did not like what he found. Allen, he believed, had strayed from established policies and misused the bureau's personnel and resources, particularly in conducting controversial studies of educational institutions. Compounding the growing tension between Allen and Cleveland was Bruere's absence as a medi-

---

[40]Bureau of Municipal Research, "The Elements of State Budget Making," *Municipal Research* 80 (December 1916): 1.

[41]President's Commission on Economy and Efficiency, *The Need for a National Budget*, 62d Cong., 2d sess., 1912, H. Doc. 854.

ator; he had already resigned in January 1914 to become city chamberlain.[42]

Matters came to a head in May 1914 in a dispute over a conditional donation from John D. Rockefeller. At this time, the bureau was sorely in need of funds as several substantial five-year grants made in 1909 were slated to expire by the end of the year. Rockefeller approached the bureau early in 1914 with an offer of $10,000 for five years plus the promise of his aid in raising a total of $100,000 a year. He later increased his offer to $20,000 a year. When Rockefeller met with bureau trustees R. Fulton Cutting and Victor Morawetz on April 10 to present his offer, he appended several conditions. As Cutting later recalled the encounter, Rockefeller

> expressed warm interest in the Bureau's local work and said that he would like to contribute to its continuance in 1915, but he said that he did not approve of the practice of the Bureau undertaking work outside of the State of New York for compensation, nor the action of the directors of the Bureau undertaking to deal with the strictly pedagogical problems involved in the management of the public schools. He stated that as he felt that these activities of the Bureau were prejudicial to its usefulness as a local institution he was not disposed to contribute to the fund of the Bureau so long as these activities continued.[43]

The bureau accepted both the money and the conditions. According to Cutting, there was no compromise of the bureau's autonomy because the board of trustees had been contemplating similar changes for a long time.[44]

Allen, however, was furious. According to him, Rockefeller also demanded that the bureau divorce the training school from the bureau and deemphasize its publicity work by discontinuing its *Efficient Citizenship* bulletins. Each of these activities was close to Allen's heart and close to his power base within the bureau. With all his accustomed passion and more than a touch of self-righteous indignation, Allen declared that accepting Rockefeller's terms would completely compromise the bureau's integrity. Cleveland, who had met with Rockefeller the day after the ini-

[42]Senate, *Industrial Relations: Final Report and Testimony Submitted to Congress by the Commission on Industrial Relations*, 64th Congress, 2d sess., Doc. no. 415 (1916), 8314 (testimony of Frederick A. Cleveland).

[43]Ibid.,7951–52 (testimony of R. Fulton Cutting).

[44]Ibid.

tial offer, was more than happy to have a powerful ally in his battle to contain the increasingly irritating Allen. Cleveland calmly but firmly supported Rockefeller's offer and eventually won the trustees to his side.[45]

Without Bruere's mediating influence, the conflict between Cleveland and Allen turned bitter. One staff member remarked at the time that "the greatest blow that could have been struck was when our friend Bruere went away because it seems that the division of authority became more marked than before between the directors."[46]

Further fanning the flames, Allen went public with his opposition. One *New York Times* headline declared, "DIRECTORS FALL OUT IN RESEARCH BUREAU—Dr. W. H. Allen Who Can Not Agree With Dr. F. A. Cleveland, May Be Ousted—Rockefeller As Factor—Report That His Domination Caused Friction Denied by Officers of the Organization."[47] By October 1914, Allen was indeed ousted. Over the years, his abrasive, headstrong manner had alienated much of the staff and several powerful trustees. His forthright and public criticism of the Rockefeller donation ensured Cleveland's victory in the power struggle that followed Bruere's departure. Allen, however, did not go quietly. True to form, with the public announcement of his resignation, he issued a pamphlet to the press titled "Reasons Why Mr. Allen Believes That Mr. Rockefeller's Conditional Offer of Support to the New York Bureau of Municipal Research Should Not Be Accepted," in which he accused Rockefeller of trying to manipulate the bureau's activities.[48]

Although Cutting denied that cessation of the bureau's publicity work was one of Rockefeller's conditions, the bureau soon replaced its snappy, accessible "Efficient Citizenship" postcard bulletins with a substantial monthly bulletin, *Municipal Research*, which presented detailed and in-depth studies of particular problems in public administration. Allen decried the changes as a betrayal of the bureau's original mission. In 1914, he wrote,

the Bureau of Municipal Research, had three paralytic strokes: (1) It decided to stop keeping the public informed about government deficien-

---

[45]Ibid., 8335 (testimony of William H. Allen). Allen also provides an account of this incident in *Rockefeller: Giant, Dwarf, Symbol* (New York: Institute for Public Service, 1930), 424–34.

[46]Statement of C. J. Driscoll, *Minutes of Proceedings at the House of Professor Seligman, 324 West 86th Street, [New York], May 17, 1914*, E. R. A. Seligman papers, Box 5 Rare Books and Manuscript Library, Columbia Univertsity, New York.

[47]*New York Times*, quoted in Senate, *Industrial Relations*, 8463.

[48]"Dr. Allen Out of Bureau of Municipal Research," *Survey* 33 (October 17, 1914): 62; Senate, *Industrial Relations*, 8465–66.

cies, breakdowns, weaknesses; . . . (2) It discontinued its school service and publicity for non-expert taxpayers; (3) Forgetting that in its teaching days it had issued a pamphlet with so startling a title as *To Hell with Reform*, it publicly renounced what it called the sensationalism of such earlier titles as *Civicity, Like Charity, Begins at Home*; *No Matter Who's Elected*, etc.[49]

For Allen, the bureau lived and died by medical metaphors. The greatest threat to the bureau's health was its new approach (or lack thereof) to publicity.[50]

During Cleveland's absence in Washington, Allen had developed "Efficient Citizenship" into a popular, easily accessible, free, and widely disseminated pamphlet series—780 issues published in quantities that ran into the millions.[51] When Cleveland returned, he was openly contemptuous of Allen's one- and two-page publications, declaring that Allen's approach "was reaching out for publicity and that it lent itself more directly to hostile criticism than it did to constructive purposes."[52] To explain the bureau's change in policy following Rockefeller's gift, Cleveland stated simply that "in order that the effects of yellow journalistic publicity might die out, the Bureau did deliberately refrain from pushing 'red' and 'yellow' cards under the noses of citizens in every morning's mail."[53]

Cleveland saw the *Municipal Research* bulletins as the right type of publicity. The new bulletins were issued less frequently (monthly), were less affordable (one dollar per issue), and were not easily intelligible to the average citizen (containing long and detailed studies, frequently over one hundred pages, of complex municipal problems). To Allen, publicity meant frequent doses of brief, simple messages for broad popular consumption. To Cleveland, it meant reasoned and sophisticated studies issued for experts and professional reformers.

In his battle with Allen, Cleveland had a formidable ally in Jerome Greene, secretary to John D. Rockefeller. Greene shared Cleveland's contempt for Allen's brand of publicity. Allen's "postal card bulletins have be-

[49]William H. Allen, "Interpreting Government to the Citizenship," in *Experts in City Government*, ed. Edward A. Fitzpatrick (New York: D. Appleton, 1919), 169.

[50]Allen sustained the medical metaphor in a 1916 article critical of Bruere, among others, whom he described as "tuberous obstacles to reform." William H. Allen, "Tuberous Obstacles to Reform in New York City," *National Municipal Review* 5 (July 1916): 419–27.

[51]Bureau of Municipal Research. "National Program," 83.

[52]Senate, *Industrial Relations*, 8317–18.

[53]Frederick A. Cleveland, "What Is Civic Education?" *National Municipal Review* 5 (October 1916): 653.

come a laughing stock," declared Greene, "[and represent] a gross perversion of the functions of the Bureau" by casting its objectivity into question. Greene was especially put out by Allen's criticisms of a Rockefeller-supported study of the New York school system, which he found to be "an atrocious bit of meddling." By March 1913, Greene was complaining that "something has got to be done" about Allen. It was therefore with ill-concealed glee that Greene confided to Paul Hanus (who conducted the original study of New York school that Allen had criticized) that he had received unofficial word of Allen's impending ouster from the bureau. In asking Hanus to keep the happy news to himself until "something comes out from other sources," Greene suggested that he "treasure this particular secret in your bosom and get what fun out of it you can."[54]

Allen's bitter experience with the bureau fostered in him a growing suspicion of expert authority and the power of philanthropists. He saw Cleveland and others like him as subverting democracy by seeking to remove the subjects of expert analysis from the realm of public discourse. Allen insisted that Cleveland's type of publicity would foster a "contempt for the public's ability and right to understand expert government." Allen believed that the bureau had become a captive of public officials and civic-minded philanthropists. With Bruere's entry into a government dominated by officials sympathetic to its program, Allen saw the bureau surrendering its independent voice to become an adjunct to city administration. With the acceptance of Rockefeller's conditional donation, he saw bureau sacrificing its intellectual autonomy for financial security.[55]

Allen, ever the savvy publicist, obtained a powerful forum to express his views in 1915, when he became a consultant to the United States Commission on Industrial Relations. Originally established in 1911 in response to rising labor unrest and radicalism, the commission also held a series of hearings in 1915 on the influence of philanthropic foundations over civic and industrial education. The commission asked Allen to conduct a study of several of the largest organizations, including two Rockefeller and three Carnegie foundations. In response to Allen's accusations concerning Rockefeller's conditional donation to the bureau, the com-

[54]"Memorandum by Mr. Jerome D. Greene concerning the Bureau of Municipal Research," March 17, 1913, Rockefeller Family Archives, North Tarrytown, N.Y., Record Group III 2 D, Box 2, Folder 5; Jerome D. Greene to E. C. Moore, November 21, 1912, Rockefeller Family Archives, Record Group III 2 D, Box 2, Folder 6; Jerome D. Greene to E. C. Moore, March 10, 1913, Rockefeller Family Archives, Record Group III 2 D, Box 2, Folder 6; Jerome D. Greene to Paul H. Hanus, June 2, 1914, Rockefeller Family Archives, Record Group III 2 D, Box 2, Folder 6.
[55]Allen, "Interpreting Government," 170–74.

mission called Allen, Cleveland, and R. Fulton Cutting to present their versions of this transaction in public hearings.[56] The dispute between Allen and Cleveland undermined morale within the bureau and the hearings undoubtedly damaged its reputation. The true turning point in the bureau's career, however, had quietly come and gone long before these more spectacular events brought its problems to light. The bureau's greatest influence came from its reputation as the country's foremost expert in municipal budget reform. When Cleveland left for Washington in 1911 to direct Taft's Commission on Economy and Efficiency, he took with him the momentum of the budget reform movement. Even after his return to the bureau in 1913, he remained deeply involved in efforts to establish the national Institute for Government Research in Washington. The Taft commission supplanted the bureau at the vanguard of the budget reform movement, redirecting its focus to national affairs. After the commission's demise, the Institute for Government Research took up the banner of national budget reform and carried it until the passage of the Budget and Accounting Act in 1921.

[56]Complete treatment of the commission's activities concerning labor unrest may be found in Graham Adams, Jr., *The Age of Industrial Violence, 1910–15* (New York: Columbia University Press, 1966), and James Weinstein, *The Corporate Ideal in the Liberal State: 1900–1918* (Boston: Beacon Press, 1968), 172–213. Neither of these studies, however, deals with the commission's investigation of foundations. For the testimony concerning the Rockefeller donation to the bureau, see Senate, *Industrial Relations*, 7951–54 (testimony of R. Fulton Cutting), 8310–25 (testimony of Frederick A. Cleveland), and 8327–71 (testimony of William H. Allen). Allen also discusses the hearings in his *Reminiscences*, 247–56.

6 IMAGINING THE STATE

In his powerful study of the political and institutional struggles that shaped the development of national administrative capacities during the late nineteenth and early twentieth centuries, Stephen Skowronek begins by contrasting contemporary awareness of government's pervasive coercive power with H. G. Wells's observation of 1906 that "the typical American has no 'sense of the state.'" Skowronek makes the important point that the emergence of new governing arrangements did not arise reflexively or automatically in response to new conditions. Rather, he argues that states change "through political struggles rooted in and mediated by preestablished institutional arrangements." He deftly analyzes the complex interplay of institutions, procedures, and intellectual talents that transformed the American state from a patchwork of long-established political and institutional relationships in which decentralized courts and parties remained primarily responsible for administration into a "New American State" with a powerful administrative arm.[1]

The story of national budget reform builds upon yet modifies some of Skowronek's insights. For all the explanatory power of his model, ironically Skowronek seems to imply that the "sense of the state" itself was the more or less reflexive response to the emergence of new administrative capacities. In contrast, an analysis of budget reform reveals the development of a "sense of the state" as prior to, or at least coordinate with, other powerful forces in actual state building. Quite simply, in order to build a state

[1] Steven Skowronek, *Building a New American State: The Expansion of National Administrative Capacities, 1877–1920* (Cambridge: Cambridge University Press, 1982), 1–18.

you must first be able to conceive it. The process of conception, of course, is modified by and, in turn, modifies experience. Through long, arduous, uncertain, halting, yet persistent attempts to explore and map the terrain of federal administration, proponents of accounting reform, and later champions of budget reform, allowed prospective state builders to make the conceptual leap from conceiving of government as a random agglomeration of administrative fiefdoms to envisioning a coherent, interrelated, and unitary state. The process of budget reform enabled Americans to imagine a new state.

President Taft's appointment of the Commission on Economy and Efficiency culminated a series of sporadic efforts to reform federal financial administration that stretched back to the Civil War. As with state and local government, financial administration at the national level during the nineteenth century was uncoordinated and disorganized: no formal budgetary system existed; revenues were not considered in conjunction with expenditures; and no administrative apparatus oversaw departmental operations.[2]

Between 1869 and 1895, Congress conducted a series of investigations into departmental business methods, first to address problems of debt and retrenchment in the aftermath of war, and later to address the concerns of citizens and organizations doing business with the government. As it began to examine specific complaints about government administration, Congress found that it had no idea as to the nature and extent of departmental operations. With each new special committee, Congress uncovered more information about personnel, supplies, and activities than it knew how to handle.

During the 1870s and 1880s, Congress was simply overwhelmed by the mass of information it had accumulated through its investigations. It perceived the need for order but could not control an administrative apparatus that it did not comprehend. Then, in 1893, a joint congressional commission, commonly known as the Dockery-Cockrell Commission, for the first time employed a staff of experts in accounting and business organization to examine and make recommendations about departmental administration.

---

[2]Arthur Smithies, *The Budgetary Process in the United States* (New York: McGraw-Hill, 1955), 11–12; Lucius Wilmerding, Jr., *The Spending Power: A History of the Efforts of Congress to Control Expenditures* (New Haven: Yale University Press, 1943), 225–34. Leonard D. White, *The Republican Era, 1869–1901: A Study in Administrative History* (New York: Macmillan, 1958), 28–29, 95–109.

The report of the Dockery-Cockrell Commission provided the first indication that government activities could be defined and classified. With order came the possibility of control. But with the possibility of control came also competition over who would exercise control. The presidency, largely dormant in administrative matters since the Civil War, came to life again shortly after the Dockery-Cockrell Commission made its report in 1895, and directly contested Congress for control over the executive branch. Theodore Roosevelt initiated the challenge with a series of presidential commissions (the most important being the Keep Commission on Department Methods) and wrested the initiative away from Congress.

President Taft maintained the initiative by creating the Commission on Economy and Efficiency in 1910. The Dockery-Cockrell and Keep commissions had provided the first sense of the scope and nature of specific government activities, but they did not attempt to integrate them into a coherent whole. They were bound by a limited concern to control the terms of isolated administrative operations such as pension claim settlement or the dissemination of agricultural statistics. The Taft Commission broke new ground by setting forth a coherent theory of organization and management that tied together all federal operations within a single plan of administration—a national budget system. A national budget system would do more than increase economy and efficiency. It would establish centralized control over the administrative apparatus of the federal government.

Federal Financial Administration: 1865–1894

During the last third of the nineteenth century, federal bureau chiefs and the appropriations committees in Congress largely set the administrative agenda. The president played almost no role in the process, and the secretary of the treasury acted as a simple conduit to compile departmental estimates and pass them along to Congress.[3] The appropriations process began with individual bureaus as they prepared their estimates for the coming year. Typically the chief clerk in the appropriate secretary's office compiled the estimates within each department. The secretary of the treasury then compiled the departmental estimates into a single "Book of Estimates," which he transmitted directly to the House Appropriations

[3]White, *Republican Era*, 95–109; Morton Keller, *Affairs of State: Public Life in Late Nineteenth Century America* (Cambridge: Harvard University Press, 1977), 108.

Committee without review or revision. Congress passed appropriations acts based on the estimates, but left to the departmental spending officers the final execution of authorized appropriations. As Leonard White notes, "No one was responsible for formulating a coordinated budgetary program for the entire government."[4]

Unlike cities such as New York, the federal government, with limited spending power and consistent revenue surpluses from 1866 to 1893, did not need to turn to finance capitalists for funding. Its primary business relations with the private sector involved instead such particularized transactions as the processing of land and pension claims. Unlike finance capitalists, land companies and Civil War veterans had little interest in the solvency of the government as a whole. They simply wanted swift and favorable responses from one or another department to their claims. They favored accounting reform and publicity, but their goal was to facilitate and regularize specific business transactions, not to assure themselves of the soundness of government administration as a whole.

The federal government was soon overwhelmed by the mass of business-related claims. Complaints over delays and confusion in processing claims grew rapidly in the decades following the Civil War. Congress was so disorganized that it did not even know what the various departments were empowered to do or how they processed land and pension claims.[5] After 1880 Congress became increasingly aware of the need for more systematic reform of departmental business methods. Between 1880 and

[4]White, *Republican Era*, 97–98; Daniel Selko, *The Federal Financial System* (Washington, D.C.: Brookings Institution, 1940), 82, 89.

[5]In 1880, 21 percent of total federal expenditures went to fund army pensions. By 1890, the amount had risen to 34 percent. Claims flooded the Pension Office, located in the Department of the Interior, reaching a peak of 635,000 in 1898. See James D. Savage, *Balanced Budgets and American Politics* (Ithaca: Cornell University Press, 1988), 132; and White, *Republican Era*, 208–20. Theda Skocpol has shown how Civil War pension benefits during the last third of the nineteenth century evolved into a sophisticated federal patronage system that reached an extraordinarily broad and diverse constituency of northerners. Theda Skocpol, "America's First Social Security System: The Expansion of Benefits for Civil War Veterans," *Political Science Quarterly* 108 (Spring 1993): 85–116. Others engaging in business transactions with the Department of the Interior included contractors for Indian supplies, land corporations, timber dealers, mining operators, and a mass of individual claimants for land under the Homestead Act, passed in 1862. The General Land Office handled most matters relating to the survey and disposition of public lands. In 1887, a congressional investigation found some 276,670 pending claims alone in the five divisions of public lands, preemption, mineral, contest, and board of review. See White, *Republican Era*, 196–201, and U.S. Senate, *Report of the Select Committee to Inquire into and Examine the Methods of Business and Work in the Executive Departments of the Government*, 50th Cong., 1st sess., 1888, S. Rept. no. 507, pt. 1, 221.

1910, Congress conducted eighty-nine investigations of various aspects of federal administration. Most investigations concentrated narrowly on single agencies or practices, but a few looked more broadly to general administrative problems in government. The first broad study was conducted by the Senate Select Committee to Inquire into and Examine the Methods of Business and Work in the Executive Departments of the Government, popularly known as the Cockrell Committee (after its chairman, Senator Francis M. Cockrell, Democrat of Missouri).[6]

THE DISCOVERY OF COMPLEXITY

In 1887, the Senate created the Cockrell Committee with the following mandate: "to inquire into and examine the methods of business and work in the Executive Departments of the Government, the time and attention devoted to the operations thereof by the persons employed therein, and generally to inquire into and report to the Senate the causes of the delays in transacting the public business said to exist in some of said Departments."[7] Initially, the Senate was more concerned with improving constituent access to government goods and services than with exploring new systems of administration. Over the course of its year-long investigation, however, the committee amassed a mountain of information about government operations that provided Congress with its first inkling of the true complexity of governmental administration.

The committee found arrearages in the war department amounting to 110,998 claims, applications, and accounts of various sorts. The treasury department had a larger backlog, including 270,872 unprocessed of veterans' pension claims. Conditions at the General Land Office were the worst. Its commissioner, William Sparks, admitted that the work of his entire bureau was one to two years in arrears, with upward of 275,000 individual cases pending. The committee found that such delays, in addition to provoking the ire of thousands of legitimate claimants, also "encouraged and emboldened speculators and spoilators to fraudulently and corruptly seize upon public lands."[8]

The committee rejected Commissioner Sparks's request for more and

---

[6]Bess Glenn, "Search for Efficiency in Federal Record Management," *American Archivist* 21 (April 1958): 159–60; Harold T. Pinkett, "Investigations of Federal Record-Keeping, 1887–1906," *American Archivist* 21 (April 1958): 163–67.

[7]U.S. Senate, *Executive Departments*, 1.

[8]Oscar Kraines, *Congress and the Challenge of Big Government* (New York: Bookman, 1958), 24–26; U.S. Senate, *Executive Departments*, 221–28.

better-paid staff, suggesting instead that the General Land Office meet the problem by getting more work out of its existing employees and firing those found incompetent.[9] The committee's entire report reflected a similarly particularistic approach to the problems of business methods in the departments. Its most significant accomplishment was to obtain passage of a bill authorizing the destruction of certain superfluous government records, tons of which had been accumulating in Washington basements for decades.[10]

Although narrow and limited in its vision of reform, the Cockrell Committee's approach nonetheless followed a certain logic of administrative development. The initial discovery and physical management of records necessarily preceded the development of more sophisticated technical and conceptual tools of organization. The committee broke new ground by calling for detailed statements of the organization of the executive departments. The resulting flood of undifferentiated facts overwhelmed the committee, which had no staff and lacked any conceptual system of accounting or classification to organize or make sense of the data. It chose, therefore, to attack the problem simply by trying to reduce the physical mass of information it had uncovered.

In the 1890s, problems of economy and efficiency in government gained a new urgency as the country entered a severe economic depression and the government began to run deficits for the first time since the Civil War.[11] In 1893, Congress took a major step toward mastering the overload of information uncovered by the Cockrell Committee when it established the Dockery-Cockrell Commission, formally called the Joint Commission to Inquire into the Status of the Laws Organizing the Executive Departments. The commission's general mandate was similar to that of the Cockrell Committee, but it was expressly authorized to make recommendations "to secure greater efficiency and economy" provided they could be made "without injury to the public service."[12]

---

[9]U.S. Senate, *Executive Departments*, 221–22, 232–33. Commissioners of the General Land Office had been requesting additional personnel all through the 1870s. See Department of the Interior, General Land Office, *Annual Report of the Commissioner of the General Land Office* (Washington, D.C.: Government Printing Office, 1881), 1–13.

[10]Pinkett, "Federal Record-keeping," 167–69.

[11]Keller, *Affairs of State*, 310; Ester Rogoff Taus, *Central Banking Function of the United States Treasury, 1789–1941* (New York: Columbia University Press), 85–96; Charles H. Stewart III, *Budget Reform Politics: The Design of the Appropriations Process in the House of Representatives, 1865–1921* (Cambridge: Cambridge University Press, 1989), 176–77.

[12]U.S. House, *A Review of the Work Done by the Joint Commission—Reorganization of the Accounting System and Business Methods in the Executive Departments*, 53d Cong., 3d sess., 1895, H. Rept. no. 2000, 1.

The commission had six members, three from each house of Congress, and employed a professional staff of up to three experts. Charles Waldo Haskins, Elijah Watt Sells, and Joseph Reinhart served the commission as the first private professional business experts ever employed by Congress in a general administrative investigation. All three had extensive experience with the major railroads helping to reorganize their systems of accounts. Haskins and Sells, of course, both later became close associates of Frederick Cleveland.[13]

Over the course of two years, the commission compiled a list of 175 laws concerning departmental business methods and conducted a census of personnel and salaries throughout the executive branch.[14] The commission's signal achievement came with the passage of the Dockery Act of 1894, which "prescribed the first major overhauling of the Treasury Department's accounting and auditing systems since their establishment in Alexander Hamilton's day."[15] The act concentrated auditing authority in the single comptroller and authorized him to prescribe the forms for keeping and rendering all public accounts (except for those of the post office). The resulting system was more centralized but reflected a concern almost exclusively for the legality, accuracy, and regularity of accounts with little thought for the wisdom or effectiveness of particular operations.[16] Despite its progress, the commission still saw accounting solely as a function of the proprietary operations of government and lacked any appreciation of accounting as a political tool to reinforce the legitimacy of representative democracy.[17]

Perhaps the commission's most important innovation was its least tangible: its expert staff provided the means of imposing order on the chaos

[13]Ibid., 1–2; Kraines, *Big Government*, 55–57; White, *Republican Era*, 89–90.

[14]Kraines, *Big Government*, 97–99; U.S. Senate, *Purchase of Department Supplies—Report to the President by the Committee on Department Methods Relative to the Purchase of Department Supplies*, 59th Cong., 2d sess., 1906, S. Doc. 106, 1–2; Senate, Select Committee to Investigate the Executive Agencies of the Government, *Investigation of Executive Agencies of the Government*, 75th Cong., 1st sess., 1937, S. Rept. no. 1275, 230–31.

[15]Kraines, *Big Government*, 70.

[16]Ibid., 70–79; Willard Eugene Hotchkiss, "The Judicial Work of the Comptroller of the Treasury" (Ph.D. diss., Cornell University, 1911), 26; Frederick C. Mosher, *A Tale of Two Agencies: A Comparative Analysis of the General Accounting Office and the Office of Management and Budget* (Baton Rouge: Louisiana State University Press, 1984), 18–19; Harvey C. Mansfield, *The Comptroller General: A Study in the Law and Practice of Financial Administration* (New Haven: Yale University Press, 1939), 60–65.

[17]U.S. House, *Review of the Work*, 15, 17; U.S. House, Joint Commission of Congress to Inquire into the Status of Laws Organizing the Executive Departments, *Methods of Accounting in the Treasury*, 53d Cong., 2d sess., 1894, H. Rept. 637, 7.

of data unearthed by the Cockrell Committee. As Leonard White observes: "The experts . . . developed the first systematic presentation of the anatomy of federal administration as a whole in two extensive compilations: a listing of all the laws creating departments, agencies, and their subdivisions, fixing salaries and regulating the employment of clerks; and a tabular statement showing the number and titles of offices, bureaus, and divisions with the number and status of their employees."[18] The experts' "anatomy of federal administration" not only helped to crystalize awareness of the nature and scope of the administrative apparatus of government but also provided the first intimations of a means to control it.

With increasing awareness of the scope and complexity of governmental operations came renewed criticisms of the patchwork administration of courts and parties. Before any change could occur, reformers had to break the hold that party machines had gained over American institutions during the time of intense party competition which had followed the Civil War. The election of William McKinley as president in 1896 ushered in a period of Republican hegemony that lasted until 1912. The resulting relaxation of party competition provided enough political stability for reformers to attempt a reconstitution of the national administrative apparatus.[19]

Augmenting the political window of opportunity presented by the era of Republican hegemony, finance capitalists reemerged as a force in national fiscal affairs during the 1890s and early 1900s. As the Panic of 1893 deepened into depression, the treasury, still under obligation to redeem greenbacks pursuant to the Resumption Act of 1875, found its gold reserves dwindling to critical levels. In early 1894, Secretary of the Treasury John Carlisle tried to sell $50 million in bonds to bolster reserves but found no takers until New York bankers bought up most of the issue. By early 1895, the banks had given all the gold they could spare, but the treasury still found its reserves dangerously low. In desperation, President Cleveland turned for emergency assistance to a consortium of leading New York bankers led by J. P. Morgan. Morgan and H. P. Belmont took $40 million of 4-percent thirty-year bonds and agreed to help stop the export of gold by controlling the exchange rate. By the end of the year, the treasury reserve was again stable and Morgan and his associates had made a handsome profit on the deal.[20]

---

[18]White, *Republican Era*, 90.

[19]Skowronek, *Building a New American State*, 40–46, 168.

[20]Taus, *United States Treasury*, 85–95; Margaret G. Myers, *A Financial History of the United States* (New York: Columbia University Press, 1970), 213–16.

In addition to bond sales, the government enacted an income tax in 1894 to raise revenue and offset growing deficits. In 1895, however, the Supreme Court declared the tax unconstitutional, and the government was thrown back on the tariff and bond sales to keep the treasury solvent. Thus, when the Spanish-American War placed new strains on government finances, Congress had little choice but to provide for an issue of $400 million in 3-percent bonds. To avoid any unnecessary risk, the treasury again turned to New York finance capitalists to underwrite the issue.[21]

The Panic of 1907 further consolidated the new ties between finance capitalists and the federal government. On October 22, the failure of the Knickerbocker Trust Company, the third largest bank in New York, precipitated a panic. To stabilize the situation, Secretary of the Treasury George Cortelyou quickly deposited $36 million in New York banks. (During the course of the panic, Cortelyou eventually deposited almost $80 million to help banks remain liquid.) In November, Cortelyou offered for sale $50 million in Panama Canal bonds and $100 million of 3-percent certificates of indebtedness authorized under an act of 1898. National banks were the main purchasers of these certificates.[22] Depression, war, and panic forged new ties between the federal government and finance capitalists, creating a powerful client group in the private sector, who had an interest in reforming government administration to secure their investments.

By the turn of the century, conditions were ripe for administrative reorganization. The congressional investigations had uncovered the complexity of government operations and set forth the technical and conceptual apparatus to control them. The Republican hegemony of 1896 to 1912 presented the political opportunity to make use of that apparatus. And newly engaged finance capitalists created a powerful client group in the private sector with an interest in seeing reform carried out.

In the decades following the Civil War, politicians had neither the inclination nor the ability to control governmental operations. Congress dominated government and the president was only marginally involved in administration. The fumbling but persistent efforts of the congressional investigative commissions, however, had raised the possibility of establishing centralized control over the ungainly federal bureaucracy. The possibility of control, in turn, raised new issues of who would exercise it.

[21]Taus, *United States Treasury*, 96–97; Myers, *Financial History*, 240.

[22]Taus, *United States Treasury*, 121–28; Myers, *Financial History*, 245–46; Donald R. Stabile and Jeffrey A. Cantor, *The Public Debt of the United States: An Historical Perspective, 1775–1990* (New York: Praeger), 72–77.

Suddenly, the president's hitherto negligible role as "chief executive" began to take on new significance.[23]

THE BATTLE FOR CONTROL BEGINS

Theodore Roosevelt's accidental accession to the nation's highest office provided America with the perfect embodiment of an imposing and engaged president. Propelled by boundless energy and guided by a vision of the president as an active steward of the people's interests, Roosevelt seized the initiative from Congress and embarked on a program of administrative reform to assert presidential control over the executive branch. His personal background, skills, and temperament prepared him well to challenge Congress for control over the growing administrative apparatus of the new American state. Roosevelt was arguably the best-prepared administrator to enter the presidency up to that time. He had served as a U.S. Civil Service commissioner and as head of the New York Police Commission. While governor of New York State, he reorganized the canal system, the correctional institutions, and factory inspection organization and procedures. As vice president, he supported both Gifford Pinchot's campaign to professionalize the forest service and Elihu Root's plan for modernizing military administration. In addition, as demonstrated in his close relationship with Pinchot, Roosevelt embraced the authority of expert opinion and could appreciate the opportunity to enhance his power which was presented by the work of the experts on the Dockery-Cockrell Commission.[24]

On January 31, 1902, Roosevelt issued an executive order forbidding all officers and employees serving under any of the executive departments

[23]As Steven Skowronek observes with respect to the broad challenge to the patchwork administration of courts and parties that occurred at this time: "After 1900, the doors of power opened to those who saw a national administrative apparatus as the centerpiece of a new governmental order. The central question in institutional development was correspondingly altered. It was no longer a question of whether or not America was going to build a state that could support administrative power but who was going to control administrative power in the new state that was to be built." Skowronek, *Building a New American State*, 165.

[24]Peri E. Arnold, *Making the Managerial Presidency: Comprehensive Reorganization Planning, 1905–1980* (Princeton: Princeton University Press, 1986), 23; Harold T. Pinkett, "The Keep Commission, 1905–1909: A Rooseveltian Effort at Administrative Reform," *Journal Of American History* 52 (September 1965): 298; Oscar Kraines, "The President versus Congress: The Keep Commission, 1905–1909, First Comprehensive Presidential Inquiry into Administration," *Western Political Quarterly* 23 (March 1970): 5.

from soliciting pay or increases or otherwise attempting "to influence in
their own interest any other legislation whatever, either before Congress
or its committees, or in any way save through the heads of the departments in or under which they serve."[25] In 1906, he extended this gag order to cover the independent agencies of government, such as the
Interstate Commerce Commission. With these orders, Roosevelt interposed his cabinet between subordinate executive department officials and
Congress, thereby disrupting the symbiotic relationship that had grown
up between bureau chiefs and committee chairmen. Forcing officers and
employees to go through department heads allowed Roosevelt a measure
of control over the flow of information between the departments and
Congress.[26]

Roosevelt also challenged Congress through his repeated use of presidential commissions to investigate government administration. Since
the end of the Civil War, comprehensive administrative reviews had been
a congressional responsibility. Roosevelt broke with tradition by ap-
pointing a total of six commissions to investigate the organization of
government scientific work, department methods, public lands, inland
waterways, country life, and national conservation. Each commission was
responsible only to the president. Roosevelt appointed them without consulting Congress or seeking statutory authorization for their activities.[27]

With the appointment in 1905 of the Commission on Department
Methods, Roosevelt asserted for the first time that the president bore primary responsibility for the proper conduct of government operations.[28]
Popularly named after its chairman, Charles H. Keep, assistant secretary
of the treasury, the commission began by examining complaints from private corporations concerning their business dealings with the government. Its first investigation confirmed allegations of irregularity and graft
in the awarding of government contracts for typesetting machines by the
Government Printing Office and led to the firing of the public printer on
the grounds of maladministration.[29]

The Keep Commission's subcommittee on accounting found the accounting system implemented under the Dockery Act of 1894 to be inco-

[25]Executive Order of January 31, 1902, reprinted in United States Civil Service Commission, *Twentieth Annual Report of the U.S. Civil Service Commission* (Washington, D.C.:
Government Printing Office, 1904), 65.

[26]Skowronek, *Building a New American State*, 177–80.

[27]Kraines, "President versus Congress," 5–6.

[28]Ibid., 5–6, 46; Pinkett, "Keep Commission," 297–98; Skowronek, *Building a New
American State*, 183; White, *Republican Era*, 90–92.

[29]Kraines, "President versus Congress," 10–12.

herent and inaccurate. The subcommittee also criticized the continued use of single-entry accounts and proposed the immediate introduction of a comprehensive system of double-entry bookkeeping as the basis for "rounding out" the present system. As no legislation was required, the secretary of the treasury adopted the new system effective July 1, 1907. This marked the first use of double-entry accounts by any office of the federal government.[30]

The Keep Commission's investigation of accounting methods was more comprehensive than the Dockery-Cockrell's, but it actually accomplished less, because Congress, resentful of Roosevelt's imperious usurpation of its prerogatives, refused to enact the commission's recommendations. In the end, every one of the Keep Commission's long-term projects for administrative reform was left to languish, victim of a congressional counterattack against the advance of presidential power. In 1909, Congress went so far as to pass the Tawney Amendment to the Supplemental Appropriations Act, which prohibited the expenditure of public funds to support presidential commissions unless the funds had been appropriated for that express purpose.[31]

Although the Keep Commission's substantive reforms met with limited success, the commission established an important precedent for presidential action in the arena of administrative management. The same year that Congress limited presidential authority to fund commissions, it also empowered the president to obtain detailed estimates of how and where appropriations exceeded revenues "to the end that he may . . . advise the Congress how in his judgement the estimated appropriations could with least injury to the public service be reduced."[32] The act granted the president only an incidental advisory authority, but it marked the first time Congress had formally included the president in the appropriations process.[33]

[30]Committee on Department Methods, Assistant Committee on Accounting, Special Committee on Treasury Bookkeeping, ["Report upon the Examination of Bookkeeping and Warrants, Treasury Department"], October 29, 1906, Papers of the President's Commission on Economy and Efficiency, National Archives and Record Service, Washington D.C., RG 51, Series 05.1, Box 33; E. F. Bartelt, *Accounting Procedures of the United States Government* (Chicago: Public Administration Service, 1941), 24; Gustavus A. Weber, *Organized Efforts for the Improvement of Methods of Administration in the United States* (New York: D. Appleton, 1919), 74–80; Kraines, "President versus Congress," 27–30.

[31]Kraines, "President versus Congress," 27, 38–40; Skowronek, *Building a New American State*, 184–86; Arnold, *Managerial Presidency*, 25; Pinkett, "Keep Commission," 312.

[32]35 U.S.C. chap. 299, sec. 7, 1909, quoted in Stewart, *Budget Reform Politics*, 179–80.

[33]Selko, *Federal Financial System*, 100; Kraines, "President versus Congress," 45.

The first decade of the new century thus saw president and Congress jockeying for position in the struggle to control government operations. Under Roosevelt the presidency again emerged as a significant force in national administration. Congress met this challenge by ignoring the Keep Commission recommendations and passing the Tawney amendment. It failed, however, to retrieve the reform initiative from the president.

SETTING THE NATIONAL REFORM AGENDA: THE TAFT COMMISSION

When William Howard Taft took office in 1909, he inherited a rapidly growing, increasingly activist government that had been regularly running deficits in the years since 1894 (including three of the preceding five years).[34] In 1910, Taft moved to make the chief executive a significant participant in the appropriations process through the creation of a national budget system. His chosen vehicle to promote reform was a presidential commission employing outside experts in conjunction with federal administrators. Taft, no doubt chastened by the Tawney amendment, took a more conciliatory approach than Roosevelt and asked Congress to authorize his project. Congress responded with an appropriation of $100,000 and the president's Commission on Economy and Efficiency was born.[35]

To head the new commission, Taft chose Frederick Cleveland, who applied his talents as the country's foremost expert on municipal budget reform to problems of national administration. Cleveland began his investigation on September 27, 1910, under the title "The President's Inquiry in re Economy and Efficiency." The inquiry lasted until March 8, 1911, when it was formally superseded by the president's Commission on Economy and Efficiency (commonly known as the Taft Commission). In addition to Cleveland, who served as chairman, the Taft Commission had four members and a secretary: William F. Willoughby, assistant director of the census and former treasurer of Puerto Rico; Walter W. Warwick, auditor of the Panama Canal and of the Government of the Canal Zone; Frank J. Goodnow, professor of administrative law at Columbia University; Harvey S. Chase, a certified public accountant from

---

[34]Henry Jones Ford, *The Cost of Our National Government* (New York: Columbia University Press, 1910), 2; Arnold, *Managerial Presidency*, 27–28.

[35]Skowronek, *Building a New American State*, 186–87; Arnold, *Managerial Presidency*, 32–38; Weber, *Organized Efforts*, 84–85.

Boston with extensive experience in local budget reform efforts; and Merritt O. Chance, auditor for the post office department.[36]

From his work with the Bureau of Municipal Research, Cleveland brought the methods of the municipal "survey" to bear on problems of national administration, using the Taft Commission to conduct the first investigation of federal administration as an organic whole.[37] As Taft put it in describing to Congress the magnitude of the commission's task, "This vast organization [of the executive branch] has never been studied in detail as one piece of administrative mechanism. Never have the foundations been laid for a thorough consideration of the relations of all of its parts."[38]

The commission divided its work into five fields of inquiry: organization, personnel, business methods, accounting and reporting, and the national budget. Again reflecting the influence of Cleveland's experience in local reform, the commission established the budget as the centerpiece of its program. In its most significant report, *The Need for a National Budget*, the commission argued that a complete budget system would provide an effective means whereby the constitutional principles of federalism and separation of powers "may be maintained with integrity and whereby the Government may be kept in constant adjustment with the welfare needs of the people; a means also whereby the economy and efficiency of the administration may be regularly brought to a test."[39] Despite its name, the commission was concerned only secondarily with economy and efficiency. Its primary focus was on ordering relations of power within the federal system.

During the first months of the inquiry, Cleveland built a staff of five accountants, a law clerk, and four stenographers. The staff eventually grew to fifty-eight and was supplemented by a board of four consulting experts drawn from eminent accounting firms: J. N. Gunn, of Gunn, Richards & Co.; Elijah Watt Sells from Cleveland's old firm of Haskins & Sells; J. E. Sterrett, of Dickinson, Wilmot & Sterrett; and Francis F. White, of Deloite, Plender, Griffiths & Co. In addition, each department appointed

---

[36]Weber, *Organized Efforts*, 84–87.

[37]President's Commission on Economy and Efficiency, "Report to the President by the Commission on Economy and Efficiency," *Circular No. 30* (Washington: Government Printing Office, 1913), 31.

[38]President's Commission on Economy and Efficiency, *Message of the President of the United States on Economy and Efficiency in the Government Service*, 62d Cong., 2d sess., 1912, H. Doc. no. 458, 4.

[39]President's Commission on Economy and Efficiency, *The Need for a National Budget*, 62d Cong., 2d sess., 1912, H. Doc. no. 854, 131, 136.

special committees of existing personnel to collaborate with the commission in compiling and analyzing data about government administration.[40]

Recognizing the potential for territorial disputes, Taft made clear to all departments his strong personal interest in the project and his desire that they cooperate fully with the commission. Taft also appointed a special board of referees with authority to resolve interdepartmental disputes and conflicts of jurisdiction arising from the commission's investigations.[41] Finally, Taft located the commission in the White House and made Cleveland a presidential aide with authority to sign directives "By Order of the President." As the direct agent of the president, the commission extended presidential authority and presence throughout the federal bureaucracy to all branches and all offices, including those in the field outside of Washington. During its three years of existence, the commission conducted 110 separate studies of administrative organization and procedures.[42]

THE POWER OF ADMINISTRATIVE TAXONOMY

To guide its work, the commission created the first comprehensive organizational charts of the federal government. These charts were based on outlines that showed in great detail not only the departments, commissions, bureaus, and offices of the government but also the sections, shops, field stations, and so on which constituted all the subdivisions through which the government performed its day-to-day activities. The outlines also classified each operating unit by character and geographical location, the number of units of like character in Washington, and the number and character of government services in each city or other point in the United States. In one circular, for example, the commission pub-

[40]President's Commission, *Circular No. 30*, 3–8; U.S. House Committee on Appropriations, Subcommittee on Sundry Civil Appropriations, *Hearings on the Sundry Civil Appropriations Bill for 1913*, 62d Cong., 2d sess., May 17, 1912 (statement of Frederick A. Cleveland), 44. The president directed the following departments and establishments to appoint committees to cooperate with the commission: State, Treasury, War, Navy, Justice, Post Office, Interior, Agriculture, Commerce and Labor, Smithsonian Institution, Interstate Commerce Commission, Civil Service Commission, and Government Printing Office. Idem, "Interim Report on Plan of Inquiry and Progress of Work from September 27 to December 31, 1910," *Circular No. 4* (Washington: Government Printing Office, 1911), 5–6.

[41]President's Commission, *Circular No. 4*, 8; idem, *Circular No. 30*, 6.

[42]President's Commission, *Circular No. 4*, 5–10; idem, *Circular No. 30*, 4; Arnold, *Managerial Presidency*, 39.

lished fifty-three charts setting forth the organization of the Department of the Navy, from its scheme of central command in Washington to the place of the supply office in the naval base at Olongapo in the Philippine Islands. Similar charts were compiled for all the cabinet departments. Outlines and charts together identified and formalized the location and interrelation of all administrative units in the federal government.[43]

A jumble of amorphous federal agencies, with ever-shifting duties and operations, had resisted comprehensive organization. Using the information it collected through surveys and inspections, the commission literally outlined each administrative unit, defining its boundaries by promulgating an official description of its proper role and assigning it a place within a comprehensive scheme of government operations. Fixing a unit's place and identity rendered it visible both to itself and to other units. Seeing one another clearly, diverse units could appreciate their interrelationships and derive a sense of belonging to a larger bureaucratic structure—a structure that, as defined by the commission, had the president at its head. Thus, in the very act of creating a cohesive executive branch, the commission worked to shift the primary orientation of the diverse bureaus and agencies of the federal government away from Congress and toward the president.

The commission matched its mania for amassing and classifying information with a passionate and repeated insistence on the need to develop a common language of accounting and reporting across all areas of government operations. As things stood in 1911, each department—sometimes each bureau within a department, and sometimes even offices within a bureau—employed diverse and often unintelligible symbols and nomenclature in their records.[44]

A transparent, normalized form of communication was essential to breaking each department's local monopoly over administrative data and to building an executive branch. The diverse vernaculars of all the particular bureaus and offices had to be replaced by a single, official administrative language. The commission, in effect, tried to create a dictionary of acceptable terms and phrases to be used in the conduct of all govern-

---

[43]U.S. House, *Message of the President*, 5, 25–38; President's Commission on Economy and Efficiency, "Organization Charts of the Department of the Navy," *Circular No. 17* (Washington, D.C: Government Printing Office, 1911). For similar charts of other departments, see Records of the President's Commission on Economy and Efficiency, Record Group 51, Boxes 75 and 76, National Archives, Washington, D.C.

[44]President's Commission, *Circular No. 4*, 11–12, 20–22.

mental affairs so that "each record and report may convey the same meaning to the one who reads as was in the mind of him who wrote."[45]

An official language also provided the basis for official recognition of government activities. Business transactions, in particular, would not be acknowledged as legitimate unless recorded in the proper fashion. Only by adopting devising and installing "documents of expenditure with prescriptions as to certification and authentication"[46] could the administrator "keep in touch with the details of current business . . . [and] obtain a true statement of the facts . . . as a basis for accounting and reporting."[47] No payments would be made or goods accepted unless they were recorded on an "authenticated" document. In this way, official accounts became, in a sense, more real than the government operations themselves.

BUILDING A PYRAMID OF AUTHORITY

Classification set boundaries. It individualized and differentiated administrative units from one another, rendering them susceptible to focused attention and analysis. The commission made clear that the purpose of the outlines of organization was "to exhibit the machinery of the entire government . . . in such a way as to indicate not only every working unit into which the Government is organized for the performance of its functions, but also the relations of such units to each other as regards direct lines of administrative authority."[48] The use of the term "exhibit" recalls the image of New York City's budget exhibits (the triumphant 1911 exhibit having occurred during the height of the commission's investigation). Like the budget exhibits, the commission aimed to create a guidebook to governmental administration, a display to reveal the inner workings of the bureaucracy. Here, however, the guidebook was a hierarchy, and the tourist was the chief executive who would use visibility, not for informed consumption, but as a basis for exercising centralized control. Moreover, by describing the "relations of such units to each other," the organizational outlines also established a basis for comparing units to

---

[45]Ibid., 23.

[46]Ibid.

[47]President's Commission on Economy and Efficiency, "Description of Expenditure Documents and Procedure for the Purchase of Supplies, Materials, Equipments, and Services Other than Personal and for the Distribution of Supplies and Materials from Stores," *Circular No. 6* (Washington, D.C.: Government Printing Office, 1911), 2.

[48]House, *Message of the President*, 25–26.

each other and for measuring all against the norms of efficiency promulgated by the budget experts.

The different connotations of "exhibiting" government through a budget reflect a basic shift that occurred as budget reform moved from the local to the national level. The Bureau of Municipal Research presented budget reform primarily as a means of improving citizen control over government (even if that control took the form of reactive consumption of preselected government services). At the national level, Cleveland gave free rein to his more technical vision of budget reform. He employed similar ideas of education, oversight, and visibility but transposed them into a wholly administrative milieu in which the president took the place of "the people" as the primary observer of government. Here, though, the president did not sit at the end of a spoke of information radiating from a budgetary hub; he presided at the top of a pyramid of authority built through successive levels of surveillance, as each level of administrative authority reported upward through a chain of command culminating in the president.

As Cleveland later wrote, the old system of administration by congressional committee led to "'invisible' and irresponsible government." A comprehensive budget system, he asserted, would render government "visible," that is, subject to the scrutiny and evaluation of both the president and the people. Cleveland characterized the budget as an "institutional method of control-without-violence."[49] Visibility in itself would control people within a hierarchical system of surveillance. Naked force would be exercised only as a last resort to coerce adherence to standards of efficiency. While subjecting administrative officers to compulsory and permanent visibility, however, the exercise of disciplinary power itself would remain largely invisible, as part of the automatic functioning of the scientific mechanism of the budget system.[50] As President Taft put it to

---

[49]Frederick A. Cleveland, "Good-Will and Economic Blockade," *Annals of the American Academy of Political and Social Science* 95 (May 1921): 235.

[50]Cleveland discusses "visible" and "invisible" government in several books and articles; see, e.g., Frederick A. Cleveland, "Budget Making and the Increased Cost of Government," *American Economic Review* 6, supplement (March 1916): 50–71; idem, "Need for Readjustment of Relations between the Executive and the Legislative Branches of Government," in Frederick A. Cleveland and Joseph Schafer, eds., *Democracy in Reconstruction* (Boston: Houghton Mifflin, 1919), 429–36; and Frederick A. Cleveland and Arthur E. Buck, *The Budget and Responsible Government* (New York: Macmillan, 1920), 390–97. For a discussion of systems of surveillance and control and classification, see Michel Foucault, *Discipline and Punish* (New York: Vintage, 1979), and idem, *The Order of Things: An Archaeology of the Human Sciences* (New York: Random House, 1970).

the commission's departmental representatives: "There is nobody investigating you, . . . you are investigating yourselves." Taft chose to ignore or obscure the fact that one purpose of the investigations was to render the departments ultimately subject to his control. Nor did he mention that outside experts had predetermined the terms and objects of their investigation. Instead, he equated applying the rules of discipline with controlling them.[51]

In discussing the power of the budget to oversee and discipline government operations, Cleveland invoked the image of a conning tower that "lifts the naval officer above the dead level of the sea and gives him breadth of vision." He urged the creation of "administrative conning towers" throughout the federal government. From their superior vantage point, elevated government officials within each department would survey all beneath them, identify inefficiency, and report their findings upward through a pyramid of authority culminating in the chief executive.[52]

Creating a unified and self-conscious executive branch threatened the special relationships that had evolved between isolated administrative units and their patron congressional committees. Previously, individual bureaus or agencies typically appealed directly to relevant congressional committees for funds. Even if they could not get direct access, their requests, as presented in the Book of Estimates, were rarely revised by superiors and were passed on to Congress more or less intact. Cleveland later described bureau chiefs as "functionalized, bureaucratic, feudal lords [who] did not look to their titular superior . . . for powers and policies. They looked to irresponsible committees."[53] A system of coordinated review would interpose a hierarchy of authority between the diverse administrative units and Congress and demand that all requests be considered together and in relation to one another.

Nothing inherent in a budget system, however, precluded Congress

[51]President's Commission, *Circular No. 4*, 8.

[52]"One of the Conditions Precedent to Efficient Management of Public Affairs: Address by Frederick A. Cleveland, Chairman of the President's Commission on Economy and Efficiency" (n.d.), Records of the President's Commission on Economy and Efficiency, Record Group 51, Box 23, National Archives, Washington, D.C., 1–12; "Memorandum Setting Forth Some of the Objections Which Have Been Raised with Respect to the President Preparing and Submitting a Budget to Congress Each Year" (n.d.), Records of the President's Commission on Economy and Efficiency, Record Group 51, Box, 125, National Archives, Washington, D.C., 10.

[53]Frederick A. Cleveland, "Responsible Leadership and Responsible Criticism," *Proceedings of the Academy of Political Science* 8 (July 1918): 31; Woodrow Wilson addressed this problem as early as 1885 in his influential study of American politics, *Congressional Government* (1885; reprint, Baltimore: Johns Hopkins University Press, 1981), 116–34.

from exercising ultimate control over the executive branch. As William F. Willoughby later noted, many people in the United States adhered to "the doctrine that the administrative power resides primarily in the legislature rather than in the executive, the latter being deemed to be but the agent of the former for carrying out its orders."[54] Indeed, during the last third of the nineteenth century, presidents had functioned as little more than clerks in administrative matters.[55] The key to changing perceptions of presidential authority lay in controlling the process that created the executive branch. While working to develop a new identity among the administrative departments, the commission, therefore, took great care to propose a system that would redirect primary orientation of the departments away from Congress and toward the president.

The commission sought the allegiance of administrative officers by presenting a budgetary system as something that would protect their credibility and enhance their discretion. Boldly inverting the implications of the system's new discipline, the commission asserted that standardized accounting and reporting practices actually would protect and strengthen an officer's position in the administrative hierarchy. Specifically, with current and accurate information, the administrator would "be able to protect himself from suspicion of infidelity and inefficiency by reason of the fact that he will not be able at all times to render a satisfactory report." Indeed, the question of fidelity could not "be settled . . . unless an adequate accounting control exists."[56] This argument subtly established a dynamic that compelled ever-greater compliance with the system once it was accepted. Without an accurate and timely accounting system there may have been mistrust, but it was generalized, without focus. The new system of accounts singled out any administrator keeping to the old ways. Previously generalized mistrust was now concentrated on the recalcitrant individual who resisted the discipline of the new system. The only way he could protect himself was to join the others and adopt the new accounting practices. Once adopted by a part of an office, the system compelled the "voluntary" compliance of the rest.

The commission also offered administrators greater operational discretion in return for acquiescing in budgetary surveillance. Uniform ac-

---

[54]William F. Willoughby, *The Problem of a National Budget* (New York: D. Appleton, 1918), 58.

[55]White, *Republican Era*, 95–109.

[56]President's Commission on Economy and Efficiency, "Conclusions Reached with Respect to Expenditure Accounting and Reporting," *Circular No. 33* (Washington, D.C.: Government Printing Office, 1913), 5.

counts and reports, submitted regularly, the commission argued, would allay Congress's suspicions and convince it to grant greater discretion to administrators. More important, the commission in effect argued that individual departments, as isolated administrative units, would remain subject to the vagaries of overspecified congressional management, while as part of a unified executive branch under a budgetary regime, they would obtain greater operational discretion, conditional only upon accepting presidential oversight.

Like the Bureau of Municipal Research on the local level, the commission urged Congress to substitute oversight for direct control of the budgetary process. Willoughby and Goodnow maintained that a budget system would enable Congress to maintain supervisory control over administrative officials even as it granted them greater discretion through more general allotment of appropriations.[57]

Finally, the commission recommended extending efficiency ratings (based on the new system of accounting and reporting) to all government offices, including local field offices throughout the country—traditionally a great source of patronage and influence for congressmen. Efficiency ratings would serve to reorient the attention (and loyalty) of job holders from the patrons who got them their jobs to the "scientific" rules and practices, concocted by experts and administered through the pyramid of authority that culminated in the president, adherence to which determined their future benefits and promotions.[58]

CONGRESS RESPONDS

The House of Representatives, newly Democratic after the elections of 1910, fought back. Led by Representative John Fitzgerald, a Tammany man from New York and chair of the still-powerful House Appropriations Committee, Congress began to rein in the commission. The first confrontation came in 1912 when Cleveland appeared before the House Subcommittee of Sundry Civil Appropriations to request additional funding. Because of a clerical misunderstanding, the official Book of Estimates

---

[57]Frank Goodnow, "The Limits of Budgetary Control," *Proceedings of the American Political Science Association* 9 (1912): 69; William F. Willoughby, "Allotment of Funds by Executive Officials an Essential Feature of Any Correct Budgetary System," *Proceedings of the American Political Science Association* 9 (1912): 78–87.

[58]William F. Willoughby, "Efficient Organization of the Personnel in Administration," *Proceedings of the Academy of Political Science* 3 (January 1913): 137.

requested only $75,000 for the commission in the coming year. Through Cleveland, the president was now requesting $250,000, which Cleveland considered the minimum necessary to carry on the commission's work effectively. Fitzgerald denied the request, stating that under no circumstances would the subcommittee report out an amount greater than that contained on the Book of Estimates. The meager grant of $75,000 crippled the commission, forcing it to curtail its investigations and cut back on staff (Goodnow and Willoughby had to retire as commissioners).[59]

Undaunted, the commission supplied Taft with enough information and support to compile a model budget. In a message to Congress on June 27, 1912, transmitting the commission's report, *The Need for a National Budget*, the president made clear his intention to submit an executive budget based on functional classifications. Taft emphasized that his budget was meant to supplement, not replace, Congress's traditional estimates. He therefore directed his department heads to prepare two sets of estimates, one following the usual line-item object classification format used in the Book of Estimates and the other employing the commission's new classifications.[60]

Taft's opponents in the House would have none of this. Fitzgerald perceived the proposed executive budget as a direct threat, declaring that "Congress knew best the character and extent of the information it desired . . . [and] that it would not be wise for Congress to abdicate, even by implication, its prerogative in this manner." In August, Fitzgerald tried to block Taft's efforts by attaching a rider to a pending appropriation bill requiring that annual estimates be submitted "only in the form and at the time now required by law, and in no other form and at no other time."[61]

The president, however, disregarded the rider, asserting that Congress had no power to interfere with his requests for information from administrative officers. On September 19, 1912, he instructed the secretary of the treasury and all the department heads to provide him with information compiled along the lines set forth in the commission's report, as the

[59]U.S. House Committee on Appropriations, Subcommittee on Sundry Civil Appropriations, *Hearings on the Sundry Civil Appropriations Bill for 1913*, 62d Cong., 2d sess., May 17, 1912, 152–55; Walter Otto Jacobsen, "A Study of President Taft's Commission on Economy and Efficiency and a Comparative Evaluation of Three Other Commissions" (M.A. thesis, Columbia University, 1941), 45–46.

[60]President's Commission on Economy and Efficiency, *Need for a National Budget*, 1–5; Jacobsen, "President Taft's Commission," 55–57; Harvey C. Mansfield, "Reorganizing the Federal Executive Branch: The Limits of Institutionalization," *Law and Contemporary Problems* 35 (Summer 1970): 476–77.

[61]John Fitzgerald, quoted in Weber, *Organized Efforts*, 89–90.

basis for compiling an executive budget.[62] With the controversy elevated to constitutional proportions, Taft had the commission gather expert opinion and write memoranda supporting his right to prepare and submit an executive budget. By the end of November, Cleveland had amassed numerous testimonials from academics and professionals across the country supporting the commission's work in general and attesting to the president's constitutional right to submit a budget.[63]

Further support came from Frank Goodnow, who had become president of Johns Hopkins University since leaving the commission. Goodnow organized a special session on the national budget at the 1912 annual convention of the American Political Science Association. Business and industry also expressed growing interest in the commission's work. In November, the Chamber of Commerce of the United States published an extensive review of the commission's report in its organ, *The Nation's Business*, and then circulated a referendum among its member organizations calling for a national budget system. The referendum passed by the near-unanimous vote of 573 to 10.[64] By the time all the letters and reports came in, President Taft was a lame duck, having lost to Woodrow Wilson in the 1912 election. Nonetheless, as one of his last acts in office, Taft sent Congress a report prepared by the commission titled "A Budget for the Fiscal Year 1914."[65]

Congress was singularly unimpressed. It was willing to concede Taft's authority to demand information from his department heads and compile a budget, but it then exercised its own rights and ignored the budget altogether. Fitzgerald tersely dismissed Taft's reasons for submitting an ex-

[62]Weber, *Organized Efforts*, 89–90; Jacobsen, "President Taft's Commission," 36–37. In his letter, Taft asserted that "in my opinion, it is entirely competent for the President to submit a budget, and Congress cannot forbid or prevent it." Quoted in Frederick A. Cleveland, "The Federal Budget," *Proceedings of the Academy of Political Science* 3 (January 1913): 120.

[63]"Memorandum Setting Forth Some of the Objections," Record Group 51, Box 125, For a sampling of supportive expert opinion, see Nicholas Murray Butler to Frederick A. Cleveland, October 24, 1912; Arthur Twining Hadley to Frederick A. Cleveland, October 23, 1912; Charles E. Merriam to Frederick A. Cleveland, October 25, 1912; John Wigmore to Frederick A. Cleveland, November 19, 1912; Walter Hines Page to Frederick A. Cleveland, October 30, 1912; Arch W. Shaw to Frederick A. Cleveland, December 7, 1912, Records of the President's Commission on Economy and Efficiency, Record Group 51, Box 126, National Archives, Washington, D.C.; R. E. Coulson, "Are $300,000,000 Worth Saving?" *System* 23 (April 1913): 363–71; Arch W. Shaw, "The Nation's Business," *System* 23 (March 1913): 247–49.

[64]Willoughby, *National Budget*, 154; Donald T. Critchlow, *The Brookings Institution, 1916–1952* (De Kalb: Northern Illinois University Press, 1985), 32.

[65]Jacobsen, "President Taft's Commission," 57.

ecutive budget as "not well founded."[66] Taft may have won a battle over his constitutional right to submit a budget, but he lost the war of getting a budget enacted.[67]

About a month after Wilson's inauguration, one last attempt was made to salvage the commission. Henry Bruere, who had kept in touch with Cleveland throughout the latter's tenure as chair of the commission, together with John Purroy Mitchel and Louis Brandeis, obtained an audience with the new president to plead for the commission. Wilson expressed sympathy for the commission's work but explained that he needed to concentrate on his own program of reform, which, at that time, did not encompass budget reform. (Mitchel, at least, could take some comfort from the meeting—Wilson soon appointed him to the powerful post of collector of customs for the Port of New York.)[68]

In the end, most of the commission's reports were left to languish in Congress. Before leaving office, however, Taft implemented many of its recommendations that called for executive action alone. The treasury department in particular adopted several of the commission's accounting reforms. The secretary of the treasury promulgated new classifications in 1911 "to make a beginning toward the standardization of accounting theory, procedure, forms, and nomenclature." (The commission, finding that many services were still using a single-entry accounting system and did not even understand the basic principles of double-entry accounting, issued a circular to explain the new treasury requirements in simple language to administrative officers throughout government.)[69]

Congress did not stop at disregarding the president's budget. Newly alive to the possibilities for centralized control over the executive branch presented by the commission's work, Congress acted affirmatively to retake the initiative. Shortly after restricting the commission's work, Congress created the Division of Efficiency within the Civil Service Commission in August 1912 to "establish a system of efficiency ratings for the classified service in the several executive departments in the District of Columbia." The division was reorganized in 1916 as the inde-

[66]Statement of Rep. John J. Fitzgerald, *Cong. Rec.*, 50th Cong., sess., June 24, 1913, 2155.

[67]As Steven Skowronek has noted, insurgent Republicans played a significant role in opposing the recommendations of the commission. Congress's refusal to enact Taft's budget was bipartisan. See Skowronek, *Building a New American State*, 190–94.

[68]Jacobsen, "President Taft's Commission," 69; Jane S. Dahlberg, *The New York Bureau of Municipal Research* (New York: New York University Press, 1966), 88.

[69]Jacobsen, "President Taft's Commission," 72; Arthur E. Buck, *Public Budgeting* (New York: Harper, 1912), 37–38; President's Commission, *Circular No. 33*, 5.

pendent Bureau of Efficiency with a broader mandate "for investigation of duplication of statistical and other work in the various branches of the government service."[70] On its face, the new division would seem to complement the work of commission. Herbert Brown, who had served on both the Keep and Taft commissions, was appointed director. Brown, however, felt little loyalty to the Taft Commission. He believed that Congress had cut the commission's funding "because of [its] utter failure to show any accomplishments of value."[71] In the coming years, Brown developed an especially close working relationship with Senator Reed Smoot of Utah and other key members of Congress. The division became a servant of the legislative branch, helping to extend Congress's oversight of administrative operations in much the same manner as the commission had been organized to serve the president.

Congress also moved toward consolidating the appropriations process into a single House committee that would better be able to make use of the information provided by the division. Again, Representative Fitzgerald led the way. As an alternative to the Taft Commission's plan, he offered a series of amendments designed "to concentrate in one committee all questions of appropriations and leave the authorizations with the legislative committees to which such authority properly belongs."[72] Fitzgerald's efforts culminated in 1920 with the reconsolidation of authority in the single House Committee on Appropriations, bringing to an end the era of fragmentation that began with the devolution of 1885.[73]

The passing of the Taft Commission did not stop the movement for an executive budget. By the mid-1910s, the idea of budget reform had taken hold across the nation. In 1915 and again in 1917 Congress introduced a number of resolutions calling for the establishment of boards or commissions to consider the problem of national budget reform. In 1916, both the Democratic and Republican parties explicitly called for budget reform in their national platforms.[74] The question now was not whether there should be a national budget, but what form it should take and who should control it—Congress or the president? In raising this question, the Taft

[70]Me Shin Chiang, "The Bureau of Efficiency" (Ph.D. diss., Harvard University, 1940), 19–20, 27.

[71]Herbert D. Brown, "Memorandum for General Burleson," July 25, 1916, Records of the Bureau of Efficiency, Record Group 51, Box 12, National Archives, Washington, D.C., 2.

[72]Statement of Rep. John J. Fitzgerald, 2159.

[73]Stewart, *Budget Reform Politics*, 202, 204–8.

[74]Willoughby, *National Budget*, 150–56.

Commission altered the battle of administrative reform from an analysis of business practices to a struggle for ultimate authority over the executive branch of government—a struggle that would not be settled until 1921, when the Budget and Accounting Act vested that authority in the president.

7 CREATING THE MODERN CHIEF EXECUTIVE

The Budget and Accounting Act of 1921 marks a fundamental shift in the theory and practice of federal governance in the United States. Up to this time, under what Woodrow Wilson had aptly termed "Congressional Government," control over the administrative apparatus of the federal government, such as it was, was lodged in the legislative branch. Congressional control reflected a long-standing American suspicion of governmental authority and a particular aversion to executive power that might contain the seeds of despotism. The Budget and Accounting Act changed this. It set responsibility for the administrative apparatus of the federal government firmly and clearly in the hands of the president. The new chief executive under the budgetary regime was a brother to the corporate chairman of the board, a rational manager well poised to lead America into the decade when the "Business of America" would be business.

Led by the Institute for Government Research (immediate precursor to the Brookings Institution), the proponents of a national executive budget system articulated a theory of delegated authority that cast the president as both an agent of Congress, carrying out its general directions, and as the best representative of the national interest, standing in opposition to the localistic interests of individual congressmen. They drew on the paradigm of citizen-government relations developed by local budget reformers, effectively giving the role of citizen to Congress while identifying local government with the president. Just as the men of the Bureau of Municipal Research had asked citizens to entrust local government with increased power because a scientific budget system would enable them to hold it accountable, so the men of the Institute for Government Research convinced Congress to delegate responsibility for public administration to the president and then use the budget to oversee his execution of its mandate.

Under the direction of William Willoughby, the institute proved remarkably adept at promoting national budget reform. It set the agenda for congressional hearings and debates over the Budget and Accounting Act and provided critical technical support to the new Budget Bureau during its first years of operation. Although animated by the work of the Bureau of Municipal Research, the national campaign for budget reform was concerned primarily with relations of power and authority within government—not between government and the people. The institute targeted elite policymakers and shed the bureau's interest in publicity and education, preferring to let other organizations take up the burden of speaking to the people at large.

The campaign for national budget reform fundamentally altered the relations of power and authority among the president, Congress, and the federal bureaucracy, but along the way it lost touch with the goal of adapting representative democracy to a mass industrial society—the goal that had animated the first proponents of local budget reform. To the Bureau of Municipal Research, a scientific budget system had meaning and value only as it served to make government more responsible and responsive to the people. To the institute, the budget was to be a neutral tool of an energetic executive, as applicable to the autocracy of Prussia as to the democracy of the United States.

A NEW VIEW OF BUDGET REFORM

Shortly after his failed appeal to President Wilson to salvage the work of the Commission on Economy and Efficiency, Frederick Cleveland turned to creating a privately funded national organization, styled on the Bureau of Municipal Research, to continue the work of national budget reform. In 1914, he helped form a steering committee to draft the organizational structure, search for a board of trustees, and arrange initial financing for such a bureau. In addition to Cleveland, the steering committee, known as the Committee of Nine, included Charles Norton, President Taft's personal secretary, who had since become vice president of the National Bank of New York; Jerome Greene, the secretary of the newly created Rockefeller Foundation; Anson Phelps Stokes, a churchman and educator; R. Fulton Cutting, a longtime patron of the New York Bureau of Municipal Research; Raymond Fosdick, who had earlier worked closely with Cleveland and Henry Bruere while he was commissioner of accounts of New York City and who was, by 1914, an adviser to John D. Rockefeller, Jr., in his philanthropies; Frederick Strauss, a banker; Charles Niell, a railroad executive and former commissioner of labor; James Curtis, Fosdick's law partner and former assistant secretary of the treasury; and Theodore Vail, the president of AT & T. The Committee of Nine later formed the basis for the board of trustees of the Institute for Government Research, which was chartered on March 10, 1916.[1]

At one early meeting of the committee, Charles Norton noted that recent changes in the tariff together with the new income tax had "called to mind with particular force . . . the subject of our national expenditures and the importance of a close analysis of them."[2] To address these changes and prepare the way for the institute, the Committee of Nine convinced the Rockefeller Foundation to fund a "Special Committee on Scientific Research in Governmental Problems" composed of Greene, Fosdick, Norton, Niell, and Willoughby, who had previously worked with Cleveland as a member of the Taft Commission. The special committee then employed Cleveland to direct a series of studies on government administration. While Cleveland was beginning his studies, the others were hammering out the details for the organization of the Institute for Government Research. During 1915, they recruited Charles Van Hise, president of the University of Wisconsin, Arthur T. Hadley, president of Yale University, and Felix Frankfurter, among others, to serve on the board of trustees.[3]

The institute was largely the child of the municipal research bureau movement. It shared the bureau's belief in the efficacy of applying scientific principles of management to public administration in cooperation with government officials. It was permanently staffed by "nonpartisan" experts who were to make known "the most scientific practical principles and procedures that should obtain in the conduct of public affairs." And

[1] Charles Thompson, *The Institute for Government Research: An Account of Research Achievements* (Washington, D.C.: Brookings Institution, 1956), 6–8; Charles Saunders, *The Brookings Institution: A Fifty-Year History* (Washington, D.C.: Brookings Institution, 1966), 13–14; Donald T. Critchlow, *The Brookings Institution, 1916–1952* (De Kalb: Northern Illinois University Press, 1985), 32–33.

[2] "Proposed Statement to be made by Mr. [Charles D.] Norton in calling to order the meeting at the Century Club on November 20th, [1914]," Rockefeller Family Archives, Record Group I.I, Series 200, Box 26, Folder 295.

[3] Saunders, *Brookings Institution*, 14–16.

finally, as the bureau had led the movement for local budget reform, the institute soon became the driving force behind the campaign for a national budget system.[4]

The institute, however, was not the same as the bureau. From the outset it began to develop its own identity and elaborate a program of budget reform that came to diverge significantly from the early vision of the municipal reformers. The first break came with the appointment of William F. Willoughby as the institute's first director. Many had assumed that Cleveland would get the job. As former chairman of the Taft Commission and current superviser of the Rockefeller-funded series of studies in government administration, he seemed the natural choice. But in the wake of Congress's rejection of the Taft Commission's report, the board of trustees believed that Cleveland lacked the political acumen to garner congressional support for budget reform. Jerome Greene, who had earlier helped to oust Allen from the Bureau of Municipal Research, later recalled that Cleveland had been slated for the directorship of the Institute for Government Research, but it soon became evident that Cleveland "lacked the ability to make a lucid presentation of his work to other people." According to Greene, the board of trustees feared that "the whole movement was likely to be brought into disrepute through Mr. Cleveland's manner of oral presentation, a defect which would have made his contacts with administrative officials and Congressional committees very difficult."[5]

Cleveland, in short, was boring, opaque, and more than a bit aloof. As Raymond Fosdick put it, he had "a rather involved way of expressing himself, which is often baffling to a person seeking the simple facts of a case."[6] Ironically, Cleveland, who had just won a battle over Allen by attacking his overly popular style of reform, now found himself being

---

[4]Thompson, *Institute for Government Research*, 9; Critchlow, *Brookings Institution*, 36; William F. Willoughby, "The Institute for Government Research," *American Political Science Review* 12 (February 1918): 52. Like the bureau, the institute placed budget reform at the center of its program. As the director of the institute wrote in 1917, "There can be no question that the greatest single reform to be accomplished in the system of administration of the national government consists in the adoption by that government of a scientific budget system. The desire to promote this reform undoubtedly constituted one of the strong motives leading to the creation of the Institute." Institute for Government Research, *Annual Report of the Director, 1917*, Annual Reports of the Director, 1916–1926, Box 1, File 1, Brookings Institution Archives, Washington, D.C., 8.

[5]Jerome D. Greene to Hermann Hagedorn, December 19, 1935, Papers of Jerome D. Greene, Box 2, Harvard University Archives.

[6]Raymond B. Fosdick to John D. Rockefeller, Jr., August 25, 1915, Rockefeller Family Archives, Record Group III 2 D, Box 2, Folder 6.

passed by because he was not popular enough. He had made a career out of addressing other experts, leaving the diplomatic work of dealing with politicians and philanthropists to Bruere and Allen. Now, as he was poised to carry his great campaign to its triumphant conclusion at the national level, he was suddenly obsolete. Cleveland continued to speak out, and many listened, but the baton of leadership had passed to William F. Willoughby and the Institute for Government Research.[7]

During his tenure at the institute, Willoughby became one of the country's most influential advocates of budget reform. He proved remarkably adept at forging close working relationships with key members of Congress and the executive branch, and he himself drafted much of the legislation that eventually became the Budget and Accounting Act of 1921.

At first glance, Willoughby appears similar to Cleveland in background and interests. Both had been university professors, Cleveland, of accounting and finance at New York University, Willoughby, of political science at Princeton, and they had served together on the Taft Commission. But whereas Cleveland and the other members of the Bureau of Municipal Research had entered public life as social and political reformers, Willoughby's formative professional experiences were as a public administrator.

On his graduation from Johns Hopkins in 1884, Willoughby joined the Department of Labor as a statistician. During Theodore Roosevelt's administration he served simultaneously as treasurer and president of the Executive Council of Puerto Rico. In 1909, he became assistant director of the census bureau, where he served until joining the Taft Commission in 1911. From 1914 until 1916, while at Princeton, Willoughby, together with his twin brother, Westel (an eminent constitutional scholar and past president of the American Political Science Association), acted as a legal adviser to the Chinese government.[8]

Throughout his career, Willoughby concentrated less on broad issues of social reform and good citizenship than on making government run efficiently. He worked as a public official from inside the government, addressing policymakers and bureaucrats, not the public at large. He expressed a distrust of popular democracy which stood in marked contrast to the bureau's focus on an educated citizenry as the ultimate goal of budget reform. William Allen, already soured toward any Rockefeller-supported enterprise through his experiences with the bureau, recognized

[7]Critchlow, *Brookings Institution*, 32–34; Saunders, *Brookings Institution*, 17.
[8]Critchlow, *Brookings Institution*, 34–36; "William F. Willoughby," *National Cyclopedia of American Biography*, vol. A (New York: James T. White, 1930), 212–13.

the difference immediately, asserting that "the institute for governmental research [was] financed by the Rockefeller foundation and associates upon a platform that unequivocally disregards, where it does not unequivocally disrespect, public ability and right to understand budgetary questions."[9]

Willoughby's attitude toward publicity reflected his disdain for the public. Publicity of the sort practiced by Allen in the budget exhibits was, according to Willoughby, "of small importance" because budgets "have to do with technical subjects; and even if they were perfectly understood by each of ten, fifty, or one hundred million people it would be necessary to provide some practical way for having issues formulated, discussed and decided."[10] Willoughby thought it far more effective and realistic to concentrate on informing Congress, as the people's representative, than to address the people themselves.[11]

Willoughby viewed public opinion as an object to be manipulated in the service of the institute's program, not as a guide for political action. "The time may come," he wrote, "when, in respect to certain proposals, it may be desirable to secure the support of public opinion. In such cases the policy should be that of getting the active support of other organizations rather than that of entering upon a campaign of propaganda."[12] Here Willoughby completely reversed the means and ends of early budget reform: the bureau had seen improved administration as a means to restore some measure of popular control over government and to address the dangers of a disaffected citizenry; Willoughby saw the public simply as a mass whose opinion might on occasion be aroused to support the institute's independent goal of improving government administration. In his hands, the people became instruments of expert reform rather than its intended beneficiaries.

Willoughby happily left the task of educating the public to other organizations—as long as they used information supplied by the institute. To augment his control over the flow of information, Willoughby served on

[9]Critchlow, *Brookings Institution*, 34–36; William H. Allen, "Serious Defects in Maryland's Budget Law," quoted in Harvey S. Chase, "The Budget Amendment of the Maryland Constitution," *National Municipal Review* 6 (May 1917): 397.

[10]William F. Willoughby, Westel W. Willoughby, and Samuel McCune Lindsay, *The System of Financial Administration of Great Britain* (New York: D. Appleton, 1917), 16.

[11]William F. Willoughby, *The Movement for Budgetary Reform in the States* (New York: D. Appleton, 1918), 1.

[12]William F. Willoughby, "Memorandum regarding the Policy and Program of the Institute," June 1916, Official Papers, 1915–1935, Box 1, File 2, Brookings Institution Archives, Washington, D.C., 3.

a variety of committees in other organizations that were committed to spreading the word of budget reform to selected segments of the public. By 1920, Willoughby's assignments included the Committee on Budget and Efficiency and the Committee on the Department of Public Works of the United States Chamber of Commerce; the Committee on Federal Legislation of the American Council of Education; the Committee on Federal Statistics of the American Statistical Association; and the Joint Committee on a National Archives Building of the American Historical, Economic, and Political Science Associations.

According to Robert Brookings, who was then chairman of the institute that would soon bear his name, Willoughby's connections enabled the institute both "to influence, and largely determine, the direction that the efforts of these organizations shall take, and . . . to secure a publicity and support for reforms which it believes to be desirable, which it could not otherwise obtain except through the expenditure of many thousands of dollars."[13] The institute, however, valued other organizations solely as they served its own interests. Brookings gave no indication that the institute had anything to learn, only to teach.

Willoughby dealt similarly with newspapers. He noted with pride that such "leading journals" as the *Saturday Evening Post*, the *New York Times*, the *New York Post*, and the *Washington Star* had developed the habit of coming to the institute for information about problems of national administration. Willoughby worked with the press so as to ensure that "these papers take a correct position in respect to the advocacy of change."[14] Willoughby, in short, trusted neither the public nor the newspapers to reach "correct" conclusions on their own.

Other groups, such as the National Budget Committee, whose board of directors included Henry Stimson, Paul Warburg, and Woodrow Wilson (as honorary chairman), readily adopted the role of propagandists for the institute's program. Testifying before the House Select Committee on the Budget, Samuel McCune Lindsay, the National Budget Committee's vice chairman (and co-author with Willoughby of a book on the British system of financial administration), described his organization's purpose as "to organize public opinion with respect to the need of a national budget system." Since many other organizations dealt with the more technical as-

[13]Robert S. Brookings, "Report of the Chairman," February 12, 1920, Official Papers, 1915–1935, Box 1, File 1, Brookings Institution Archives, Washington, D.C., 8–9.
[14]Institute for Government Research, *Annual Report of the Director, 1920*, Annual Reports of the Director, 1916–1926, Box 1, File 1, Brookings Institution Archives, Washington, D.C., 10.

pects of budget reform, Lindsay felt that the National Budget Committee "might perform a useful service by attempting to focus discussion" and helping these diverse groups to cooperate in lobbying Congress for reform.[15] The committee's chairman, John Pratt, was even more direct about manipulating public opinion. Through educating the public about the true meaning of a budget system, Pratt believed that his organization would prevent "any interference on the part of the public in trying to bring to bear political pressure in a way that will interfere with that budget system."[16]

Throughout 1918 and 1919, as Congress began seriously to consider budget legislation, the National Budget Committee published a fortnightly newspaper, *The National Budget*, devoted entirely to promoting budget reform. The committee also built a network of "budget clubs" in which "small groups of men and women throughout the country" could debate topics of public interest "with the object of creating added interest in questions that affect citizens as voters and taxpayers." By December 1919, some 250 budget clubs were functioning or in the process of formation in the states of New York, Pennsylvania, Connecticut, Illinois, and Missouri. Soon thereafter, the fourteen state governors accepted honorary chairmanships of state branches of the National Budget Committee. The movement grew steadily until March 1922, by which time the committee had organizations operating in over half the states in the Union. Though often composed of businessmen and bankers, the clubs also formed independent "Women's Fortnightly Budget Clubs" and reached out to local philanthropies, such as settlement houses. National Budget Committee members in New York City, for example, helped to arrange a debate on the budget between the children of the Christie Street Settlement House and the College Settlement House.[17] Through such activities, the committee hoped to "excite and marshall" public opinion in support of proper budget reform legislation.[18]

Willoughby and his allies saw public opinion as something to be managed and tactically mobilized to secure particular goals that the budget

[15]U.S. House Select Committee on the Budget, *National Budget System: Hearings before the Select Committee on the Budget*, 66th Cong., 1st sess., September 23, 1919, 149.

[16]Ibid., 103.

[17]"Opening Budget Club Campaign," *National Budget*, October 15, 1919, 6; "Miss Parke Defines 'Kitchen Mindedness,'" *National Budget*, November 15, 1919, 8; "Clubs to Debate Budget," *Budget*, December 1, 1919, 8; "Missouri Forms Budget Clubs," *Budget*, December 15, 1919, 2; "National Budget Committee Growing Throughout Country," *Budget*, February 1, 1920, 1; "Announcement," *Budget*, March 1, 1922, 2.

[18]"After a Budget Bill, What?" *Budget*, February 1, 1920, 2.

experts, not the public, had determined were desirable. They thereby subordinated public opinion to the ends of the experts. Willoughby did not
want to inform the public so much as to arouse public opinion when it
suited his purposes.[19] His approach to publicity shared more with the official World War I propaganda of George Creel's Committee on Public Information than with William Allen's "Efficient Citizenship" pamphlets.
Through films, short speeches given by "four minute men" at theaters
across the country, and tens of millions of pieces of patriotic literature,
the Committee on Public Information mobilized public opinion in support of the war effort. Like Willoughby, Creel sought less to educate than
to persuade. Both appealed to the public primarily to secure its endorse-
ment of policies already decided on by governing elites.[20]

In relegating publicity to a secondary status, Willoughby broke decisively with the early advocates of local budget reform. Like so much reform of the early Progressive era, the work of the Bureau of Municipal
Research was originally animated by the belief that objective information,
compiled by neutral experts, could educate and empower the people to
make responsible decisions about public affairs. All too easily, however,
the logic of basing public opinion on expert information led to a conviction that public opinion *had to* be based on expert information to be legitimate. Willoughby took the next step and fully inverted the relationship
between experts and democracy. For Willoughby and the men of the Institute for Government Research, experts would define the appropriate
goals of government and then selectively marshal public opinion to support their goals. Where Allen had used budget exhibits to "advertise" the
public policy options from which citizens might choose, Willoughby (and
Creel) used publicity to obtain the acquiescence of the people in decisions
already made by experts. In Willoughby's hands, the research bureau
evolved from the Bureau of Municipal Research's patronizing but sincere
efforts to educate people for responsible citizenship into the modern think

[19]Willoughby displayed his elitism and disdain for popular democracy early in his career
as a member of the governing Executive Council of Puerto Rico. In justifying the rule by the
nonelected council, Willoughby explained that the Puerto Ricans' long history under the
Spanish monarchy had not provided them with the habits of mind or practical political experience "necessary to the successful working of complete self government." William F.
Willoughby, "The Executive Council of Puerto Rico," *American Political Science Review* 1
(August 1907), 567.

[20]For a brief discussion of George Creel's activities during World War I, see David M.
Kennedy, *Over Here: The First World War and American Society* (New York: Oxford University Press, 1980), 59–66. Creel recounted his own impressions of his propaganda work
in *How We Advertised America* (New York: Harper, 1920).

tank, which disdained public opinion and sought only the attention of elite policymakers.

To Allen and the men of the bureau, true budget reform meant using budget information to connect citizens to the government, making it more responsible and responsive to their needs and concerns. Without publicity, the technical aspects of accounting and reporting were worthless. Hence Allen's idea of "socialized intelligence": he wanted to use the budget to create informed voters capable of holding the government officials accountable for their acts. Allen, moreover, was wary of expert authority as a threat to democracy. "Expertness," he asserted, could become a "menace" to democracy where "men of science fail to keep in touch with unscientific minds [i.e., the public]."[21]

The men of the bureau may have developed a model of publicity that cast the citizen as a reactive consumer, but this was to be a consumer who was capable of exercising informed choice. Moreover, as a tool of representative democracy, publicity was to be constant, subjecting all government activities to the light of day, every day. (Willoughby, in contrast, aimed to publicize government activities selectively and sporadically.) Although the bureau intruded the budget as an essential referent into all authoritative political discussion, it nonetheless engaged citizens in political discussion.

As originally envisioned by the men of the bureau, there were three stages to budget reform: first, adopt a budget system; second, use the new system to improve government administration; and third, publicize the information about government operations gained through improved administration to connect the people to their government, thereby revitalizing representative democracy. The budget, in short, was to be a means toward the greater end of a revitalized representative democracy.

In Willoughby's hands, the means devolved into an end in itself. He certainly believed that budget reform *could* be an instrument of democracy, but he was primarily concerned to get congressmen and administrators to accept only the techniques and the form of a budget system. Willoughby's attitude was broadly reflected in the hearings conducted by Congress on budget reform in 1919 and 1920. Nicholas Murray Butler, president of Columbia University and a member of the institute's board of trustees, summed up the new view in his assertion that "a properly formulated national budget is not an end in itself, but a means, and a very important

---

[21]William H. Allen, "Interpreting Government to the Citizenship," in Edward A. Fitzpatrick, ed. *Experts in City Government* (New York: D. Appleton, 1919), 174.

means to improving the whole administrative organization of government."[22] Butler, like Willoughby and like most of the forty people who testified before Congress on the adoption of a national budget, considered the budget a tool to improve government administration but lost sight of the ultimate goal of making government more directly responsive to the will of the people.

To men such as Willoughby, public debate had value only as it aided them in their private discussions with policymakers.[23] It was but a small step to conclude that the principles of scientific budgeting existed independently of any particular political system. As Willoughby remarked of the British budgetary system, its procedures "are not necessary consequences of the adoption by that country of the responsible type of government, but may be put into practice by any government." From the outset, then, Willoughby framed the campaign for national budget reform in terms that cut it free from its original moorings in democratic theory.[24]

THE CAMPAIGN FOR A NATIONAL BUDGET SYSTEM

As Cleveland was working to establish the institute, the idea of budget reform was taking hold across the nation. In 1915 and again in 1917, Congress introduced resolutions calling for the creation of boards or commissions to consider the problem of national budget reform. In 1916, both the Democratic and the Republican Party explicitly called for budget reform in its national platform. That same year, Democrats in the House of Representatives held a special caucus to consider the discarded recommendations of the Taft Commission. Although they reached no conclusions, their work was followed in 1917 by several resolutions in the House and Senate calling for the creation of a commission to study and prepare

[22]"Testimony of Nicholas Murray Butler, January 12, 1920," U.S. Senate, *Hearings before the Committee on Consideration of a National Budget*, 66th Cong., 2d Sess., 1920, 74.

[23]On the tendency of think tanks, such as the Institute for Government Research, to be used as vehicles to remove contentious political issues from public debate, see David Eakins, "The Development of Corporate Liberal Policy Research in the United States, 1885–1965" (Ph.D. diss., University of Wisconsin, 1966), 142–55; and idem, "The Origins of Corporate Liberal Policy Research, 1916–1922: The Political-Economic Expert and the Decline of Public Debate," in Jerry Israel, ed., *Building the Organizational Society* (New York: Free Press, 1972), 163–79.

[24]William F. Willoughby, *The Problem of a National Budget* (New York: D. Appleton, 1918), 62.

a plan for a national budget system. The following March, Representative Medill McCormick of Illinois introduced a series of bills to establish a national budget system. The county's entry into World War I, however, diverted attention from domestic reform, and none of McCormick's bills was enacted that session.[25]

The men of the institute appreciated that they would have to hold their campaign for budget reform in abeyance until the end of the war. But this did not mean that they were inactive. To the contrary, they saw the war years as an opportunity to position themselves to spring into action with even greater force after the conclusion of hostilities. Willoughby had his staff conduct administrative surveys of various federal departments and offered their services to a number of bureaus to help them prosecute the war effort, including the Council on National Defense, the American Red Cross, several offices in the war department, the Bureau of Education, the Bureau of Foreign and Domestic Commerce, the War Risk Insurance Board, and the state department. Willoughby himself assisted General Herbert M. Lord, head of the Department of Finance of the war department (and a future director of the Bureau of the Budget), in recasting the department's scheme of appropriations and allotments to correspond to proper budgetary principles.[26]

Willoughby recognized that in the aftermath of war, the entire executive branch of the government might be reorganized. Already such wartime measures as the Overman Act had endowed President Wilson with extraordinary powers over government operations.[27] Politicians and citizens alike were beginning to view the potential for coordinated government activity in a new light. As Willoughby saw it, "No more opportune time could be had for the introduction of a budgetary system. . . . It is fortunate, therefore, that the Institute will, by that time, have rendered available such a body of information regarding the subject, and will be in a position actually to assist in the taking of the action that will be required."[28] Willoughby proved remarkably prescient. After the conclusion of the war, work on establishing a national budget system began in earnest

[25]Ibid., 150–56; Saunders, *Brookings Institution*, 14–16.

[26]Institute for Government Research, *Annual Report of the Director, 1917*, 15–16; *Annual Report, 1918*, 4; Brookings, "Report of the Chairman," 3–4; William F. Willoughby, *Interim Report, October 1, 1917* (Washington, D.C.: Institute for Government Research, 1917), 6–19.

[27]Steven Skowronek, *Building a New American State: The Expansion of National Administrative Capacities, 1877–1920* (Cambridge: Cambridge University Press, 1982), 198–200.

[28]Institute for Government Research, *Annual Report of the Director, 1917*, 11.

in both chambers of Congress, with Willoughby and his staff guiding the process at every step.

World War I did not cause any major innovation in the ideology or techniques of budget reform, but it did affect its trajectory and pace of development. The demands of sustaining the war effort had transformed the public economy. Federal expenditures rose from approximately $700 million in 1916 to well over $18 billion in 1919. Similarly, the federal civilian work force more than doubled, from just under 400,000 in 1916 to 845,500 in 1920.[29]

To finance the war effort, the federal government turned to the new income tax and to war bonds. Between 1913 and 1915, only 2 percent of the U.S. population was liable to any income tax. The revenue needs of the war led the government to raise income tax rates and extend them across more of the population. During World War I the income tax raised nearly 60 percent of all current federal revenue at its peak, but remained steeply progressive, drawing most heavily on people with incomes over $20,000. For example, of the nearly $170 million collected under the 1916 Revenue Act, over 95 percent came from people with incomes over $20,000. From 1917 to 1919, the upper income group paid an average of 75 percent of the income taxes although it comprised less than 1 percent of those filing returns.[30]

Tax revenues, however, were only a drop in the bucket of war finance. The enormous expenses of fighting a total war required the federal government to borrow money on a massive scale not seen since the Civil War. Fortunately, the government was well positioned to float new bond issues because by 1915 its per capita debt was almost at its lowest point since 1861. With its strong credit position and the place of the United States generally as a safe haven for investment in a time of turmoil, the government had little trouble obtaining loans. Between 1916 and 1920, the federal government's interest-bearing debt increased from $1 billion to over $24 billion.[31]

War bond drives made creditors out of millions of citizens, giving them

[29]Peri E. Arnold, *Making the Managerial Presidency: Comprehensive Reorganization Planning, 1905–1980* (Princeton: Princeton University Press, 1986), 53; Louis Fisher, *Presidential Spending Power* (Princeton: Princeton University Press, 1975), 32.

[30]Charles Gilbert, *American Financing of World War I*, (Westport, Ct.: Greenwood, 1970), 113–15; John Witte, *The Politics and Development of the Federal Income Tax* (Madison: University of Wisconsin Press, 1985), 79–86; Carolyn Webber and Aaron Wildavsky, *A History of Taxation and Expenditure in the Western World* (New York: Simon and Schuster, 1986), 421–22.

[31]Gilbert, *American Financing of World War I*, 230.

a new and direct interest in their government's finances. The total sales of five Liberty Loan and one Victory Loan drives topped $21 billion. The third and fourth Liberty Loans alone had a combined total of close to forty million subscribers. Although millions of Americans participated in the loan drives, over 80 percent of the total amount subscribed was in denominations over $100 (with the bulk of that being in amounts over $1,000) that were largely taken by banks and other large institutional investors. The U.S. Steel Corporation, for example, took over $128 million of the four Liberty Loans.[32]

The steeply progressive income tax and massive bond sales to large institutional investors transformed the relationship between financial elites and the federal government. First, major bondholders had a powerful interest in protecting their investment by ensuring that the government remained solvent. Second, all wealthy individuals and corporations had a new incentive to protect their incomes by ensuring that government waste and inefficiency did not precipitate unnecessarily high tax rates. Budget reform, by then well known throughout the country, provided a ready solution to these concerns. The oversight of a budget system would effectively audit bondholders' investments while improved efficiency helped to keep taxes to a minimum.

The financial changes of the war thus consolidated a new and powerful constituency for budget reform. Upon the conclusion of hostilities this consistency was ready to throw its weight behind the final push to establish a national budget system. Inspired by "the vast increase in expenditure due to the war," which had "given rise to a heavy burden of taxation . . . and to government borrowing hitherto unknown and never anticipated," the United States Chamber of Commerce, for example, adopted a resolution (drafted in part by Willoughby) calling on local chambers of commerce across the country to campaign for national budget reform.[33]

Politicians felt the pressure and responded. Representative James W. Good of Iowa, the Republican chairman of the House Appropriations Committee and a leader in the movement for national budget reform, noted that the enormous cost of prosecuting the war had "brought about a radical change in the fiscal affairs of the United States," requiring the government to raise "practically all of its revenue through a system of direct taxation," the result being "that from the taxpayer is coming a demand

---

[32]Donald R. Stabile and Jeffrey A. Cantor, *The Public Debt of the United States: An Historical Perspective, 1775–1990* (New York: Praeger, 1991), 80–81; Gilbert, *American Financing of World War I*, 136–42.

[33]"A Business-Like Government," *Nation's Business* 7 (June 1919): 56, 61.

that is both increasing and constant for greater economy and efficiency in the Government's fiscal affairs."[34] The "taxpayers" Good spoke of came overwhelmingly from the upper tiers of society.

In 1919 both the House and the Senate established select committees to study and propose plans for a national budget system. Medill Mc-Cormick, now a member of the Senate, served as chairman of that body's committee, while James Good became chairman of the House committee. Reviewing the defects of the existing system of national finance, the House Select Committee on the Budget reported that

> expenditures are not considered in connection with revenues; that Congress does not require of the President any carefully thought-out financial work program representing what provision in his opinion should be made for meeting the financial needs of the Government; that the estimates of expenditure needs now submitted to Congress represent only the desires of the individual departments, establishments, and bureaus; and that these requests have been subjected to no superior revision with a view to bringing them into harmony with each other, to eliminating duplication of organization or activities, or of making them, as a whole, conform to the needs of the Nation as represented by the condition of the Treasury and prospective revenues . . . The various bureau chiefs act independently of each other. Bureaus of executive departments doing similar work are thus stimulated into rivalry, and so far as the estimates go, very little effort has been made to coordinate the activities of the several departments and bureaus, and in practice this method has resulted in extravagance, inefficiency, and duplication of service.[35]

The concern for duplication, lack of coordination, administrative rivalry, and the absence of a presidential work program all reflect the thought of the Taft Commission. This is not surprising considering that the report was largely written by none other than Willoughby himself.

True to his plan, Willoughby had successfully positioned the institute to take the lead in budget reform after the war. Already well connected in

[34]Rep. James W. Good, "An Address Delivered before the Illinois Manufacturers' Association in Chicago, Friday evening, January 9, 1920," submitted to the U.S. House by Joseph Cannon, *Cong. Rec.,* 66th Cong., 2d sess. (Appendix), 1920, vol. 59, pt. 9, 8733. See also Charles H. Stewart III, *Budget Reform Politics: The Design of the Appropriations Process in the House of Representatives, 1865–1921* (Cambridge: Cambridge University Press, 1989), 197–99.

[35]U.S. House Select Committee on the Budget, *National Budget System,* 66th Cong., 1st Sess., 1919, H. Rept. no. 362, 4.

Washington, Willoughby had come to the attention of Representative Good in 1917 through his book, *The Problem of a National Budget*. Thus, when in 1919 Good became chairman of the House Select Committee on the Budget, he naturally turned to Willoughby to advise him in conducting hearings and writing a budget bill and its accompanying report.

Willoughby did more than advise; he dominated the process from start to finish. In September and October of 1919, the committee held hearings at which, according to Willoughby, "the great majority of [the thirty-seven] witnesses were summoned at the suggestion of the Institute." Willoughby attended all the hearings and suggested many of the questions asked. He was gratified (though probably not surprised) to find that a considerable number of the witnesses called were familiar with the publications of the Institute on Budget Reform and "had been largely influenced by them in reaching their opinions regarding the character of the action that should be taken." Indeed, the committee's report stated that there was a "remarkable uniformity of opinion" in support of adopting a budget system "as a central feature of [the federal government's] system of financial administration."[36]

Upon the conclusion of the hearings, Willoughby assisted drafting the bill to be reported by the committee and the report to accompany it. At Good's suggestion, Willoughby softened some of the more stringent provisions of the bill to make it more palatable to a larger number of congressmen. The final version did not do everything Willoughby wished, but, as he wrote to Charles Norton, "everything that it does do is, I think, in the right direction."[37] Specifically, the bill, commonly referred to as the Good Bill, adopted an executive budget plan under which the president would be responsible for transmitting a budget to Congress each year. It provided for a Bureau of the Budget, located in the president's office, to serve him as his agent in compiling, reviewing, and revising departmental estimates of appropriations.

The Good Bill also created an accounting department, overseen by a new office of comptroller general, to provide an audit independent of the Department of the Treasury. Legislators who worried that the bill would expand presidential powers at the expense of Congress insisted on such

[36]Ibid., 2–3.

[37]Institute for Government Research, *Annual Report of the Director, 1919*, 3–4; Brookings, "Report of the Chairman," 6; William F. Willoughby to Charles D. Norton, May 21, 1919, Correspondence of the Board of Trustees, 1915–1925, Box 1, File 1, Brookings Institution Archives, Washington, D.C.

an auditing agency to provide a counterbalance to the Bureau of the Budget. The comptroller general was to be Congress's man in financial administration. The bill was almost immediately called up for consideration in the House and passed with only minor changes by the nearly unanimous vote of 285 to 3, on October 21, 1919.[38]

The Good Bill then went to the Senate, where it was referred to Senator McCormick's Select Committee on the Budget. The Senate was then in the midst of extensive discussion of the Treaty of Versailles, so McCormick was unable to get his committee together for hearings before December 15. Meanwhile, on December 3, President Wilson came out strongly in support of executive budget reform in his annual message to Congress, expressing his hope "that Congress will bring to a conclusion at this session legislation looking to the establishment of a budget system."[39]

The hearings before McCormick's committee largely recapitulated the more extensive hearings conducted by Good. Most of the witnesses had already appeared before the House committee and more or less repeated their statements to the Senate. Willoughby was called as a witness, but he had his greatest impact on the Senate committee after the hearings concluded on January 14, 1920. McCormick then requested Willoughby's help in framing a budget bill. Willoughby welcomed the invitation, all the more so because he found that the committee "was giving consideration to a bill that was almost in every respect unsatisfactory." Fortunately, he found the committee "more than willing to receive the suggestions made by him. It in fact permitted him practically to rewrite the bill with the result that the bill which will come before the Senate for action is in respect to most of its features a very satisfactory measure."[40]

McCormick's bill, as it turned out, differed from Good's in several important respects. Most significant, it placed the Bureau of the Budget in

[38]Stewart, *Budget Reform Politics*, 202–4; Frederick C. Mosher, *A Tale of Two Agencies: A Comparative Analysis of the General Accounting Office and the Office of Management and Budget* (Baton Rouge: Louisiana State University Press, 1984), 28–29; Charles Wallace Collins, "Historical Sketch of the Budget Bill in Congress," *Congressional Digest* 2 (November 1922): 37. Representative Tinkham, of Massachusetts, also asked for Willoughby's assistance in drafting a bill to supplement the Good Bill by providing for changes in the rules of the House of Representatives to ensure proper handling of the budget after it was received from the president. Willoughby reported to Charles Norton, "I drafted such a resolution which he introduced precisely as prepared by me." Willoughby to Norton, May 21, 1919.

[39]"Message of the President of the United States Communicated to the Two Houses of Congress at the Beginning of the Second Session of the Sixty-Sixth Congress," 66th Cong., 2d sess., 1919, H. Doc. no. 399, 3.

[40]Institute for Government Research, *Annual Report of the Director, 1919*, 5.

the treasury department under the direction of the secretary of the treasury, not the president. The bill also called for the creation of an independent general accounting office with the authority to prescribe accounting methods and supervise the financial activities of all government agencies. The Senate passed the bill on May 1, 1920, without a dissenting vote.[41]

Conferees from the House and Senate met to resolve the differences and reported out a revised bill to Congress on May 26. The conference bill adopted a strong, independent general accounting office, locating the Bureau of the Budget in the treasury department and making the secretary of the treasury himself the director of the bureau. Although President Wilson continued to express support for budget reform, he vetoed the bill on June 4 on a technicality concerning the power of the Congress to remove the comptroller general by concurrent resolution without the president's approval. Wilson believed that this amounted to an unconstitutional infringement on his powers of appointment and removal.[42]

In the meantime, a small revolution occurred in Congress, as James Good shepherded a rules change through the House which reconsolidated appropriations authority in a single committee, thus closing a chapter of congressional financial administration which had begun in 1885 with the devolution of appropriations authority to numerous congressional committees. Good presented the consolidation as an essential balance to the president's new power under an executive budget system. Good's proposal was greeted with far more opposition than any of the budget bills. It directly challenged the power of representatives serving on the diverse appropriating committees. After considerable acrimonious debate, the resolution was approved by a vote of 200 to 117. The Senate eventually followed suit in 1922.[43]

By the time Congress passed an amended version of the budget bill in April 1921, Warren Harding had replaced Wilson in the White House. The new bill addressed Wilson's concerns by providing for removal of the comptroller general only by joint resolution of the House and Senate, which required the signature of the president to go into effect. On June 10, President Harding signed the Budget and Accounting Act of 1921 into law. The act had four main provisions. First, it placed on the president the responsibility for compiling and submitting a budget to Congress annu-

[41]William F. Willoughby, *The National Budget System* (Baltimore: Johns Hopkins Press, 1927), 30–31.

[42]Ibid., 27–31; Steven Skowronek, *Building a New American State*, 206–8.

[43]Stewart, *Budget Reform Politics*, 207–15; Willoughby, *National Budget System*, 34–38.

ally. Second, it created the Bureau of the Budget, with its own director, technically located in the treasury department, but in fact responsible only to the president, serving as his agent in all budget-related matters. Third, it prohibited any other officer or employee of the government from submitting to Congress a request for an appropriation, except at the request of either house of Congress. Fourth, it provided for an independent auditing service, the General Accounting Office, under the direction of the comptroller general, to take over all the duties formerly vested in the comptroller of the treasury.[44]

It may be asked why, if budget reform was so popular, did it take so long for the federal government to adopt it? Walter Warwick, the comptroller of the treasury when the Budget and Accounting Act finally passed, suggested that, ironically, the very lack of opposition to the reform retarded its progress. "Sometimes," he mused, "I think such a movement is hastened by a little opposition. Moreover, a few of the men who are clamoring for a budget system are insisting that none but a perfect system will satisfy them. And perfection is a difficult thing to attain immediately."[45] Actually, the time involved was just under ten years, not an unusually long period for a major restructuring of government. The idea of a national budget system did not gain currency until the publication of the Taft Commission's report, *The Need for a National Budget*, in 1912. The Democratic Congress's antipathy toward a lame-duck Republican president prevented the adoption of any plan that might increase executive power. When Woodrow Wilson took office, he expressed his strong support for budget reform, but he had his own ambitious agenda for domestic reform, and it seems unlikely that he would have wanted one of the early defining acts of his administration to be the adoption of a Republican plan of administrative reform. By 1916, however, the forces behind budget reform were regaining momentum, and all major parties adopted budget reform in their campaign platforms. Then, of course, the United States entered the war, and all major domestic initiatives, especially those calling for government austerity, were put on hold. With the conclusion of hostilities, budget reform came once again to the fore and would have been adopted by Wilson but for a constitutional technicality. Finally, in 1921, Warren Harding signed the Budget and Accounting Act. Federal administration would never be the same.

[44]Budget and Accounting Act, 1921 (June 10, 1921, chap. 18, § 1, 42 stat. 20).

[45]Walter Warwick, "The Budget, Just Common Sense," *Nation's Business* 9 (May 1921), 20.

A New Theory of Executive Power

The Budget and Accounting Act passed with such ease in part because its proponents cast it more as a means to help Congress in its conduct of the business of government than as an aggrandizement of executive power. Congress retained ultimate authority over appropriations and had the power to revise estimates as it saw fit. In addition, the newly consolidated House Appropriations Committee seemed to provide an adequate counterweight to the new Bureau of the Budget. The General Accounting Office also eased fears of possible executive usurpation by providing for an independent audit of all administrative activities.

More generally, the groundwork laid by a decade of agitation for budget reform across the country had developed the strong support of powerful constituents across the country. Organizations such as John Pratt's National Budget Committee mobilized public opinion through its budget clubs and general propaganda activities. The Institute for Government Research did its part by helping the U.S. Chamber of Commerce to organize several hundred local budget committees in 1919 to lobby Congress for budget reform. That same year, the American Federation of Labor passed a resolution calling for a federal budget system at its thirty-ninth annual convention. Samuel Gompers, president of the American Federation of Labor, asserted that "labor always welcomes any reform that is progressive and tends toward efficiency. I believe that the great army of laboring men in this country would receive immediate and concrete benefits by the adoption of a National Budget System." Major magazines, from the *Nation* and the *New Republic* to *Harper's* and the *Saturday Evening Post* also ran articles in support of budget reform.[46]

More powerful than particular endorsements or general popular support for the bill, however, was the reformers' articulation of a new theory of executive power which allayed Congress's fears of creating an overpowerful executive. Briefly stated, the theory asserted that the federal government had grown too complex to be effectively administered by Congress. Only a single chief executive sitting atop a pyramid of bureaucratic authority clearly exposed to public scrutiny could ensure efficient

---

[46]William F. Willoughby to Charles D. Norton, June 21, 1919, Correspondence of the Board of Trustees, 1915–1925, Box 1, File 1, Brookings Institution Archives, Washington, D.C.; "Labor Chiefs Endorse Plans for Budget," *National Budget*, September 1, 1919, 4; for a partial listing of some of the many popular articles written on budget reform during this time, see the bibliography to Willoughby, *National Budget System*, 328–35.

and responsible government. Congress therefore had to delegate its authority over administrative operations to the president. The president would thus become the agent of Congress in conducting governmental business operations. A scientific budgeting system would enable Congress to oversee the president's exercise of his delegated authority and hold him responsible for his actions. For effective oversight, Congress had to make a clear, direct, and substantial delegation of administrative authority to the president and give him the means to assert that authority. Only then could it legitimately hold him responsible for the performance of the federal bureaucracy. According to this logic, the more power Congress gave to the president, the better it would be able ultimately to control him. Tentative or uncertain delegations of authority would undermine congressional power. A budget system thus transformed a strong executive from a potential tyrant into an efficient and responsible administrator.

The new theory of executive power had its roots in the work of the Bureau of Municipal Research and its campaign for local budget reform. The bureau had developed a model of relations between citizen and government in which the citizen delegated authority to government to meet the demands of modern life in return for increased oversight exercised through a comprehensive budgetary system. Men such as Willoughby effectively transposed this model onto the national scene, setting Congress in the place of the people while the president took the place of the government itself. At the national level, the model became a matter of restructuring the separation and balance of powers in the federal government and assigning new roles and responsibilities to Congress and the president. As Allen, Bruere, and Cleveland had used the budget to legitimate the growth of local government in the eyes of the citizenry, Willoughby used the budget to facilitate congressional acquiescence in the expansion of presidential powers.

The Taft Commission asserted that the executive should possess "powers of initiation and leadership," while the legislative authority should primarily exercise "powers of final determination and control." In the commission's opinion, the president was "the one officer of Government who represents the people as a whole," while Congress was composed of a myriad of diverse individuals representing the localistic interests of their particular constituencies. The president, therefore, was "in a better position than anyone else" both to present a comprehensive budget to Congress and "to dramatize the work of government" to the people.

Congress, like citizens at the local level, was to have the power to accept or reject the budget but not to formulate or administer it.[47]

On taking his position at the institute, Willoughby placed the Taft Commission's ideas at the center of his work. He confidently assumed that the nation would adopt some form of budget system but believed it was by no means a foregone conclusion that it would be an executive budget. Willoughby saw federal administration as a distinct fourth branch of government. A proper *executive* budget was needed to assign both the president and the Congress their "true position and function in our political system," with the president responsible for "the formulation of a work program and the determination of the agencies through which it is to be put into effect," and the legislature "restrict[ing] its action to that of general direction, supervision and control."[48]

In his influential book, *The Problem of a National Budget*, Willoughby went even further, declaring that "the legislature should exercise no power of initiating budget proposals" because "the executive alone is in a position to determine in detail the administrative needs of the government." Like the citizen at the local level, Congress's proper role was that of reactive consumer, approving or rejecting the president's proposals but exercising no control over the compilation or presentation of the proposals themselves.[49]

Willoughby's vision of a national budget system rested on a novel theory of delegated authority that departed dramatically from the ancient maxim of "delegata potestas non potest delegari" (delegated power cannot be delegated). To John Locke's statement that the legislature "cannot transfer the power of making laws to any other hands, for it being but a delegated power from the people, they who have it cannot pass it on to others,"[50] Willoughby could counter that "under modern conditions the conduct of governmental affairs is special work requiring special abilities, training and knowledge, and therefore one to be performed by a special body having these special qualifications." The people delegated their sovereign authority to Congress because they were "impotent to exercise it

---

[47]President's Commission on Economy and Efficiency, *The Need for a National Budget* (Washington, D.C.: Government Printing Office, 1912), 10, 143–45.

[48]William F. Willoughby, "The Budget as an Instrument of Political Reform," *Proceedings of the Academy of Political Science* 8 (July 1918): 59. For Willoughby's views on the administrative as a fourth branch of government, see William F. Willoughby, *An Introduction to the Study of the Government of Modern States* (New York: Century, 1920), 270–77.

[49]Willoughby, *National Budget*, 29–30, 39.

[50]John Locke, quoted in Louis Fisher, *Constitutional Conflicts between the Congress and the President*, 3d ed., rev. (Lawrence: University of Kansas Press, 1991), 85.

except in the most general way." By the same logic, Congress could legitimately delegate its authority to the president, and the president to expert administrators. Expertise thus became the basis for a tiered delegation of authority that potentially could extend as far from its source in the people as the need for "special abilities" dictated.[51]

The prospect of an executive budget did elicit some opposition, both from Congress and within the reform community itself. Among the most vehement opponents was Edward Fitzpatrick, the director of the Wisconsin Society for the Promotion of Training for Public Service. Fitzpatrick fully appreciated the broader implications of budget reform, asserting that "when you have decided upon your budget procedure you have decided on the form of government you will have as a *matter of fact*." An executive budget was not merely a way to rationalize chaotic financial administration; it was a "change in emphasis in our whole system of government from legislative to executive." Fitzpatrick, writing in 1918, was particularly concerned that the current schemes for an executive budget did not adequately provide for increased popular control to balance increased executive power. He therefore concluded that if you "make the executive the dominating and controlling factor in budget-making . . . you [will] have, irrespective of what label you put on it, an autocratic actual government."[52]

In Congress, Senator Reed expressed similar concerns, declaring that the purpose of what became the Budget and Accounting Act was "to enable Congress once more to abdicate its powers and transferring them to the Executive." He went on to warn his colleagues that "by passing the bill you have transferred to the executive government a great fundamental power of the representatives of the people."[53]

Willoughby's eminent brother Westel tersely dismissed arguments that an executive budget undermined representative government by degrading Congress. The president, he pointed out, was also elected by the people. Indeed, Westel argued, in one sense he was "a truer representative than [congressmen], for he alone is the choice of and represents the interests of the whole, while the members of Congress each represents but a relatively small constituency."[54] To assuage further any fears of executive usurpa-

---

[51]Willoughby, *Modern States*, 83–85.

[52]Edward A. Fitzpatrick, *Budget Making in a Democracy* (New York: Macmillan, 1918), viii, 47–55.

[53]Remarks of Senator James Reed, *Cong. Rec.*, 66th Cong., 2d sess., June 5, 1920, vol. 59, pt. 8, 8626–27.

[54]Westel W. Willoughby, "Budgetary Procedure in Its Relation to Representative Government," *Yale Law Journal* 27 (April 1918): 752.

tion, William Willoughby assured the members of Congress that in creating an executive budget system, it would be making the president their agent, not their master. Congress, he asserted, should act as a board of directors of a holding corporation that did not seek to manage all the affairs of government directly but merely oversaw and gave final sanction to the actions of its agent, the chief executive.[55]

In a report largely written by Willoughby, the House Select Committee on the Budget similarly assured fellow congressmen that an executive budget as proposed in the Good Bill did not "in the slightest degree give the Executive any greater power than he now has over the consideration of appropriations by Congress." It merely provided that the president should initiate the budget, and Congress would retain the power to accept or reject it.[56]

By enacting an executive budget, Congress decisively located authority over the administrative apparatus of the federal government in the hands of the president. Locating budgetary authority, however, was only the first hurdle. To be fully effective, an executive budget system had to endow the president not only with responsibility for formulating a budget, but also with the actual power to do so. If the president was not made strong enough to control the administrative branch, there could be no basis for holding him accountable for its operation. Each version of a budget bill reported out of the Senate and the House therefore included a provision for a Bureau of the Budget that would assist the president in exercising his authority over the bureaucracy. Senator McCormick's bill, however, stipulated that the new bureau should be under the secretary of the treasury, while Representative Good's version placed the bureau under the direct control of the president. Proponents of Good's version argued that placing the bureau in the treasury would divide responsibility for government administration, thereby undermining the whole theory of an executive budget. Supporters of the McCormick bill countered that its provisions would relieve an already overburdened president of the burdensome details of financial management.[57]

The Budget and Accounting Act of 1921 represented a compromise, placing the Bureau of the Budget technically in the Department of the

---

[55]Willoughby, *National Budget*, 42, 76–80.

[56]U.S. House, *National Budget System*, 7.

[57]For a contemporary debate among budget reformers on the issue of presidential power, see "The Good versus the McCormick Budget Bill," *National Municipal Review* 9 (April 1920): 219–33. See also U.S. Senate Special Committee on the National Budget, *National Budget System*, 66th Cong., 2d sess., 1920, S. Rep. no. 524, 2.

Treasury but making it directly responsible to the president alone. With the budget bureau to serve as his personal agent in dealing with the forty-three administrative departments and independent establishments of the federal government, the president would have both authority over government administration and the means to exercise that authority. Mere formal establishment of an executive budget system, however, meant little unless the men running it took advantage of its potential for administrative control. It remained for the first administrators of the Bureau of the Budget to define the meaning and scope of presidential power under the new system.

8 THE NEW NATIONAL GOVERNMENT

During the 1920s, the new Bureau of the Budget created a unitary executive branch by promulgating standard accounts and procedures and establishing a variety of coordinating agencies to build an sense of solidarity and common identity among officials throughout the federal government. Just as the Budget and Accounting Act provided the means to create a cohesive executive branch, so it also decisively located control over the administrative apparatus of the national state in the hands of the president. The Bureau of the Budget was the president's agency. It was in his name that the bureau compiled estimates and imposed uniform practices. No longer could officials appeal directly to Congress for support. Under the new budgetary regime, all requests for funds had first to be reviewed and accepted by the president before being passed on to Congress.

As result, under the otherwise lackluster administrations of Warren Harding and Calvin Coolidge, the directors of the Bureau of the Budget created a unified and self-conscious executive branch that looked first to the president, not to Congress, for its identity and support. They recast the conceptual world of the federal bureaucracy and established the president on top of the pyramid of administrative authority which had only been imagined by Frederick Cleveland and his colleagues at the Taft Commission.

COMPLETING THE NEW AMERICAN STATE

The 1920s, normally viewed as time of quiescent, laissez-faire government, actually was a period of intense state building. The national budget system created a new executive branch with potentially great powers. That this power was not actively projected outward into society until the 1930s does not lessen the accomplishments of the Bureau of the Budget under Harding and Coolidge. Their work of internal state building was essential to the later expansion of government powers by Franklin Roosevelt. Thus, by the time the United States entered the Great Depression, the movement for budget reform had already laid the foundations for the coordinated exercise of national power under presidential direction which enabled the Roosevelt administration to implement the New Deal.

Before you "build" a state, you must be able to conceive it. To conceive a state, you must understand it as more than a random agglomeration of distinct functions and offices; you must envision it as a coherent whole, composed of distinct yet interrelated parts. During the nineteenth century, Americans had no such vision of the state. In the twentieth century, budget reform provided a new picture of government that enabled politicians and bureaucrats alike to conceive and realize a new type of unified state that was more than just the sum of its parts.

Budget reformers understood that state building was as much a matter of manipulating information as it was of struggling to enlarge this bureau or that department. The budget identified the components of national government and tied them together into a single state. With the passage of the Budget and Accounting Act, Congress and the president formally recognized the power of the budget to centralize control over governmental administration. Administrators themselves, however, continued to operate in isolated bureaucratic fiefdoms, looking after their own interests with little more sense of the "state" than their grandfathers had had. The new national budget system changed all this. It broke down administrative walls and built bridges between estranged offices. It removed blinders from bureaucratic eyes, and forced government officers to see themselves as part of a larger governing apparatus—as part of a new national state.

Many analysts of the Bureau of the Budget (BOB) have argued that during the 1920s it made only minimal use of the potential authority granted by the Budget and Accounting Act. The BOB, they contend, reflected a negative view of government which characterized the "return to normalcy" under Harding and Coolidge. Herbert Lord, who served from 1922 to 1929 as the BOB's second director, in particular is portrayed as a small-minded bureaucrat obsessed with economy and retrenchment. What meager achievements the BOB did manage during its early years, analysts attribute more to the unique personality of Charles G. Dawes, its first director, than to any structural changes he initiated.[1]

The early BOB did, in fact, proudly focus on cutting expenses. But even as the BOB was trying to pare down the size of government as measured in expenditures, it was building a new structure to centralize government administration. Under the early BOB, the government became more activist internally, even as it appeared to withdraw from involvement in the affairs of society at large. The great contribution of Charles Dawes and Herbert Lord was to realize the Taft Commission's vision of building a coherent and self-conscious executive branch oriented primarily toward the president rather than toward Congress. The degree to which the presidents of the 1920s actually exercised control over the administrative apparatus of government is less significant than that the work of the BOB made such control possible.

The Budget and Accounting Act granted broad authority to the Bureau of the Budget to assist the president in coordinating, analyzing, and revising the estimates of the departments and independent establishments and then compiling them into a single comprehensive budget to represent the president's work program for the following year. Budgetary procedure during the 1920s began with the president's indicating his general fiscal policy for the coming year and the maximum appropriations he intended to recommend to Congress. The BOB then requested all the departments and independent establishments to send in preliminary estimates of their financial needs for the coming fiscal year. After reviewing the preliminary estimates, the BOB indicated the maximum amount that would be al-

---

[1]See, for example, Louis Kimmel, *Federal Budget and Fiscal Policy, 1789–1958* (Washington, D.C.: Brookings Institution, 1959), 85–98; Aaron Wildavsky, *The New Politics of the Budgetary Process* (New York: Harper Collins, 1988), 61–65; Fritz Morstein Marx, "The Bureau of the Budget: Its Evolution and Present Role, I," *American Political Science Review* 39 (August 1945): 668–80; Allen Schick, "The Budget Bureau That Was: Thoughts on the Rise, Decline, and Future of a Presidential Agency," *Law and Contemporary Problems* 35 (Summer 1970): 520–23; Percival Brundage, *The Bureau of the Budget* (New York: Praeger, 1970), 14–18; Horace Wilke, "Legal Basis for Increased Activities of the Federal Budget Bureau," *George Washington Law Review* 11 (1943): 268–72; Larry Berman, *The Office of Management and Budget and the Presidency, 1921–1979,* (Princeton: Princeton University Press, 1979), 3–8; Norman M. Pearson, "The Budget Bureau: From Routine Business to General Staff," *Public Administration Review* 3 (Spring 1943): 131–33; Paul L. Van Patten, Jr., "B.O.B. and F.D.R.: A Stage in the Growth of the Institutional Presidency" (Ph.D. diss., University of Notre Dame, 1983), 85–106; Frederick C. Mosher, *A Tale of Two Agencies: A Comparative Analysis of the General Accounting Office and the Office of Management and Budget* (Baton Rouge: Louisiana State University, 1984), 40–42. For a forceful presentation of a contrary view, see Leonard D. White, *Trends in Public Administration* (New York: McGraw-Hill, 1933), 147–74.

lowed and directed the departments and establishments to reconsider their estimates to conform with this amount. The departments and establishments submitted revised estimates to the BOB, which then conferred with each department's budget officer about further revisions. Following the conference, the BOB made its final recommendations to the president and prepared the budget document for presentation to Congress. The estimates submitted by the president were binding upon the department heads, who were forbidden to advocate any different figures before Congress.[2]

Charles G. Dawes, Harding's choice for director of the BOB, was a prominent banker from Chicago. Dawes had previously served as general purchasing agent for the American Expeditionary Forces in France during World War I where he attained the rank of brigadier general. After the war, Dawes stayed on as a member of the U.S. Liquidation Commission, which disposed of millions of dollars of war surplus. Coordinating wartime purchases and postwar liquidation prepared Dawes well for the task of building an executive branch under a budgetary regime.[3]

The Budget and Accounting Act limited Dawes to one assistant director and four assistants. The bureau's staff remained small throughout the 1920s, growing only to twenty-eight by the end of the decade. To cope with the demands of his new job, Dawes drew on wartime precedent to bring in a number of dollar-a-year men from the business world to assist him. The most important support, however, came from the Institute for Government Research, which provided an entire supplemental staff to the BOB during its critical early years.[4]

Willoughby used his contacts in Congress to gain access to the BOB. The powerful James Good aggressively lobbied Dawes on Willoughby's behalf, declaring that he knew of "no one in the country better qualified to speak on the subject" of the national budget and assuring Dawes that he would "find [Willoughby's] suggestions very practical."[5] Taking Good's advice, Dawes called on Willoughby his first day in office. He

[2]White, *Public Administration*, 151–52; Herbert M. Lord, "The Preparation of the Budget," *Congressional Digest* 2 (November 1922): 44–45.

[3]Edward Goedeken, "Charles G. Dawes Establishes the Bureau of the Budget," *Historian* 50 (November 1987): 40–45; idem, "Charles G. Dawes in War and Peace, 1917–1922" (Ph.D. diss., Iowa State University, 1984), 233–48.

[4]Mosher, *Tale of Two Agencies*, 35–38; White, *Public Administration*, 147–48; Donald T. Critchlow, *The Brookings Institution, 1916–1952* (De Kalb: Northern Illinois University, 1985), 38–40; Goedeken, "Charles G. Dawes in War and Peace," 233–48.

[5]James W. Good to Charles G. Dawes, June 25, 1921, Bureau of the Budget, Central Subject Files, Record Group 51, Series 21.1, Box 122 National Archives, Washington, D.C.

gratefully accepted not only Willoughby's assistance but much of his scheme for implementing the new budget system. As Dawes's assistant, William T. Abbott, described the encounter to Good: "It certainly lifted a great weight off the minds of both of us to find what a wonderful amount of real helpful work [the institute has] accomplished. I feel as if the railroad had already been surveyed for us."[6]

The institute immediately dispatched several staff members to the BOB to assist in working out the technical aspects of compiling a budget. Among the most important was Henry Seidemann, an accountant, who continued to work intimately with the BOB for the next several years and had a profound impact of the development of its accounting and reporting practices. (Dawes later acknowledged a debt of gratitude to Seidemann, telling him that the "value of the cooperation of the Institute for Government Research and your own in the budget work of the last year and a half cannot be overemphasized.")[7] Seidemann and the other volunteers from the institute prepared the entire first part of the 1922 budget (with the exception of the president's budget message), containing all the summary and analytic tables.[8]

The institute's influence continued to grow under Herbert Lord, who succeeded Dawes as director of the BOB in July 1922. In a letter to Robert Brookings, Lord wrote,

The assistance of your Institute has been invaluable and could not be obtained from any other source. In giving this assistance there has been no formality, as the entire services of your Institute with its vast store of information and experienced and highly trained personnel have been placed at our disposal. I must here refer particularly to Doctor Willoughby and Mr. Seidemann, whose services to this Bureau merit individual mention. Dr. Willoughby has a vast store of knowledge concerning Budget procedure and I have availed myself most frequently of his counsel and advice, which he has so freely given. As regards Mr. Seidemann, I am afraid that I look upon him as a member of my own force. I know that he has probably devoted practically his entire time to work per-

[6]William T. Abbott to James W. Good, June 29, 1921, ibid., Box 68. In 1921, Willoughby reported, "The Institute has thus been instrumental, not only in securing the adoption of the budget system, but in determining the character of that system." Institute for Government Research, *Annual Report of the Director, 1921,* Annual Reports of the Director, 1916–1926, Box 1, File 2, Brookings Institution Archives, Washington, D.C., 8.

[7]Charles G. Dawes to Henry P. Seidemann, 12 December 1922, General Correspondence Files, 1916–1932, Box 1, File 1, Brookings Institution Archives, Washington, D.C.

[8]Institute for Government Research, *Annual Report of the Director, 1922,* 4–5.

taining to this Bureau and I owe to your Institute for his services, a debt of gratitude. He possesses that ideal combination of ability and adaptability, and it would be most difficult for me to tell you in words how valuable his services have been to this Bureau.[9]

As Dawes and Lord went about creating an executive branch, the men of the institute were at their side every step of the way. By 1924, Willoughby was able to report that the institute had obtained the confidence of key officials in both the legislative and administrative branches, with the result that "in no case has the government entered upon the improvement of its administrative system or procedure in any important particular without calling upon the Institute for its advice and assistance."[10]

The BOB's work of forging a common identity among the diverse departments of the administrative branch had two components. First, they built on the work of Taft's Commission on Economy and Efficiency to create a shared language of accounting and reporting. Second, they developed new organizational structures to promote communication and cooperation among the diverse departments and establishments of the federal government. While building the new executive branch, the BOB reoriented its focus away from Congress and toward the president. As with the Taft Commission, all directives emanating from the BOB were signed "by direction of the President" so that there was no doubt as to who was imposing these changes on the administrators.[11]

In many ways, the tenets of national budget reform paralleled Herbert Hoover's model for ordering relations between government and private enterprise. In Hoover's voluntaristic vision, the government was to collect and distribute economic data and provide guidance to producers on how best to reduce costs and minimize wasteful product differentiation. Similarly, Dawes and Lord saw the BOB as a means of collecting data on departmental administration and disseminating new accounting and reporting practices among the bureaucrats. Just as Hoover sanctioned trade associations to coordinate private enterprise, so the BOB developed coordinating agencies within government to harmonize public enterprise.[12]

[9]Herbert M. Lord to Robert S. Brookings, 8 September 1922, Bureau of the Budget, Central Subject Files, Record Group 51, Series 21.1, Box 137, National Archives, Washington, D.C.

[10]Institute for Government Research, *Annual Report of the Director, 1923*, 5.

[11]Charles G. Dawes, *The First Year of the Budget of the United States* (New York: Harper, 1923), 21.

[12]On Hoover's economics, see William J. Barber, *From New Era to New Deal* (Cambridge: Cambridge University Press, 1985).

Seidemann took the lead in formulating and installing a new uniform system of accounting and reporting for the national government. In 1922, he devised a scheme of listing and classification for the General Accounting Office which the comptroller general adopted without change. Dawes praised it as an "outstanding achievement" and a model for future work.[13] By 1925, Seidemann had supervised the installation of accounting systems in services throughout the administrative branch, including the Department of Agriculture, the Department of Justice, the Bureau of Foreign and Domestic Commerce, the Bureau of Mines, the General Land Office, and the Bureau of Public Roads.[14]

Throughout the 1920s, the BOB also developed uniform practices for transacting business with the private sector. Through the Federal Specifications Board, it promulgated specifications to regularize governmental purchases of commodities, while the Interdepartmental Board of Contracts and Adjustments developed standardized forms for dealing with private enterprise.[15] The BOB employed three basic tools to help administrative officers develop a new institutional identity as part of a coherent executive branch. First, coordinating boards were established in Washington through the BOB to promote the coordination of federal administrative activities. At the local level, the BOB fostered the formation of "Federal Business Associations" across the country, in which administrative officers assembled, exchanged information and ideas, and simply became acquainted with one another. Finally, Dawes instituted semiannual meetings at which he and the president together assembled all the key administrative officers of the government, including Cabinet members, as the "Business Organization of Government" and addressed them on subjects of budgetary administration.

During the 1920s, the BOB established a large number of coordinating boards to regularize business operations in various parts of the government. On June 27, 1921, it created the offices of chief coordinator and,

[13]Institute for Government Research, *Annual Report of the Director, 1922*, 6; Bureau of the Budget, *[First Annual] Report to the President of the United States by the Director of the Bureau of the Budget* (Washington, D.C.: Government Printing Office, 1922), 7.

[14]Institute for Government Research, *Annual Report of the Director, 1924*, 6; idem, "Memorandum to Dr. Willoughby from H. P. Seidemann, February 13, 1924," Administrative Correspondence and Reports, 12916, 1928, Box 2, File 5, Brookings Institution Archives, Washington, D.C., 1.

[15]By 1925, the Federal Specifications Board had promulgated some 300 specifications. Bureau of the Budget, *Fourth Annual Report of the Director of the Bureau of the Budget to the President of the United States* (Washington, D.C.: Government Printing Office, 1925), 19.

to cover activities in every region of the country, nine subordinate area co-ordinators, each corresponding to one on the nine corps areas of the Army. Then, in rapid succession, the BOB established eleven specific coordinating committees, including the Federal Specifications Board and the Interdepartmental Board of Contracts, as well as the Federal Purchasing Board, the Federal Liquidation Board, the Federal Board of Hospitalization, and the Federal Personnel Board. By 1929, the BOB had established a total of sixteen coordinating committees. Each committee was composed of a representative from each department and establishment concerned with the particular activity being coordinated and had a chairman who was directly appointed by or responsible to the chief coordinator. The immediate purpose of these committees was to provide interdepartmental contact and to develop business information in common.[16]

More broadly, the committees constituted the BOB's first step toward building a self-conscious executive branch. Before one assembly of government administrators, President Harding drove home the point that the coordinating boards "emphasized the great need to consider the Government's business as a whole rather than as an uncorrelated organization of loose parts." Harding urged all administrators to develop a "broader vision" of government activities. "Every one of you," he declared, "needs to realize that your services belong to the Government as a whole, and not to the subordinate part of it to which you happen to be attached." The great achievement of the coordinating boards was to develop "a real *esprit* which was formerly almost completely lacking."[17]

The coordinating committees provided a concrete structural basis on which to construct a new institutional identity for the diverse administrative departments. In doing so, they projected the president's authority into every corner of the federal administrative apparatus. According to Dawes, the BOB served as the "conduit for the transmission of Executive authority in routine business matters to the coordinating agencies for transmission to all departments and establishments." Departments had the right to appeal orders that came through the coordinating agencies, but all appeals had to be directed to the BOB, or finally to the president

---

[16]For general descriptions of the composition and work of the coordinating committees, see William F. Willoughby, *The National Budget System* (Baltimore: Johns Hopkins Press, 1927), 188–220; Carroll H. Woody, *The Growth of the Federal Government, 1915–1932* (New York: McGraw-Hill, 1934), 15–40; White, *Public Administration,* 159–61.

[17]*Addresses of the President of the United States and the Director of the Bureau of the Budget at the Second Annual Meeting of the Business Organization of Government* (Washington, D.C.: Government Printing Office, 1922), 2.

himself. There was no doubt as to where ultimate authority over their operations lay.[18]

Federal Business Associations were established in every major city across the country with the purpose of "bringing [local administrators] together from time to time in order that they might know each other personally and meet in common counsel . . . for an exchange of ideas and the development of cooperative teamwork." The BOB meant for these associations to foster tangible human bonds of community throughout the federal service, providing a concrete and immediate counterpart to the more abstract ties of uniform accounting and reporting—all with the aim of getting the field service "to think in terms of the Government as a whole rather than with reference to particular departments."[19]

The Federal Business Associations were organized and coordinated through the nine area coordinators, who, in turn, reported to the chief coordinator and through him to the director of the Bureau of the Budget. Their proliferation reveals an activist federal government steadily building its internal organizational structure throughout the 1920s. In 1922, the first 69 associations were established. In 1925, there were 124 associations representing 128 cities, and by 1929 their numbers peaked at 293, with a total of some thirteen hundred members. The associations engaged in a variety of activities to promote economy and efficiency, most of which involved coordinating federal activities in such areas as real estate allotment and transportation. Their primary value to Lord, however, was in their contribution to "welding the Government into a unified whole."[20]

Many associations also mounted extensive publicity campaigns to inform the local citizenry of how the national government operated in their communities. The publicity committee of the Boston association, for example, worked with the *Boston Globe* on a series of eighteen articles describing federal activities in the Boston area published under the caption "Uncle Sam in His Boston Office." In Los Angeles, the local association inaugurated a weekly radio talk to describe the work of the various government agencies in the area. Some of the larger offices maintained speak-

---

[18]Dawes, *First Year*, 134; Bureau of the Budget, *[First Annual] Report*, 1–2.

[19]Bureau of the Budget, *Third Annual Report of the Director of the Bureau of the Budget to the President of the United States* (Washington, D.C.: Government Printing Office, 1923), 165.

[20]Bureau of the Budget, *Fourth Annual Report*, 38; Bureau of the Budget, *Ninth Annual Report of the Director of the Bureau of the Budget to the President of the United States* (Washington, D.C.: Government Printing Office, 1930), 9; White, *Public Administration*, 160–61; Willoughby, *National Budget System*, 217–18.

ers' bureaus to make presentations in public schools and before church organizations, chambers of commerce, and Rotary and Kiwanis Clubs.[21] Through their activities, the associations imparted a new understanding and awareness of the federal government to citizens across the country. No longer was the government simply to be identified with Washington; it reached into every community and affected many aspects of citizens' lives. The associations fostered popular acceptance of expanded federal activities and perhaps also placated taxpayers who wanted to know what services they were getting for their money. The associations' brand of publicity was not intended, like the early budget exhibits, to create informed voters; nor did it emulate Willoughby's strategic use of the press to rally public opinion around a particular program. For the associations, publicity served primarily to project the presence of the federal government into people's daily lives. It asked for neither approval nor support, only the tacit recognition that the federal government had a place in their communities. Thus projecting the presence of the federal government throughout society, budget-related activities helped pave the way for Franklin Roosevelt's more interventionist New Deal programs.

Finally, there were the semiannual meetings of the Business Organization of Government. To establish his authority as director of the BOB immediately on taking office, Dawes conceived of the idea of bringing together the directing personnel of the government at Washington in a single meeting where, with the president at his side, he would inform them of their rights and duties under the new Budget and Accounting Act. On June 29, 1921, in an auditorium at the Department of the Interior, Dawes and Harding presided over a meeting of some two thousand federal officials, including the vice president, Cabinet members, the Joint Congressional Committee on Reorganization, the heads of independent governmental establishments, and diverse subordinate officials.[22]

With the president's blessing, Dawes launched upon a long and impassioned speech. Striding across the stage and forcefully gesticulating to punctuate his statements, Dawes impressed on the congregation of government officials his special status as the president's direct agent. In all matters of budgetary administration, he was superior to the Cabinet mem-

---

[21]Bureau of the Budget, *Third Annual Report*, 144; Bureau of the Budget, *Sixth Annual Report of the Director of the Bureau of the Budget to the President of the United States* (Washington, D.C.: Government Printing Office, 1927), 51; Bureau of the Budget, *Seventh Annual Report of the Director of the Bureau of the Budget to the President of the United States* (Washington, D.C.: Government Printing Office, 1928), 73–77.

[22]Dawes, *First Year*, 3–5; White, *Public Administration*, 160–61.

bers and was to be granted direct access both to information and to officers under their jurisdiction because he acted "as the eyes and ears of the Chief Executive." Dawes concluded his speech by extracting a dramatic pledge of unity and cooperation from the assembled mass of bureaucrats: "Fellow Bureau Chiefs," he cried, "are you willing, after hearing what I have said, that I should now represent you in addressing myself directly to the President of the United States with an assurance of your co-operation in his request for a reduction of government expenditures? If you so agree, if you are willing, will you indicate it by standing?"[23] The entire audience rose and applauded, committing itself en masse to budget reform and symbolically subjecting itself to Dawes's authority. Technically, Dawes was calling for help in reducing expenditures, but, as he later put it, the true purpose of such a meeting was "to create a feeling of solidarity among all the members as belonging to a single business organization [and] . . . emphasize in the mind of every man there his relation to the President as the head of the business organization." That is, the meetings were meant, first, to create a self-conscious executive branch, and, second, to place that branch under the direction of the president.[24]

Lord continued to hold semiannual meetings of the Business Organization of Government while establishing other informal "clubs" to promote economy. The Two Percent Club contained all administrators who were able to save 2 percent of the money available for personnel by not filling vacated positions; and in 1927, Lord instituted the Woodpecker Club (so called because "the woodpecker always works with his head and tells the world what he is doing") "for the sole purpose of affording the opportunity for the rank and file of our army of employees to enlist in a 100 percent campaign for small savings." The Loyal Order of Woodpeckers contained all administrators who committed to minor daily economies, from saving office supplies to turning off lights. As petty or even ludicrous as the Woodpecker Club may sound, it served further to foster and extend a sense of esprit de corps throughout the administrative service. The clubs realized only minor savings in relation to the overall budget, but they did engage average office workers and made them aware of their place as part of an organic, administrative whole.[25]

---

[23]Dawes, *First Year*, 18–19.

[24]Ibid., 154–55.

[25]*Addresses of the President of the United States and the Director of the Bureau of the Budget at the Fourteenth Regular Meeting of the Business Organization of Government, January 30, 1928* (Washington, D.C.: Government Printing Office, 1928), 16; Bureau of the Budget, *Seventh Annual Report*, 20.

The BOB also had more direct means of projecting the president's authority throughout the federal administrative apparatus. The Budget and Accounting Act directed each department and independent establishment to designate a budget officer to prepare estimates and act as liaison with the BOB. In regular meetings, the BOB brought together all the budget officers so that each one would "become thoroughly familiar with the financial problems of the Government as a whole, thus gaining the viewpoint of the President and the Bureau of the Budget as well as that of his immediate chief."[26] The BOB itself had a staff of investigators who dealt directly with each department's budget officers so as "to form a direct channel of communication and information from them to the Bureau of the Budget."[27] The investigators gathered information as a basis for the director of the BOB to review and revise departmental requests for appropriations. They could not give administrative directions, but their reports directly affected funding decisions. Moreover, Dawes directed that their investigations should cover not only questions of economy and efficiency but "should extend to . . . policy itself, with a view to advising the Director of the Bureau of the Budget, for the information of the President, as to whether limitations should be put upon existing policy and what, if any, new policies should be recommended."[28]

The investigators played a central role in implementing the system that later became known as "central clearance"—the process by which the president used the BOB to screen all agency proposals for coordination and advice on their relation to the president's program. Ironically, the impetus for central clearance actually came from Congress. In November 1921, the chairman of the House Appropriations Committee called to Dawes's attention that certain departments were making requests directly of his committee and suggested that properly they should be channeled first through the BOB and included in the president's budget.[29]

Dawes followed up in December by issuing Circular No. 49, ordering that

before any request or recommendation of this character, originating in or sponsored by an executive department or independent establishment

[26]Bureau of the Budget, *Second Annual Report of the Director of the Bureau of the Budget to the President of the United States* (Washington, D.C.: Government Printing Office, 1923), 35.
[27]Bureau of the Budget, *[First Annual] Report*, 7.
[28]Dawes, *First Year*, 191–92.
[29]See Richard E. Neustadt, "Presidency and Legislation: The Growth of Central Clearance," *American Political Science Review* 48 (September 1954): 641–43.

of the government is sent to either House of Congress, or to any committee thereof, it shall first be presented to the Director of the Bureau of the Budget, who shall make recommendations with respect thereto, to the President. And no such request shall be submitted to either House of Congress, or to any committee thereof, without having first been approved by the President.[30]

Through Circular No. 49, Dawes clearly attempted to assert central control over agency views on pending and proposed legislation. Richard Neustadt has pointed out that during the 1920s, presidents exercised central clearance narrowly, focusing only on the cost, not the substance, of agency proposals.[31] The greater significance of central clearance in the 1920s, however, lies not in the extent to which it was substantively, exercised by the BOB, but in the way it served to extend a new awareness throughout the federal government that administrative activities were not legitimate if they were not in accord with the president's program. Circular No. 49 informed departments that there was no secure administrative existence independent of the president's ultimate approval. It thus firmly interposed the president between the federal bureaucracy and Congress. No longer could administrators go directly to congressional committees with requests for funding. Under central clearance, they had to look first and foremost to the BOB and the president for support.

To develop executive control over deficiencies, the BOB issued Circular No. 51 in December 1921, requiring all departments and independent establishments to furnish the BOB with periodic reports relating to the apportionment of their appropriations and their operations thereunder. In addition, the following August, Circular No. 77 ordered that the director of the BOB be informed of the "character, purpose, scope, and probable duration" of any proposed new departmental activity.[32]

Dawes found some resistance to his assertion of central control. When addressing a testimonial dinner held in his honor by the National Budget Committee, Dawes complained of certain arrogant bureau chiefs who insisted on "maintaining their right to do as they . . . damned pleased in the interest of their department, irrespective of the interest of the great coun-

[30]Dawes, *First Year*, 162.

[31]Neustadt, "Presidency and Legislation," 646. See also Norman M. Pearson, "The Budget Bureau: From Routine Business to General Staff," *Public Administration Review* 3 (Spring 1943): 131–32, 138.

[32]Daniel Selko, *The Federal Financial System* (Washington, D.C.: Brookings Institution, 1940), 105–7.

try of which they were but a part."[33] Dawes proceeded to describe an encounter with the chief of operations of the Navy, who asserted that he had a duty to the American people to maintain the Navy that was superior to the BOB's claims upon him. In typical fashion, Dawes shot back, "The hell you do. . . . You are a subordinate official." Any duty he owed was to the president, who decided policy for the people, and to the president's agent, the BOB. "That little conversation," Dawes concluded, "saved the United States $10,000,000."[34]

In other instances Dawes could be more accommodating, as when several powerful senators approached him to demand in increase in the estimate for the Mississippi River Commission (an important source of public works projects and patronage). Dawes readily acceded to their requests and added $1.8 million to the original estimate of $4.87 million.[35] Richard Neustadt goes so far as to characterize Dawes as beating a retreat from aggressive application of central clearance in the face of departmental opposition, "leaving interpretation and compliance to departmental discretion."[36] Dawes's goal, however, was not so much to interfere with departments' discretion as to reorient their attention away from Congress and toward the president.

Harding, for example, was unequivocally committed to enforcing the basic principles of central clearance. He cautioned recalcitrant officials that "advocacy of an estimate before the congressional committee in excess of the Executive recommendation will be looked upon as sufficient reason to give consideration towards severance of employment with the Government."[37] Harding was less concerned to change the substance of departmental estimates than to ensure that administrative officials recognized the president, not Congress, as the office to which they owed their

[33]"Address of Brigadier General Charles G. Dawes," *Budget*, November 1, 1922; 15.

[34]Ibid., 15–16. Dawes also complained directly to President Harding of the Navy's resistance, asserting that "there is a desire on the part of subordinate officials [in the Navy department] to handicap, in every way, coordination, in defense of the old status quo." Charles G. Dawes, "Memorandum to the President, February 25, 1922," Bureau of the Budget, Central Subject Files, Record Group 51, Series 21.1, Box 280, National Archives, Washington, D.C., 1. See also Harold D. Smith, "The Bureau of the Budget," *Public Administration Review* 1 (Winter 1941): 109.

[35]Charles G. Dawes, "Memorandum to the President, November 19, 1921," Bureau of the Budget, Central Subject Files, Record Group 51, Series 21.1, Box 280, National Archives, Washington, D.C., 1.

[36]Neustadt, "Presidency and Legislation," 645–46.

[37]*Addresses of the President and the Director of the Bureau of the Budget at the Fifth Regular Meeting of the Business Organization of Government, June 18, 1923* (Washington, D.C.: Government Printing Office, 1923), 4.

primary allegiance. Those who disregarded this allegiance would be subject to the ultimate sanction of dismissal.

Coolidge reiterated Harding's position in an address before the Seventh Regular Meeting of the Business Organization of Government. He commanded his audience to give "their loyal support" to his official budget estimates and "served notice" as chief executive that he proposed to "protect the integrity" of his budget.[38] Congress, for its part, accepted central clearance apparently because the process did not interfere with its power ultimately to revise estimates or prohibit Congress from calling administrative officials to testify before congressional committees.

Under Lord's direction, the BOB freely and regularly exercised its power to revise and reduce preliminary departmental estimates. Between 1924 and 1929, the BOB consistently reduced them by 3.5 to 10.5 percent. As a result, congressional activity in reducing or revising estimates declined drastically. Between 1925 and 1930, the variation between congressional appropriations and the president's budget never exceeded 0.35 percent.[39] By 1927, Lord was happily reporting that it was no longer necessary to remind departmental officials of the requirements of Circular No. 49, "as universal compliance was made with its requirements."[40]

The 1920s were not years of government intervention in the economy but of executive intervention in government administration. Measured in terms of spending or number of personnel, government activity declined steadily during the decade.[41] But even as he was reducing estimates, Lord recognized that government was becoming increasingly activist in terms of internal coordinating activities. The new systems of accounts and standards specifications, the diverse coordinating agencies and associations, and the acceptance of central clearance transformed federal governance. By the end of the decade, the new budget system had decisively located authority over the administrative apparatus of the government in the hands of the president, relegating Congress to the status of a reactive spectator whose primary duty was to oversee the exercise of the authority it had delegated to the president.

[38] *Addresses of the President and the Director of the Bureau of the Budget at the Seventh Regular Meeting of the Business Organization of Government, June 30, 1924* (Washington, D.C.: Government Printing Office, 1923), 5–6.

[39] White, *Public Administration*, 182–83.

[40] Bureau of the Budget, *Fifth Annual Report of the Director of the Bureau of the Budget to the President of the United States* (Washington, D.C.: Government Printing Office, 1927), 12.

[41] See Louis Kimmel, *Federal Budget and Fiscal Policy, 1789–1958* (Washington, D.C.: Brookings Institution, 1958) 89–98; Carolyn Webber and Aaron Wildavsky, *A History of Taxation and Expenditure* (New York: Simon and Schuster, 1986), 413–27.

THE NEW MEANING OF THE BUDGET

The men of the Bureau of Municipal Research originally conceived of the budget as a means to reconnect citizens to their government by displacing corrupt party machines as the primary mediating institution between government and the people. As budget reform moved to the national level, its leaders and its meaning changed. National budget reformers concentrated almost exclusively on reordering relations of power and authority within government. Willoughby and his associates lost sight of the distinctively republican functions of a budget system. Perhaps they were less concerned with problems of democratic representation in part because national government itself was physically more removed from its constituents. Broader forces, however, also contributed significantly to the emergence of a new meaning for budget reform at the national level.

Local reform developed in large part as a response to corruption, both of the political machine and the private corporation. The men of the bureau envisioned the budget as a means of protecting the public realm of government from private power. The budget, they believed, would expose government operations to public scrutiny and thereby discourage the misappropriation of public power by private interests. Widespread, ongoing, and accessible publicity was essential to achieve this goal.

Fears of corruption played only a small role in the campaign for a national budget. The Taft Commission set the agenda, with its focus on centralizing administrative power in the executive. Issues of discipline and control guided the movement, not corruption. Whereas local reformers presented budgets as a means to connect citizens to their local government, national reformers viewed budgets primarily as a means to build a new national state.

The national government did not need protection from external threats; it needed internal reform to set its own house in order. The inward focus of national budget reform fostered a very different attitude toward publicity, as evidenced in Willoughby's condescending attitude toward the press. Public opinion mattered to Willoughby (and later to BOB directors Dawes and Lord) only as it furthered his program of reorganizing government.

National budget reform did retain the Bureau of Municipal Research's emphasis on using the budget to establish clear boundaries between the public and private spheres, but here also the nature and purpose of those boundaries took on a wholly new meaning. Local budget reformers sought to use the budget to protect government from private influence. National budget reform sought the exact reverse: to use the budget to protect private enterprise from government interference. The foremost instrument of administrative state building was to be used to contain the newly powerful leviathan it helped to create.

Local governments had long held broad police powers to regulate and direct the lives of their citizens. People were accustomed to being taxed to pay for sewers, water, and gas, for sanitation and police protection. Budget reform enabled a local government to provide these services more efficiently in part by protecting it from corruption. In the eyes of municipal reformers, government was not a threat or a burden but an instrument to further the public good.

The national government had no such tradition of police powers (and would not fully begin to develop one until the New Deal). Massive federal intervention in the national economy during World War I, therefore, unsettled many Americans, especially businessmen. Increased levels of federal taxation and debt further impressed upon financial elites the magnitude of the national government's newfound power to affect their lives. In contrast to earlier attitudes toward local government, wealthy Americans began to perceive the national government as both a burden and a threat. The threat, however, came less from the old bugbear of outright tyranny than from waste and mismanagement.

During the 1920s, government officials used the budget to reassure skittish taxpayers and bondholders. The budget, they avowed, would protect them from excessive taxes or defaulted loan repayments by ensuring that the government was run in the most efficient and businesslike manner possible. Calvin Coolidge, together with his director of the BOB, Herbert Lord, and the powerful secretary of the treasury, Andrew Mellon, forthrightly espoused the virtues of the new national budget system as a bulwark against excessive government interference in private economic affairs.

The Coolidge administration took aim first and foremost at taxes. "There is scarcely an economic ill anywhere in our country," declared Coolidge, "that cannot be traced directly or indirectly to high taxes." Together with Lord and Mellon, the president engaged in an "intensive campaign for economy" with the sole purpose of reducing taxes. Lord soon recast the budget system to address Coolidge's (and big business's) concerns. In an article published in the magazine of the U.S. Chamber of

Commerce, Lord asserted that "there is one reason for economy in the public service—reduction in taxation."[42]

Fifteen years earlier, Henry Bruere had similarly promoted economy to local business leaders, but for very different reasons. He argued that the purpose of economy in government was not to lessen the burden of taxation on the wealthy but to enable government to meet all legitimate social needs.[43] Economy, to Bruere, was a means to expand government activity in the community. By the mid-1920s, in the hands of a president who had declared that "the business of America is business," economy had become a means to protect large corporations and wealthy individuals from high taxes.

Mellon, above all, led the Coolidge administration's attack on high taxes. In his book *Taxation: The People's Business*, Mellon relied heavily on information provided through the budget system to support his campaign for lower taxes. He portrayed taxation and the national debt as threatening the very "spirit of business adventure" that was the heart of American enterprise. Mellon used the budget to identify "unnecessary" government programs to be cut, thereby enabling the government to devote more of its resources to retiring the debt and lowering taxes. He valued the budget ultimately as a means of protecting the private taxpayer and businessman from excessive burdens imposed by unnecessary government activity. The budget provided the essential prerequisite to Mellon's campaign. Without specific facts and figures, he could not have made as forceful an argument for contracting the scope of government intervention in the private sphere.[44]

If "economy" meant protecting business from government, it did not necessarily mean a return to laissez-faire. To the contrary, constructive economy in government, according to Coolidge, was not "a policy of negation," but "made ample provision for things that must be done" and "call[ed] for positive action" to meet social needs such as public buildings, internal improvements, and national defense. Coolidge recognized that, far from being laissez-faire, government should actively intervene in

---

[42]President, *Addresses of the President of the United States and the Director of the Bureau of the Budget at the Sixth Regular Meeting of the Business Organization of Government, January 21, 1924* (Washington, D.C.: Government Printing Office, 1924), 2–3; Herbert M. Lord, "'Business in Government' at Work," *Nation's Business* 12 (June 1924): 12.

[43]Henry Bruere, *The Cost of Government in New York City: A Discussion of City Business for Taxpayers* (New York: Record and Guide, 1913), i.

[44]Andrew Mellon, *Taxation: The People's Business* (New York: Macmillan, 1924), 14–22, 41–43, 93–107, 19–199.

its own administration to make improvements that would redound directly to the benefit of the people.[45]

Coolidge could embrace an activist conception of government precisely because the budget domesticated any possible threat government action might pose to business interests. Neither he nor Mellon denied a place for government in the economy. Rather, they used the budget to set boundaries to government activity so as to maximize protection of corporate elites, especially those with a financial stake in the federal government.

Coolidge's activist view of government administration, however, differed fundamentally from the original vision of local reformers such as Allen, Bruere, and Cleveland, who had used publicity to present the budget as a guide to the honest and efficient expansion of government to meet social needs. At the national level, administrators used the budget to *limit* government intrusion into the private sphere. Therefore, questions of political accountability and responsiveness to public opinion faded in significance because the logic of reform simply did not call for extensive justification of *less* government interference in people's lives.

The budget had originated as an instrument of democratic accountability but devolved into a simple, though powerful, symbol of legitimacy. In an era of contracting external government activity, the mere presence of a budget was sufficient to assure the people that public business was being carried on in an acceptable manner. The substance of the budget and its accessibility lost relevance. The budget thus gradually ceased to function as an instrument of popular control over government and became simply a measure of assurance that government activity was being conducted according to certain professionally recognized principles of public administration.

As the republican underpinnings of budget reform receded from political consciousness, Coolidge's business administration developed a new affirmative meaning for the budget. In the place of democratic accountability, the new budget would enhance material prosperity. The president asserted that as the basis for material prosperity, "the meaning of the Budget system of the United States" was "to promote [the] mental, moral, and spiritual welfare of the people."[46] The budget was not intended to empower the people but to enrich them. The path to Coolidge's new materialist view of the budget had been blazed by Willoughby and the men of

---

[45] *Addresses of the President . . . Fourteenth Regular Meeting*, 5–6.
[46] Ibid., 1–2.

the Institute for Government Research, who, by emphasizing relations of power and authority within government, first divorced budget reform from issues of representative democracy. As Coolidge told the Business Organization of Government, the "true purpose" of its meetings was "to establish the correct relations between needs and resources." "This purpose," he continued,

> is immediately translated into concrete results, not only for the people at large but for the people in the Government service. For the unemployed it makes the prospect of employment more certain. For the employed it makes hours shorter, tasks lighter, wages higher, and positions more permanent. It makes the cost of food and clothing less. It reduces rents. It makes the home easier to buy, and, having been bought, easier to pay for. It makes investments give better returns and increases the opportunity for saving. The margin for the comforts, and even the luxuries, of life is widened. The ability comes for broadening educational advantage. Leisure is secured for the better appreciation of literature, music, and art. Means exist for the ministration of charity. Contentment and peace of mind come under these conditions, because people have the feeling of success and the consciousness that they are rising superior to their environment.[47]

Democratic accountability and responsible government did not enter into Coolidge's world of budget administration. He saw only a material basis to budget reform. Prosperity was the payoff for a people whose leaders in important ways had ceased to care about democratic accountability and responsible government.

For Coolidge, the budget system enabled government to meet social needs and so provided "the material groundwork on which the whole fabric of society rests," including everything from railroads and hospitals to telephones and automobiles. Moreover, "it has given to the average American a breadth of outlook, a variety of experience, and a richness of life that in former generations was entirely beyond the reach of even the most powerful princes."[48] Like the commercial advertisements of the 1920s, Coolidge here presented the budget as enabling the government to fulfill an image and lifestyle—it made people's lives fuller and more satisfying

[47]Ibid.
[48]*Addresses of the President of the United States and the Director of the Bureau of the Budget at the Tenth Regular Meeting of the Business Organization of Government, January 30, 1926* (Washington, D.C.: Government Printing Office, 1926), 5–6.

in ways that the immediate substance of the product did not make self-evident.[49]

The men of the Bureau of Municipal Research had a consumerist model of citizenship in which people used their vote to buy government services. For them, however, government services were *public* goods, and good citizenship involved educating oneself about government activities and community needs through the budget to promote the common welfare. Political discourse remained a significant part of this process even as it was structured by reference to the budget. Citizens still realized themselves most fully as they participated in the affairs of their community.

Coolidge and the national budget reformers went further and reduced citizenship to consumption itself. The purpose of the budget was not to empower the people as citizens but to fulfil them as consumers of private goods. Arguably, political discussion had become irrelevant to citizenship and governance. People realized their identity as citizens through the private act of possessing personal goods, not through public action. By the end of the 1920s, budget reform told citizens that the legitimacy of government derived less from its responsiveness to the public will than from its ability to gratify material needs. The new national state was to be therapeutic: its purpose was to make people feel good.

THE LEGACY OF BUDGET REFORM

In a representative democracy, people will allow government to rule over them as long as they believe it is responsive to their will. In a small, homogeneous society, the people entrust politicians with power because they feel connected to them by shared interests and experiences. Periodic elections ensure accountability, but the common bond of community provides the primary basis for responsible and responsive government. As a society becomes larger, more complex, and more diverse, the bonds of community attenuate and the legitimacy of governing institutions weakens accordingly. To shore up the viability of the political system, mediating institutions develop to assure the people that government remains in touch with their concerns.

In late nineteenth-century America, political parties emerged as powerful institutions to sustain representative democracy in an urban, indus-

---

[49]For a discussion of advertising in the 1920s, see Roland Marchand, *Advertising the American Dream* (Berkeley: University of California Press, 1985).

trial society. The urban political machine, in particular, proved extremely effective in gaining the allegiance of new immigrants and the working class, convincing them that it understood their needs and shared their concerns. To the native-born white middle class, however, the machines constituted an intolerable foundation for a true representative democracy. Good government reformers worked diligently to devise alternative methods of adapting representative democracy to mass society. Some, through electoral reforms such as the initiative, the referendum, and the Australian ballot, sought to reestablish direct ties between respectable middle-class citizens and government. But electoral reforms alone only minimally improved accountability and were no substitute for the sense of shared interests and experience projected by the machine. The reforms facilitated the unmediated delegation of power to representatives but supplied no further connection between citizen and government.

In the early twentieth century, a group of reformers proposed budgets as a new type of mediating institution. A budget system would displace the machine by establishing a new foundation for legitimate representation based on continuous oversight and measurement of public activities against the yardstick of "objective" principles of financial administration. Under this budgetary regime, accountability gained force and eclipsed shared interests and experiences as the primary basis for entrusting representatives with power.

Under the new budgetary regime, first proposed by the men of the Bureau of Municipal Research, the budget ensured that government would exercise its delegated power according to certain rules of financial administration. As the system developed, however, the substance of particular rules or how they were administered became less important than that they were certified by experts as the right rules for managing government. At the national level, men such as Willoughby, Coolidge, and Mellon used the budget to legitimate power by assuring the people that it enabled government to meet their needs with economy and efficiency. People soon took budgets for granted. By the end of the 1920s, the budget had devolved from an instrument of democratic accountability into a simple but powerful symbol of legitimacy: the mere fact that they existed implied that government was accountable and hence legitimate.

As public budgets helped to create the modern American state, they also helped to create the modern American citizen—or rather citizens—because as local and national budget reformers each invested budgets with distinctive meanings and purposes, so too did they develop dual models of citizenship: the local citizen, who acted in concert with fellow citizens to form a community of educated consumers of government services that met public needs; and the national citizen, who acted as an individual consumer and judged government's effectiveness by its ability to gratify his or her personal needs. The two models of citizenship, one oriented toward public goods, the other toward private, were both fundamentally reactive and were bound together by their common image of the citizen as consumer. The national citizen did not supplant but rather coexisted in tension with the local citizen. At different times and in different places, one or the other model might seem more prominent, but both were always present.

At the local level, the men of the Bureau of Municipal Research used budgets to displace urban machines and weaken party ties while providing a new bond between the government and the people. In so doing, they redefined the boundaries between public and private, between the state and society. The budget, as government in miniature, clearly demarcated the scope of governmental responsibilities. Authoritative political discourse therefore required reference to the state via the budget document, and political action involved using one's vote to purchase government services. Local budget reform thus commodified government and made citizens into consumers. Yet even as it undermined seemingly freer and more active forms of citizen activity, local budget reform continued to emphasize the importance of political discussion—as circumscribed by the budget.

At the national level, reformers concentrated on ordering relations within government. First, budget and accounting reform revealed to public officials the nature and extent of government activities and provided a mechanism to control them. Second, in adopting an executive budget, the government firmly and clearly lodged responsibility for the administrative apparatus of the national government in the hands of the president. Third, in implementing the new system, the Bureau of the Budget, following the ideas of the Taft Commission, used the budget to impose a common identity upon the federal bureaucracy and establish a hierarchy of authority that culminated in the president.

National reformers deemphasized the importance of using the budget to maintain a bond of representation between citizen and government. As far as they were concerned, the purpose of the national budget was to enable government to satisfy people's individual needs, both material and spiritual. The community, as such, had no needs apart from those of its individual constituents. Thus public discussion was almost irrelevant to the budgetary process and, by extension, to citizenship itself. The citizen was to judge the efficacy of the national budget not by examining and debating how it promoted the common good but by assessing how it affected his or her own personal prosperity.

Budget reform, then, while helping to restructure government in the United States, also bifurcated citizen identity between a local model of citizens as civic consumers of government services and a national model of citizens as individual clients of a therapeutic state. Local government maintained its legitimacy as it served the community; national government did so by meeting individual needs. The national model readily served the national government during the relative prosperity of the 1920s. Individuals did well, and so, according to the logic of federal budget reform, they believed that the government was fulfilling its duties. This same logic, however, could thoroughly undermine the government when times were hard.

It was the peculiar genius of Franklin Roosevelt to use both the structural and conceptual changes wrought by budget reform to bolster the legitimacy of the national state in the face of the Great Depression. The budget reforms of the 1920s made the executive-driven programs of the New Deal possible. Before the Budget and Accounting Act of 1921, there was no coherent executive branch to speak of; only a loose collection of autonomous departments and independent establishments that looked directly to Congress for financial support and owed no particular loyalty or duty to the president. Under Harding and Coolidge, the Bureau of the Budget imposed a structure of accounting and reporting that promoted a common identity among the diverse federal administrative units and assigned them a clear place within a well-defined pyramid of authority that culminated in the president.

Roosevelt was the first president to make full use of the potential presented by the newly self-conscious executive branch. The new budgetary system provided Roosevelt with critical information about the nature and organization of the federal bureaucracy while establishing his authority over the bureaucracy as chief executive. Thus, when it came time to take the initiative, Roosevelt was well positioned to launch the dazzling array of programs that became the New Deal.

Roosevelt deftly played on both the local and national models of citizenship to shore up the crumbling legitimacy of governmental institutions. The New Deal's multifarious regulatory schemes, including the Agricultural Adjustment Act, the National Industrial Recovery Act, and the National Labor Relations Act, asserted national police powers on the model of state and local governments. For the first time, citizens could look to the national government to purchase with their votes the type of services that previously had been available only at the state and local level. Moreover, concentrating administrative responsibility in the hands of the president, the executive budget focused citizen attention on the chief executive. The more power Roosevelt exercised, the more he provided a bond between citizens and the state. He became the people's direct and personal representative in the federal government.

Roosevelt also combined traditional patronage programs such as the Civil Works Administration and the Works Progress Administration with more radical redistributive initiatives such as the Social Security Act and income tax reforms to address the immediate material needs of individual citizens. More powerful, however, Roosevelt himself, through his fireside chats, his speeches, and his personal style, made individuals feel good. Dr. New Deal did more to heal the spirit than to fill the belly of America during the Depression. The first modern "personal president,"[50] Roosevelt used himself as a means to legitimate the government in times of crisis. Roosevelt thus become the living embodiment of budget reform's therapeutic state.

Budget reform ultimately resolved the problem of maintaining a viable representative democracy in urban industrial society by reframing the basis of legitimate government. It began as an attempt to re-create the relationship of citizens to their government by providing a new connection based on education and surveillance of government activities. It culminated in a new vision of the state, unitary and autonomous, deriving it legitimacy less from its accountability than from its ability to meet citizen needs.

Casting the national state broadly as a source of material benefits set the stage for the full emergence of interest group politics during the New Deal. If the purpose of government was to meet needs, then it made sense to organize politically according to distinct economic interests rather than according to party affiliation.

Together, the weakened but still substantial party system and the new budgetary regime forged an amalgam of legitimating services, institutions, rationales, and symbols sufficient to sustain the creation the new national state. The state expanded steadily from Roosevelt's New Deal to John-

[50]The phrase is Theodore J. Lowi's; see *The Personal President* (Ithaca: Cornell University Press, 1985).

son's Great Society. In recent decades, however, with the continued decline of the party system and the growth of persistent budget deficits and national debt, citizens once again are questioning the basic legitimacy of our governing institutions.

The taxpayer revolts of the 1970s and 1980s (led by California's infamous Proposition 13) may be viewed as manifestations of a crisis of representation. Proposition 13 was not simply anti-government or anti-tax; it expressed the feelings of citizens who no longer trusted the government to spend their money in a responsible manner. People will pay taxes when they feel the revenues are being spent responsibly to further legitimate public goals. They can even accept a certain amount of waste and inefficiency. But Proposition 13 revealed that voters could not accept a government that no longer responded to their needs or desires. The taxpayer revolts implicitly indicate a decline in popular belief in the ability of the budget system to discipline government in the public interest.[51]

The legitimacy conferred by the budget as a symbol of responsible government has eroded in recent years, and there is nothing to take its place. Into the institutional vacuum have rushed frenzied campaigns for term limits, balanced budget amendments, and talk radio. Each catch phrase and quick fix capitalizes on the growing popular sense that government is no longer responsive to the will of the people. Similar sentiments gave rise to the movement for budget reform. The movement was flawed in many ways. It had a naive faith in supposedly objective principles of financial administration. Its commitment to representative democracy existed in profound tension with its reliance on experts. And its use of publicity to educate the citizenry all too easily degenerated into a cynical manipulation of public opinion. Yet, for all this, as the century comes to a close and we confront the problems of sustaining a viable representative democracy in an increasingly large, complex, and diverse society, we might do well to pause and consider how a group of well-meaning, intelligent, and articulate citizens used budget reform to address very similar problems as the century was born.

[51]For a general discussion of recent taxpayer revolts, see Clarence Y. H. Lo, *Small Property versus Big Government: Social Origins of the Property Tax Revolt*, (Berkeley: University of California Press, 1990).

INDEX